Flash for Programmers

Flash for Programmers

James Smith

SouthLondon
Publishing

First published in Great Britain,
2004 by South London Publishing

ISBN 0-9547066-0-9

Designed by Sally Green.

3 —

Contents

Contents

Preface

"... though prudence, intrepidity, and perseverance united are not exempted from the blows of adverse fortune, yet in a long series of transactions they usually rise superior to its power, and in the end rarely fail of proving successful."
Lord Anson

The purpose of this book is to encourage the use of Flash movies in a functional and data driven role.
A Flash movie can communicate with server processes, written in any language, in the most straightforward manner. As well as server side interaction, Flash movies can also replace much 'dynamic' HTML and JavaScript and my aim is to encourage this practice too.

I call this book 'Flash for Programmers', but it is really not just for programmers, at least not in the strictest sense. It is for anyone who wants to use Flash for utilitarian purposes, as opposed to frivolous ones. It is aimed at 'programmers' who have not used Flash before but have belatedly realised its usefulness in authoring data-driven websites, as well as at existing Flash 'designers' who have, well, belatedly realised its usefulness in authoring data-driven websites.

There is a support website for this book and no accompanying CD. The website contains a wealth of material that did not make it into the book for one reason or another, such as sample chapters omitted for the purposes of brevity; or subjects of such a transient nature that committing them to hard copy would make this book dated before its time.
You should definitely consider the website an adjunct to this book. So, the URL:

http://www.flashforprogrammers.com

This book is driven by the example movies and components in the accompanying source distribution. They constitute about nine-tenths of the effort and invention that has gone into this project and to ignore them is to completely and utterly miss the point. Even those chapters that do not relate to a specific example movie or component project (and they are rare) are the results of a distillation of ideas from those that do. You must therefore download the source distribution, install the components and get the examples movies up and running with a web server and server side language before proceeding much further. The source distribution can be found at the following URL:

http://www.flashforprogrammers.com/download/

One note about the source distribution: the HTML and many of the text files were automatically generated from source XML using a small utility called SiteGen, which I have included (together with the necessary project files) for the convenience of anyone interested in XSLT.

SiteGen currently only works on Windows, although the XSL style sheets (the files that define the rules translating the XML into HTML or whatever) are also provided and could conceivably be adapted for another program.

The text assumes that you are familiar with at least one method of server side programming or are prepared to learn. Some basic knowledge of HTML and JavaScript is also assumed. If you do not have access to a web server and some server side language such as PHP, you need to get stuck in and install them on your own machine. There is simply no way to avoid this. If you are not interested in writing Flash movies that interact with servers then you have picked up the wrong book.

If you have bought this book already and are now rueing your decision, it is worth bearing in mind that working commercially with Flash these days almost certainly means that you will have to get to grips with communicating with a server at some point. This book provides a quick and easy way to get you started. The examples distribution includes the source code for several popular, freely available server side languages and there are sufficient instructions in the text to get you up and running.

How should you read this book? If you are new to Flash, read the first chapter, 'The basics'. It is designed for neophytes and comes before any discussion of the example movies or components. Experienced Flashers can probably skip it altogether, once they have noted my use of a dynamic text field for debugging.

The next chapter, 'The examples distribution', describes how to configure and run the example movies with a web server and comes as close to being compulsory as any chapter in this book. The remaining two chapters are also pretty important, outlining both the significant aspects of data driven movies and my own (slightly idiosyncratic) approaches to them.

You can then attempt the example and component chapters, which form something of a continuous tutorial. Apologies to the more experienced Flash developers who might find the going a little pedantic to begin with. Subjects are covered once and once only as I work through the projects and therefore I would suggest that the chapters are read in roughly the right order. I would also advise that when reading these chapters, you keep one eye on the source code for the relevant example or component project.

Acknowledgements

I would never have gotten this far without the patience and support of the following people (they are listed in order of their financial contributions!): Clive Davie, Christian Köerner, Chris Hind and Marcos Bulgheroni. Special thanks (in no particular order, other than alphabetical) to: Adele Fielding, Allan Young, Dougal Cawley, Giles Richardson, Ian McGhie and Lynn Dunlop. Thanks to flashcomponents.net, a site that has probably put more traffic my way than any other; and many thanks to Mark, Paul and Chris at az2lab, who gave me a desk to work at during the final stages of this book and generally kept me sane. Also, thanks to Sally Green, who appreciated more than most what this project means to me.

Finally, thanks to my parents. This book is dedicated to them, with love.

James Smith
South London, Autumn 2003.

Part 1
Getting Started

1.1: The Basics

Starting a project

Launch Flash. It should look something like Fig. 1.1:

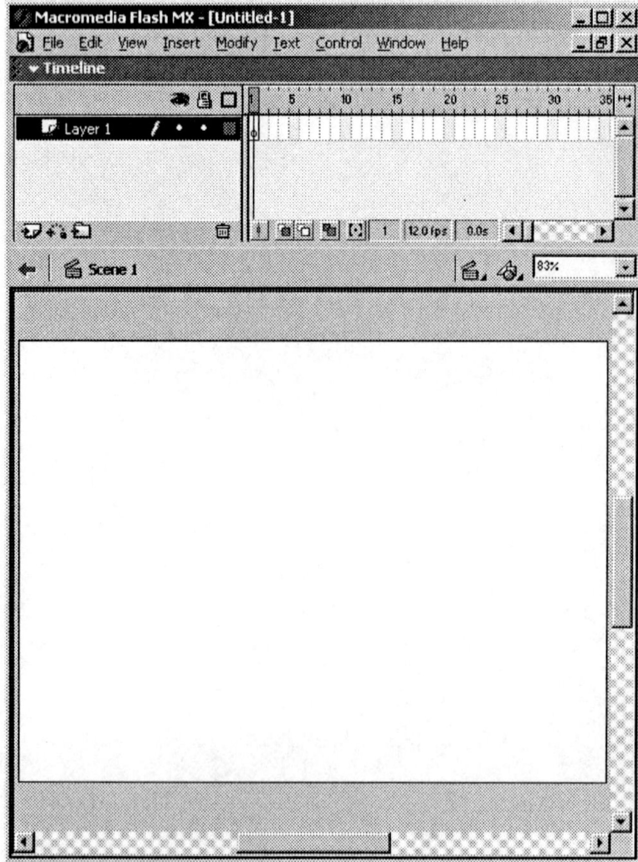

Fig. 1.1: Flash on startup with an empty project window.

The project window fills the main application window here and is made up of two distinct parts: the stage and the timeline. The stage is where graphic elements that appear in the movie are drawn. The timeline represents the progression of the movie over time during playback, with each small upright rectangle representing a frame.[1] The pink rectangle in the 'ruler' part of the timeline represents the playhead.

1 Not once in the course of this book will you ever see a movie or movie clip that uses more than the first frame, with the exception of the skin elements of some components. This is a major departure from the standard way of writing a movie, where even if the movie does not continually loop through the frames, they at least represent the various movie 'states' and changing the appearance of the movie in response to user input usually means jumping from one labelled frame to another.

Right-click on the stage and choose 'Properties' from the bottom of the resultant popup menu to bring up the properties inspector (Fig. 1.2):

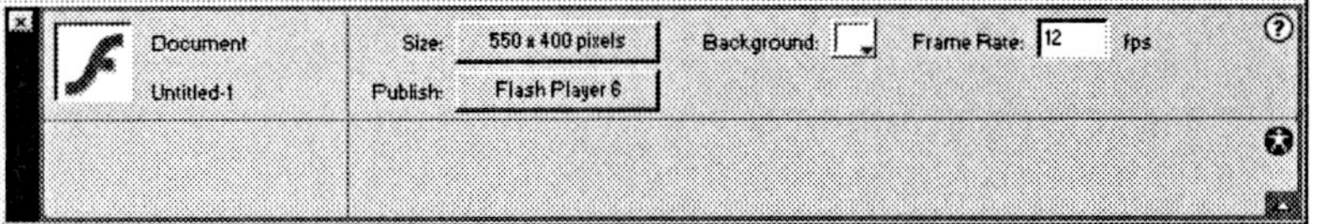

Fig. 1.2: The properties inspector showing the stage properties.

The frame rate, the size of the stage and the background colour can each be altered with the properties inspector whenever the stage is selected. The frame rate is not absolute, by the way; it can be affected during runtime by factors outside of the Flash player's control, such as the complexity of the movie or the load placed on the operating system by other applications running concurrently.

The movie dimensions set here are overridden by attributes of the HTML elements that embed the movie in a web page, though the attributes in the HTML generated by Flash when the movie is published will inherit the values set here. If the HTML page in which the movie is to be embedded is not the one that is generated by Flash during publishing (and this is usually the case), the two sets of dimensions (those set in the properties inspector and those set in the attributes of the HTML elements) should normally remain the same.[2] The background colour specified here is also overridden by the attributes of the HTML elements.

2 An exception to this rule is discussed in the 'Simple Form' example chapter.

Save the project in a place where it can be gotten at easily and publish the movie by choosing 'Publish' from the 'File' menu. Note that publishing a movie does not automatically save it - it is best to get into the habit of saving a project immediately after publishing it. Open the directory containing the saved project – it should contain two files, apart from the project file. One is the published movie, the other is the corresponding HTML file (the one generated during publishing). Take a look at the HTML file, or rather alter it by taking out the superfluous comments and adding a little indenting until it looks something like the following:

```
<HTML>
<HEAD>
<TITLE>Movie1</TITLE>
</HEAD>
<BODY bgcolor="#FFFFFF">

<OBJECT classid="clsid:D27CDB6E-AE6D-11cf-96B8-444553540000"
        codebase="http://..."
        WIDTH=550 HEIGHT=400>

  <PARAM NAME=movie VALUE="Movie1.swf">
  <PARAM NAME=quality VALUE=high>
  <PARAM NAME=bgcolor VALUE=#FFFFFF>

  <EMBED src="Movie1.swf"
         quality=high
         bgcolor=#FFFFFF
         WIDTH=550 HEIGHT=400
         TYPE="application/x-shockwave-flash"
         PLUGINSPAGE="http://..."/>

</OBJECT>

</BODY>
</HTML>
```

The values of the 'codebase' and 'PLUGINSPAGE' attributes have been shortened here, for readability. Note the presence of the attributes for the movie dimensions and background colour based on the values set in the properties inspector, as expected. Otherwise there is nothing much to note apart from the references to the movie itself, given as the 'src' attribute in the 'EMBED' element and the 'PARAM' element's 'VALUE' attribute in the 'OBJECT' element. Open the HTML file in a browser and keep it in the background. Each time the movie is revised and republished, the changes can be viewed by refreshing this page.[3]

[3] The reason for previewing a movie in this manner rather than testing it within Flash is that in real-world situations, movies cannot easily be divorced from the web pages in which they are embedded. A movie rarely ends up embedded in the page generated by Flash during publishing and in fact, this option is usually turned off. All of the example movies in this book, for example, are embedded in actively generated pages and configured via the (actively generated) movie URL. More on this later.

Symbols, instances and edit mode

Returning to Flash, click on the small white rectangle representing the first frame in the movie timeline and then click on the stage. Choose the rectangle tool from the 'Tools' toolbar and draw a relatively small rectangle. Switch back to the arrow tool and try selecting the rectangle's various constituent elements, namely its filling and four individual sides. Clicking on the stage at any time de-selects any currently selected elements, by the way.

Select all the elements either by dragging a selection box across the whole rectangle or by holding down the shift key and selecting each element in turn. Choose 'Convert to Symbol...' from the 'Insert' menu. The 'Convert to Symbol' dialog box should appear (Fig. 1.3):

Type 'FBox' in the 'Name' field and click 'OK'. This converts the rectangle shape into an instance of a symbol. Symbols are the basic building blocks of movies and come in three flavours: movie clips, buttons and graphics. Movie clips are basically mini movies, each with its own independent timeline; buttons have a special timeline with frames corresponding to the various button states; and graphics are simple elements with less functionality generally and a timeline that is synchronised with the main movie timeline.

Once the rectangle shape has been turned into a movie clip, its appearance on the stage changes. When selected, there is a blue bounding box around it and a black circle with a cross positioned at its top left-hand corner representing the coordinate centre. Try moving it around on the stage. Note that it is a single entity now whereas the previous rectangle shape had several constituent elements. Symbols can be reused as many times as needed and represent distinct elements in a movie. Their definitions are stored in the project library, which can be viewed by choosing 'Library' from the 'Window' menu (Fig. 1.4):

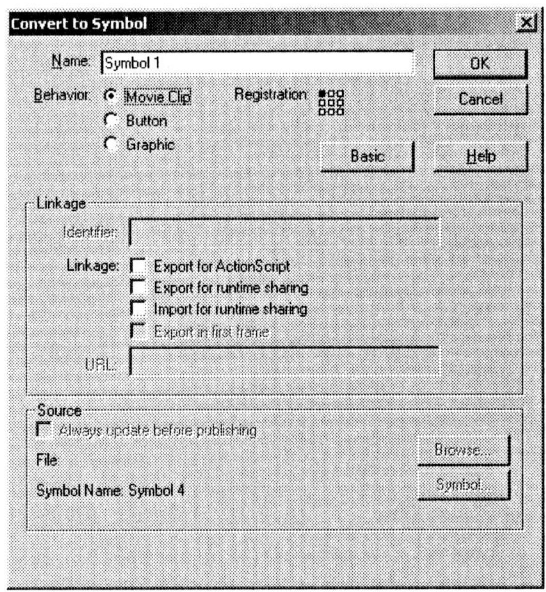

Fig. 1.3. The 'Convert to Symbol' dialog box.

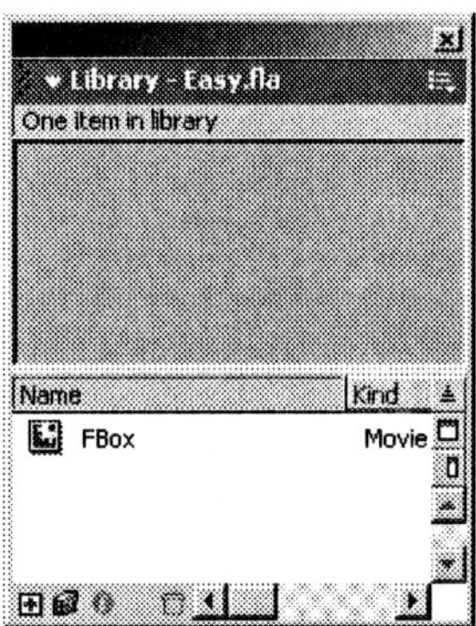

Fig. 1.4. A pint-sized library window.

Once a symbol (of any flavour) has been created, its definition stays in the library until it is explicitly deleted from there. In particular, removing the last instance of a symbol from the stage will not remove its definition from the library. Try removing the 'FBox' symbol from the stage and then dragging a couple of instances of it back from the library to prove this.

Right-click on the symbol in the library or on one of the instances on the stage and choose 'Edit' from the popup menu. Flash is now in edit mode (Fig. 1.5):

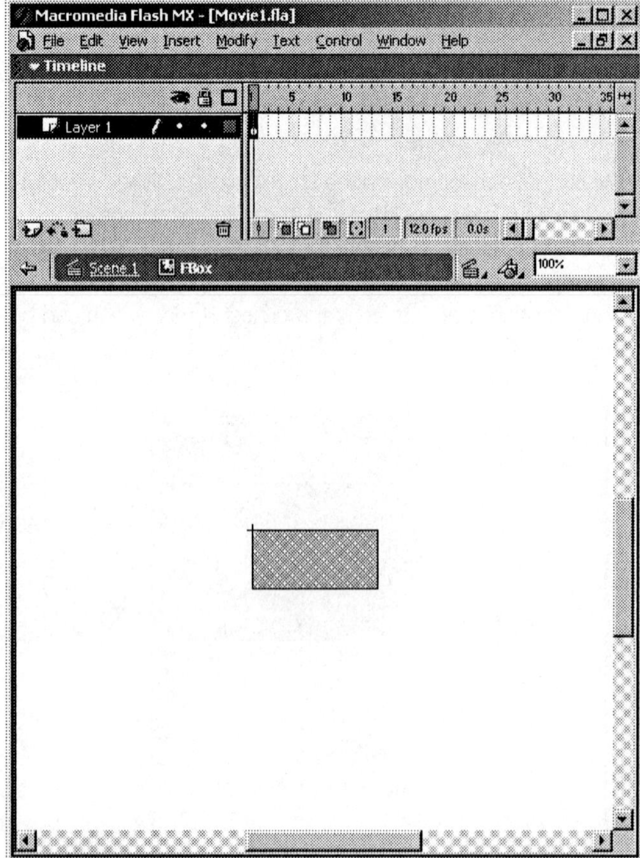

Fig. 1.5. Flash in edit mode.

The name of the symbol is visible under the timeline, next to the 'Scene 1' link. Select the fill and change its colour. Return to the stage view now by clicking on the 'Scene 1' link. Note how the appearance of both instances of the symbol reflects the changes made during edit mode. Double-clicking on a symbol or choosing 'Edit In Place' from the popup menu will put Flash into edit mode whilst keeping the stage visible, if a little transparent.

Layers, buttons and key frames

Delete one of the box instances, leaving just one on the stage. Double-click on the name of the layer in which it sits and rename it 'Box'. Create another empty layer by clicking on the small icon that looks like a folder with a plus sign next to it, just below the timeline. Call this new layer 'Button'. Make sure it is selected and draw another rectangle on the stage. Select it and turn it into a symbol, but a button this time, not a movie clip. Call it 'Button' and edit it. It should look something like Fig. 1.6:

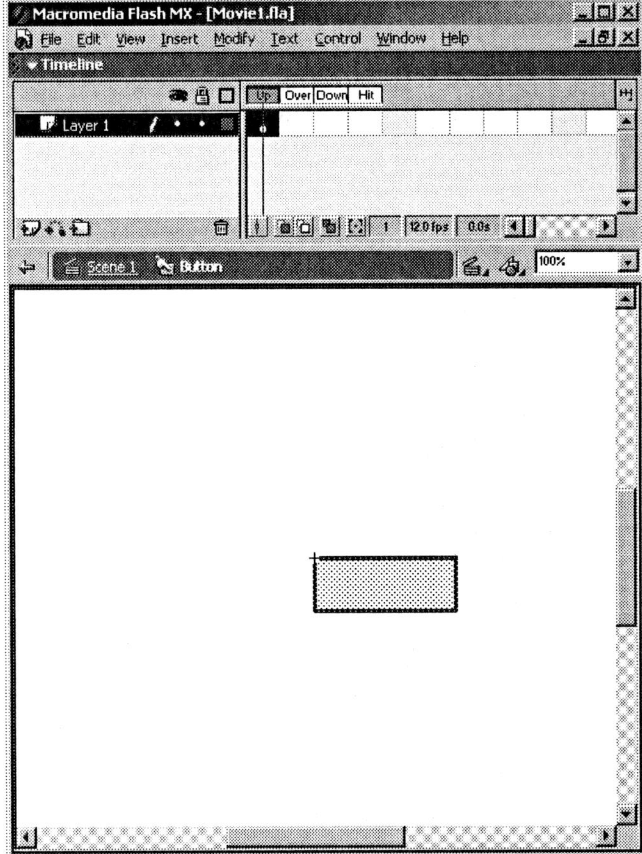

Fig. 1.6. An edited button with a button's timeline.

The timeline here differs from that of a movie clip symbol in that it has only four frames, each of which represents a button state. The fourth 'Hit' frame represents the hit area of the button and does not appear in the movie. If this frame is left blank, the hit area of the button is taken to be the amalgam of the contents of the other three frames. These frames do not necessarily have to contain graphics – they can be left blank and the appearance of the button will stay the same when activated or pressed.

Note that the graphic in the first frame still remains visible when the other frames in the button timeline are selected. The first frame is a special type of frame, known as a key frame, with frames that follow it continuing to show its contents until another key frame is created. If the 'Over' and 'Press' frames are to contain different graphics to the 'Up' frame then, key frames must be created to hold them. To do this, select the 'Over' frame in the timeline, say, and choose 'Blank Keyframe' from the 'Insert' menu. A white rectangle with a small empty circle will appear in the previously empty frame space. Do the same with the 'Press' frame.

Now, when these frames are selected, the initial graphic disappears. Fill these frames with the contents of the first frame by selecting it in the timeline, copying the contents to the clipboard, selecting one of the other frames and pasting the graphic in place by choosing 'Paste in Place' from the 'Edit' menu. This ensures that the pasted element occupies precisely the same place on the stage as the original. Select the 'Over' frame and change the colour of the graphic's filling there. Come out of edit mode and republish the movie to see the button in action.

Text fields, object script and button handlers

Create another layer, call it 'Debug' and drag it below the box layer. Make sure it is selected and choose the text tool from the 'Tools' toolbar. Click on the stage and drag the mouse down and to the right. Releasing the mouse button leaves a text field selected on the stage. Note how the appearance of the properties inspector changes to reflect the type of element selected. Choose 'Dynamic Text' from the drop-down list near the top left of the inspector and type 'debug' in the 'Var' field towards the bottom right. Change the text font to something easily readable such as Verdana and the text colour to red.[4]

Bring up the actions panel by choosing 'Actions' from the 'Window' menu. Hide the 'Actions toolbox' on the left side of the panel by clicking on the small elongated arrow button sitting halfway down the divider. Click on the small white icon just below the 'close' button in the top right of the panel and choose 'Expert mode' from the popup menu. Select the button on the stage and type the following into the actions panel:

```
on ( pressed ) {

    _root.debug += "button pressed\n";
}
```

Script associated with instances of symbols on the stage in this manner is called object script. Only event handlers are allowed in object script – stand-alone variable and method definitions are not.[5] Handlers are executed when certain events are triggered. The handler here is triggered when the button is pressed, obviously.

The body of the handler alters the contents of the debug field by changing the value of its associated variable, which was set in the properties inspector above. The prepended '_root' keyword signifies that the variable sits in the root timeline – in essence, it is a reference to the movie as a whole. Republish the movie and check that the button works.

4 I've found this simple debug field to be the most convenient way to print debug messages and use it in all the example and component projects. In particular, it replaces the use of the native trace( ) method, which I find laborious. Keep this debug field even in finished movies – it is easy enough to hide by simply moving it off the stage and it can then be brought back in the likely event that the movie behaves unexpectedly in a production environment.

5 Object script has a few idiosyncrasies. Read the 'Scope' appendix for further details.

Movie clip events

Event handlers can also be assigned to movie clips, where they relate to events such as the movie clip being unloaded or receiving data; or the frame head entering the frame in which the movie clip resides. The form for movie clip event handlers is slightly different to that for button handlers, the 'onClipEvent' keyword being used instead of just the 'on' keyword.

Select the box symbol on the stage and type the following script into the actions panel:

```
onClipEvent ( enterFrame ) {

	_x += 1;
	_y += 1;
}
```

The box should now move diagonally across the screen from its initial position when the movie is republished, the 'enterFrame' handler being invoked every time the playhead enters the frame in which the box resides. The direction of travel will be from left to right (as expected) and from top to bottom – the origin of Flash's coordinate system being the top left-hand corner of the stage, with y coordinates increasing in a downward direction.

Instance names and frame script

Select the box on the stage again and remove the associated object script from the actions panel. On selecting the box, the contents of the properties inspector should change (again). Towards the top left of the inspector will be a text field containing the greyed text '<Instance name>'. Replace this with 'box_mc'.

Create another layer, name it 'Actions' and drag it above the box layer. Click on its leftmost frame in the timeline and type the following into the actions panel:

```
_root.box_mc._x = Stage.width / 2;
_root.box_mc._y = Stage.height / 2;
```

Script associated with a frame in this manner is called frame script. Event handlers cannot be defined within frame script, they are never needed – frame scripts are simply executed every time the play head enters the frame. Unlike object scripts, frame scripts can contain variable and method definitions.

In this case, the box movie clip is referenced and positioned in the centre of the stage. It will not sit exactly in the centre however, because its own coordinate system is centred at its top left-hand corner. This can easily be rectified by editing the movie clip once more and centering its contents using the 'Align' panel (Fig. 1.7):

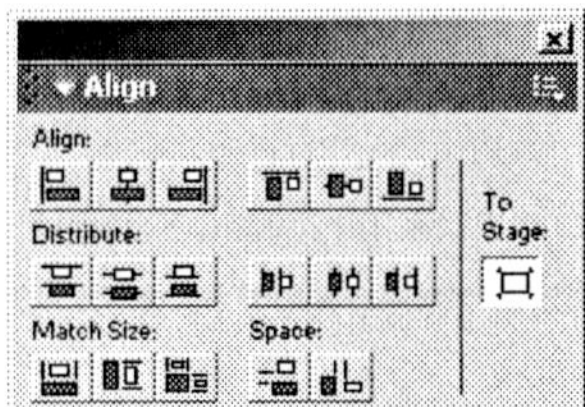

Fig. 1.7. The 'Align' panel.

Select the entire contents of the movie clip (these should be selected by default when the movie clip is first edited), make sure that the 'To Stage' toggle button is pressed and then press the second and fifth buttons in the top 'Align' row. Republish the movie and the box should appear exactly in the middle of the stage, as expected.

Generating movie clips dynamically

Delete the box movie clip again (for the last time) by deleting the layer in which it sits. Also delete the button layer, leaving just the debug and actions layers. The button definition can also be removed from the library at this stage, in fact, as it will not be needed again.

Right-click on the box movie clip definition in the library and select 'Linkage…' from the popup menu. The 'Linkage Properties' dialog box should appear (Fig. 1.8):

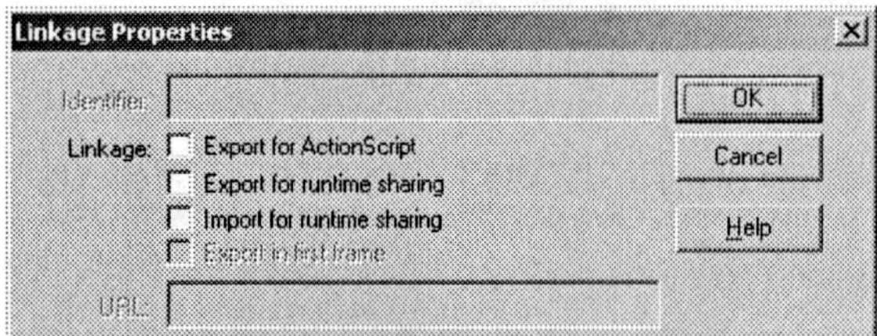

Fig. 1.8. The 'Linkage Properties' dialog box.

Check the 'Export for ActionScript' box, type 'FBoxSymbol' into the 'Identifier' text field (which will become active once the box is checked) and click 'OK'. Linkage identifiers give the movie clip definition a name and allow it to be referenced in the script, for various purposes. It is also possible to specify a linkage identifier in the 'Convert to Symbol' dialog box when a symbol is first created.[6]

Return to the actions panel, make sure the first frame in the actions layer is selected and type the following above the existing frame script:

```
_root.attachMovie( "FBoxSymbol", "box_mc", 0 );
```

Run the movie again – it should look identical. Instead of the box movie clip being present when the movie is published however, it has been created dynamically at runtime with the attachMovie( ) method. This method takes three parameters: the first is the linkage identifier of the movie clip definition in the library; the second is the instance name of the resultant movie clip instance; and the third is its depth, movie clips with higher depths appearing in front of those with lower ones. Depths must be unique – if two movie clips are created with the same depth, the one initially created will be unloaded to make way for the next.

Use of the prepended '_root' keyword here places the newly created box movie clip in the root timeline of the movie. Because movie clip instances created using the attachMovie( ) method become children of the movie clip instance on which the method is invoked, newly created movie clips can, in fact, be attached to any existing named movie clip instance. Components (which are usually comprised of many child elements) are usually built up in this way, for example.

6 I've covered this subject extremely briefly here but its importance is worth a little emphasis. Naming a symbol on the stage by way of the properties inspector identifies just that instance of the symbol, not the symbol definition itself. Assigning a linkage identifier on the other hand, identifies the symbol definition in the library. The obvious analogy is a Java or C++ class name (read 'linkage identifier'), as opposed to the name of a class instance (read 'instance name', clearly). Being able to reference the definitions of the symbols themselves is absolutely central to much of what follows.

Defining a class and associating it with a movie clip

Edit the box movie clip again, renaming the existing layer 'Graphic' (it will be called something like 'Layer 1' by default) and creating an actions layer above it. Make sure that the actions layer is selected and type the following script into the actions panel:[7]

```
#initclip

function FBoxClass()
{
    this.init();
}

FBoxClass.prototype = new MovieClip();
Object.registerClass( "FBoxSymbol", FBoxClass );

FBoxClass.prototype.init = function () {

    this.onEnterFrame = function () {

        this._x += 1;
        this._y += 1;
    }
}

#endinitclip
```

This script creates an FBoxClass class, associates it with the corresponding box movie clip definition and adds a class method for good measure. All the code is contained within an initialiser block, delimited by what appear to be two preprocessor instructions, #initclip and #endinitclip. Flash has no preprocessor as such but the inclusion of these instructions does ensure that this script will be executed at runtime before any frame or object script in the movie.

The class is created implicitly by way of defining its constructor, the constructor definition itself simply being a function definition, and the name of the method being the required name of the class. In the body of the constructor, the init( ) class method is invoked using the 'this' keyword, use of the 'prototype' keyword in the init( ) method definition here ensuring that it can be invoked on every instance of the class.[8]

The two most important lines lie between the definitions of the constructor and init( ) method. The first line calls the Object.registerClass( ) method with the linkage identifier of the movie clip definition and the name of the class, unquoted. This allows the 'this' keyword to be associated with both the movie clip and class instance simultaneously. The second line allows the class to extend the built-in MovieClip class, which defines all the properties and methods of movie clips.

The use of these two methods forms the backbone of most advanced Flash programming, and is absolutely essential to the working of complex movie clips and especially components. They amply demonstrate the duality of graphic elements and script that gives Flash its power. *I cannot stress enough that you must familiarise yourself completely with the full significance of these two lines of code.*

---

7 This chapter is not a comprehensive lesson in Flash object-oriented programming any more than it is a exhaustive tutorial on Flash design. Read the Flash documentation if the explanations here seem insufficient. Some other chapters may help your understanding of Flash classes if you are new to the subject, in particular the 'Profiling' and the 'The trouble with Flash class inheritance' appendices. The most important technique to grasp, which is explained in some detail here, is the symbiotic relationship between ActionScript classes and movie clip definitions.

8 Again, look at the appendices or the Flash documentation for further explanation.

The Flash event model and function objects

The init( ) method here sets the 'onEnterFrame' handler of the movie clip to an anonymous method that performs the same task as the object script previously associated with the instance of the box on the stage (since removed). Using a function object and the 'onEnterFrame' keyword (or any other keyword corresponding to a movie clip event, for that matter) is entirely analogous to using object script. Button handlers can also be defined in this way and can be applied directly to movie clip instances as well as button instances.

These constructs have replaced the use of object script in most cases, with the various event names used in this 'event model' closely resembling the corresponding names in the object script event handlers. The 'onEnterFrame' keyword corresponds to 'enterFrame' for example, 'onPress' to 'press' and so on.[9]

[9] Object script is not entirely obsolete, however. Defining movie-clip and button handlers in this 'old-fashioned' way can often reduce the complexity of frame script. See the 'Prices' and 'Volumes' movies for usage examples.

Using components

Components are basically complex movie clips that implement an interface to allow their configuration via the properties inspector when they are placed on the stage.[10] They are usually packaged into extensions and can be installed using Macromedia's extension manager.[11] Once installed, they are available from the components panel, shown in Fig. 1.9:

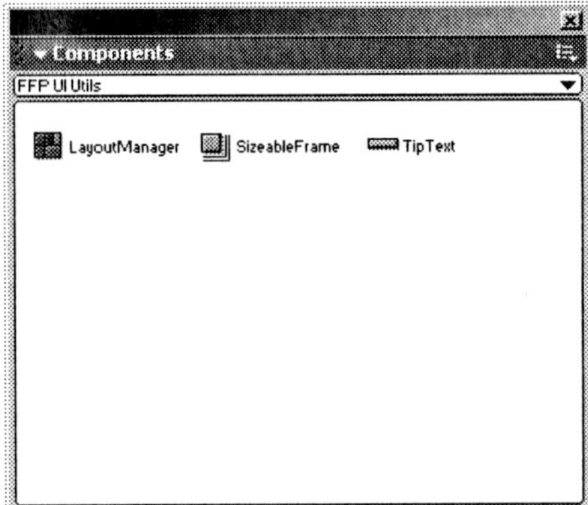

Fig. 1.9. The 'Components' panel showing the three 'UI Utils' components.

Flash comes preconfigured with several component extensions and there are many more available from the Macromedia exchange and third-party websites. This book also adds four more of its own: 'UI Utils', 'Lightweight', 'PopUp' and 'MultiListBox'.[12]

Components can be used by dragging them onto the stage from the components panel in much the same way that a symbol is dragged from the library. Being little more than complex movie clips, their definitions become available in the library once they have been dragged onto the stage and, in fact, they can be dragged directly into the library from the components panel if there is no need for instances to be left on the stage in the first place.

Most components are made up of several child elements and these are held by the components themselves as assets. These assets will also appear in the library when the component is used but will usually (if the component is well designed) appear in separate child folders.

When an instance of a component is selected on the stage, the appearance of the properties inspector will change to show the various properties that are available to configure it (Fig. 1.10):

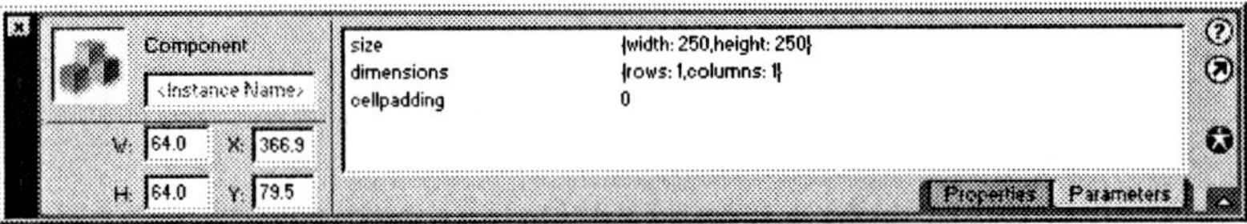

Fig. 1.10. The properties inspector showing some component properties.

---

10 Diverse definitions and explanations are given in the sections of this book dealing with both the example movies and the components themselves. For now, this definition will suffice when referring to component use as opposed to component design.

11 This is a free utility available from the Macromedia site. It comes with its own documentation and no instructions for its use are given here. It can also be used to package new extensions, and instructions for its use in this capacity are given in the 'Packaging extensions' appendix.

12 The components from these extensions are widely used in the example movies as well as being discussed in the components chapters and you should install all four before reading much further. Using a component in a project places it in the project library so there is actually no need to install all the components to get the example movies running, but it is a good idea to familiarise yourself with using the extension manager, nonetheless.

Here the size, dimensions and cellpadding of the 'LayoutManager' component are all available in the properties inspector and can be set directly without recourse to ActionScript. Other properties can be set by calling methods on the component instance once it has been given an instance name. Definitions of these methods should be listed in the reference panel (again, if the component is well designed), brought up by choosing 'Window>Reference' from the main menu.

If new revisions of existing components become available, these can be reloaded into Flash using the extension manager.[13] This does not mean that the projects in which they are used are automatically updated, however. The revised components should be dragged onto the stage or into the library, forcing Flash to update both the components and their child elements. The existing component instances will be updated and Flash will probably ask for confirmation that the child elements should be replaced too (Fig. 1.11). Always select 'Replace existing component (not undoable)' from this dialog.

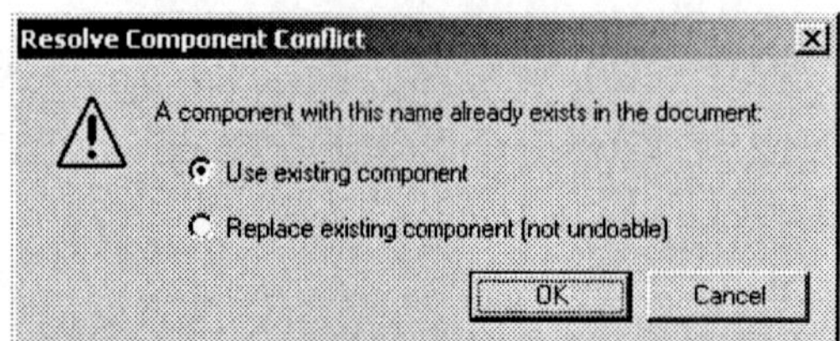

Fig. 1.11. The 'Resolve Component Conflict' dialog box.

Components have linkage identifiers and can therefore be created at runtime using the attachMovie( ) method, as long as the component definition itself is already present in the library. The fourth, optional argument of the attachMovie( ) method is useful when instantiating components, with the elements of the associative array effectively replacing the properties available in the properties inspector:

```
_root.attachMovie( "FLayoutManagerSymbol", "layout_mc", 0, {cellpadding:10} );
```

13 The components that come with the examples distribution are probably not the latest versions. I suggest you use the versions that come with the examples distribution when reading through this book and upgrade to the latest ones when using the examples (or your own movies) for real-world applications.

Applying style properties

Many components, including the pre-installed ones provided by Flash together with most of the components written for this book, admit the use of style properties. These allow certain aspects of components such as colour and font metrics to be altered programmatically. The complete list of styles available in the Flash UI extensions is given in the Flash documentation, with the components in this book adding a couple more.

There are two main methods of applying styles to components. Firstly, they can be applied to all the components in a movie at once by using the 'globalStyleFormat' object. The following code will set the background colour and font of all components in a movie:

```
globalStyleFormat.background = "0x336666";
globalStyleFormat.textFont = "Verdana";
globalStyleFormat.applyChanges();
```

The applyChanges( ) method must be called once the style properties have been set in this manner before the changes will take effect. Alternatively, style properties can be applied to individual component instances by invoking the setStyleProperty( ) method:

```
input_mc.setStyleProperty( "highlight", "0xcccccc" );
```

Note that there is no need for an applyChanges( ) method here. A style property set using the setStyleProperty( ) method will override the equivalent global style, if it has been set.

1.2: The Source Distribution

Choosing a web server and a server side language

Download and unzip the source distribution and place it somewhere handy. There are very few situations when the directory structure cannot be left exactly as it is.[14] The example and component movies themselves are presented as active websites and will not work without the supporting server side processes. You must therefore install and configure (or have access to) a combination of a web server and a server side language and be wholly satisfied that it is running properly before attempting to configure the source distribution itself.

Movies can interact with any combination of web server and server side language. It makes no more sense to ask whether or not a movie can communicate with, say, Apache or ASP than asking whether or not a particular browser can do so. It is important to bear this fact in mind when choosing a server solution and not choose one in the belief that it can communicate with Flash more easily than any other. In particular, proprietary server solutions (the ones that cost money) will not do a better job of communicating with Flash than the well-known and freely available ones.

The choice of web server software is therefore completely arbitrary – it simply does not matter which one is used. The choice of server side language, on the other hand, is limited to those which the source distribution supports. The options are Perl, PHP, Java servlets and ASP.[15] No particular configuration is needed for any of these languages, with the exception of Java, where both the 'config' directory and the GNU regular expressions package contained in the 'lib' directory must be included in the classpath.

Given the number of combinations of web server software, platforms and languages available, it is beyond the scope of this book to provide detailed instructions on how to install and configure any of them, with one exception.[16]

For web servers running locally for the express purpose of running the source distribution, the document root can simply be set to point to the topmost 'ffp' directory of the source distribution and the default page should be set to the 'Index.html' file found therein. If the web server was previously tested after installation by typing 'localhost' into a browser (on whatever port) and viewing something along the lines of an introductory page from the server vendor, the 'Index.html' file of the source distribution should now be visible instead.

In the case of shared access to a web server, or with several applications running on the same local server, it probably needs to be configured to run the source distribution as a 'web application' rather than as the root site. The default page of the web application should still point to the 'Index.html' file however, regardless of where the 'ffp' directory needs to be placed.

14 Some servlet engines may insist that you move the 'classes' directory containing the Java source files into a 'WEB-INF' directory in order to conform to the servlet specification. Otherwise, I cannot think of a situation when the original directory structure needs any alteration at all. You can easily break the examples by moving things around without due care so try to avoid do doing so unless you familiarise yourself fully with the server code first.

15 These are the available options as the book goes to press. If you want to use another language, you will have to write the code yourself. The implementations are functionally equivalent and well documented so you should be able to port them to your language of preference without too much difficulty.

16 The exception is the Resin servlet engine and instructions for installing it on a Windows box are given below. I cannot do a better job of explaining how to install any particular web server or server side language than the relevant documentation and if things do not go according to plan, it is to the relevant FAQs and user groups for that you need to turn for help, not this book.

Installing and configuring Resin

If the thought of setting up a web server and a server side language is simply too daunting to even contemplate, this section gives instructions on how to install and configure Resin,[17] a lightweight servlet engine for Windows that also doubles as a web server. It can be downloaded from the Caucho site at the following URL:

http://www.caucho.com/download/

Resin needs the Java SDK and not just the Java runtime. Download and run the relevant Java SDK setup program if necessary. It can probably be obtained at the following URL:

http://java.sun.com/j2se/

There is no install program for Resin – just unzip it and place it in its own directory. The 'C:\Program Files' directory is one option but a better alternative is to place it somewhere like 'C:\resin', giving easy access to the configuration files and avoiding troublesome spaces in the directory path. There is a setup binary in the 'bin' directory of the distribution but this is a helper program for configuring web servers to run Resin as a servlet runner and can be safely ignored. Uninstalling Resin pretty much means just deleting the installation directory.

Open a DOS box and navigate to the 'bin' directory. Run the stand-alone web server by typing 'httpd' and hitting return. If this fails to run, almost certainly it cannot find the correct path to the Java distribution. By far the easiest way to fix this is to use the 'java_home' command line argument. Try typing 'httpd –java_home C:\java', for example, if the Java SDK is installed in the 'C:\java' directory.[18]

Type http://localhost:8080/ into a browser to bring up the welcome page served by Resin. It uses the default 'doc' directory and displays the 'index.html' file in there. Check that the servlet examples work correctly, and if they do Resin is fully installed.

17 Resin is not free, except for hobbyists, students, etc.

18 Or you can set the 'JAVA_HOME' environment variable, if you prefer. I've never known Resin not to run successfully once it can find the Java distribution.

To run the source distribution, Resin's configuration file needs to be changed. It is called 'resin.conf' and can be found in the 'conf' directory of the install directory. Replace it with the one supplied in the 'resin' directory of the source distribution. Resin keeps a copy of the default configuration file in the 'conf/samples' directory so it can always be restored at a later date, if required. The configuration file itself is an XML file:

```
<caucho.com>

    <http-server>

        <!-- application directory-->
        <app-dir>d:\ffp\</app-dir>

        <!-- the http port -->
        <httpd-port>8080</httpd-port>

        <!-- application classpath, with source directory for re-compilation -->
        <classpath id='classes' source='classes' compile='true'/>

        <!-- how often to check servlets for changes -->
        <class-update-interval id='2'/>

        <!-- configuration classpath -->
        <classpath id='config'/>

        <!-- GNU regex classpath -->
        <classpath id='lib/gnu-regexp-1.1.4.jar'/>

        <!-- error log -->
        <error-log id='log/error.log'/>

        <!-- special mapping so /servlet/<servletName> invokes <servletName> -->
        <servlet-mapping url-pattern='/servlet/*' servlet-name='invoker'/>

    </http-server>
</caucho.com>
```

The value of the 'app-dir' element will probably have to be altered to reflect the install directory of the source distribution but otherwise, this configuration should work as-is. Note that a port number of 8080 is specified explicitly here even though this is the default. It can be changed to 80 (the default port for HTTP) if preferred.

The path for the servlet class files is given next in the first 'classpath' element. Resin can compare the time stamps of a servlet class file to its corresponding source file and recompile the latter if necessary. This option is turned on here by setting the 'source' attribute to point to the directory containing the relevant Java source files (the same directory that contains the class files, in fact) and setting the 'compile' attribute to 'true'. The following 'class-update-interval' element specifies how often Resin compares these two set of files, in seconds. A second 'classpath' element enables Resin to find the source distribution configuration file, namely 'java.config'; and a third element enables it to find the GNU regular expressions package included in the source distribution.

An error log is specified in the 'error-log' element, which should be the first place to look if Resin appears to be working but the source distribution is not. Lack of a trailing slash in the filename means the file is placed relative to the Resin installation directory. The last element instructs Resin to match any name to the same servlet class name when it is preceded by 'servlet/'. The relative URL 'servlet/helloworld' will run the 'helloworld' servlet, for example.

Once the necessary changes have been made to the configuration file Resin can be restarted, and refreshing the browser should bring up the source distribution's static index page.

Configuring the source distribution

The index page contains four sets of links, corresponding to each of the server side languages supported by the source distribution. Being statically generated,[19] the links contained therein are essentially hardcoded and it is doubtful whether they will work with all but a minority of possible server configurations. Regardless of whether they work or not however, a useful first step in configuring the source distribution is to manually edit the index page and remove all the links that do not relate to your particular choice of server side language, leaving just one set of four links.

The remaining links must be altered (manually, again) to work with your particular server configuration. If the right set of links has been chosen, probably the only task necessary is to prepend the path corresponding to the web application. Get the topmost 'Hello, world!' link working first. It points to the most vacuous of server side processes that does nothing but print out an HTML page. *You must get both this link and the server process to which it points working before proceeding any further*. Once you have done this, amend the other links accordingly.

In order to get the source distribution to work with your server setup, its internal configuration will most likely need changing. The configuration variables are held in a file in the 'config' directory (one for each server side language, in fact). The following listing is in pseudo-code but the contents of the files corresponding to each server side language will be similar:

```
CONFIG{ "rootDir" } = "D:/ffp/"
CONFIG{ "appPath" } = "/"
CONFIG{ "procPath" } = "servlet/"
CONFIG{ "procExt" } = ""
```

All the data needed to deduce the values of these variables for any particular server configuration is already available in the form of where the source distribution has been placed, which set of links has been left undeleted and which path has been prepended to those links in order to get the 'Hello, world!' link working.

The topmost variable points to the location of the source distribution. It has nothing at all to do with the web application, it is simply the full path name of the 'ffp' directory and must include a trailing slash. The remaining three variables can all be deduced by inspecting the values of the amended hyperlinks. Consider the following cases, for example. Each link points to the 'Hello, world!' server process, but running on various server configurations:

```
/cgi-bin/helloworld.cgi
/servlet/helloworld
/examples/servlet/helloworld
/usr/jones/helloworld.php
/helloworld.asp
```

19 Statically generated by the web server that is, not the file system – you should have a web server up and running by now, with the index page being shown as the default page.

Firstly, the 'appPath' variable. This is essentially the default, relative URL of the web application. If the index page is set to be the root document of the web server, its value may just be a forward slash. Otherwise, it is the full path of the relative URL to the left of 'helloworld', minus any directory or alias that is specific to the server side language, such as 'cgi-bin/' or 'servlet/'. In the first, second and fifth cases above for example, its value is '/'; in the third case, '/examples/'; and in the fourth case, '/usr/jones/'. Note the use of forward slashes at both the start and at the end of the variable. The convention for the source distribution is that it always includes a leading forward slash and a trailing forward slash as well, if necessary.

The 'procPath' variable should be set to the relevant alias or directory of the server side process. It should not include a leading forward slash but must include a trailing one. In the first case, its value is 'cgi-bin/' for example; in the second and third cases, 'servlet/'; in the fourth and fifth it remains empty.

The 'procExt' variable should be set to the extension of the server side process (if it has one) and should include a leading dot if necessary. In the first case its value is '.cgi'; in the second and third cases it is empty; in the fourth case it is '.php'; and in the fifth case, '.asp'.

Make a note of the three last configuration variables once they have been deduced. Concatenate them in order and include 'helloworld' between the 'procPath' and 'procExt' variables. The result should be a correctly formed URL matching exactly the URL in the topmost hyperlink. Place the values in the relevant configuration file and click on the 'Test movie' link. This page contains a simple test movie that queries a server process and reports the results:

```
The request URI is '/servlet/test?data=all'
The loaded variables are 'Hello,' and ' world!'
```

The first line shows the request URL that the embedded movie has generated from the configuration variables. Here the server process name is 'test', not 'helloworld', otherwise the principle is precisely the same. The second line shows that the movie has successfully queried the server and obtained the values of two variables. Of course, the request URL here will differ according to your own server configuration, this being just an example.

Once this movie works, the whole source distribution will work without further ado. Go back to the index page and click on the links for the examples and components sites and bookmark these pages.

1.3: Getting into the Details

Loading data into a movie

Flash has an efficient and robust technique for loading data into a movie at runtime, namely the loadVariables( ) method. It works by populating a target symbol with variable definitions contained in a data stream conforming to a specific format. The first argument specifies the URL of the resource containing the variable definitions, known as the request URL, whilst the second argument specifies the symbol instance which receives them when the method is invoked.

Open the test movie project in the 'movie/Test' directory of the source distribution. The loadVariables( ) method is called at the end of the loadVars( ) method in the root script. For now, comment out the line setting the 'uri' variable, adding a line that references a local text file instead:

```
function loadVars () {

/// var uri = app + "?data=all";
    var uri = "Test.txt";

    debug += "The request URL is '" + uri + "'\n";

    loadVariables( uri, loader );
}
```

Edit the movie publish settings by choosing 'Publish settings...' from the 'File' menu, check the 'HTML' box to generate the corresponding HTML page, republish the movie and launch the HTML page. The movie should now display the following in the debug field:

```
The request URL is 'Test.txt'
The loaded variables are 'Hello,' and ' world!'
```

The first line of the debug field is set in the loadVars( ) method before the actual call to the loadVariables( ) method, then there is a short pause (a very short pause in fact, since the data is loaded from a source sitting right next to the movie on the local file system) before the variables themselves become available in the target symbol.

Target symbols are by convention left empty, with an instance being placed in the exact, top left-hand corner of the stage. It is also good practice to place them in their own layer and to lock it once the required object script has been added. Empty symbols are represented on the stage by a white dot with a black border, by the way.

The object script attached to the target symbol contains an event handler for the 'data' event, triggered when the last remaining variable has been loaded into the movie. Variables should never be used until this event is triggered. In this case, the data handler calls the displayVars( ) method in the root script, passing the values of the two variables defined in the data file:

```
onClipEvent( data ) {

    _root.displayVars( var1, var2 );
}
```

Note that there is no processing of the variables as such – they simply appear 'as if by magic' and can be used immediately the 'data' event has been triggered. Open the 'Test.txt' data file to see the two variable definitions:

```
var1=Hello%2C&var2=+world%21&
```

The format is identical to GET requests and should be familiar from countless URLs in any browser address bar. All the definitions must appear on the one line – carriage returns in a data file are anathema to Flash.[20] The variable definitions themselves are delimited by ampersands (including a trailing one, for safety's sake), the name and value of each being encoded and placed either side of an equals sign.

Encoding variable names and values in this way ensures that they do not break the data format. Both the ampersand and equals signs have a special significance for example, so they cannot be used in variable names and values without first being encoded. Generally, most non-alpha numeric characters are encoded. The specific rules are:

1. The ASCII characters 'a' through 'z', 'A' through 'Z', '0' through '9', and '.', '-', '*', '_' remain the same.
2. The space character is converted into a plus sign '+' (the plus sign is encoded according to the third rule below).
3. All other characters are converted into the 3-character string '%xy', where xy is the two-digit hexadecimal representation of the lower 8-bits of the character.

Returning to the text file above, the comma after the 'Hello' is encoded to '%2C', the space before the 'world' to a plus sign and so on. It is possible to relax these rules a little for Flash data, but it is not recommended.

Although the Flash data format does not support arrays or dot syntax, arrays (even multidimensional ones) can be mimicked by including indices in the variable names, as in 'var1' and 'var2' above. Furthermore, the movie need not be written knowing the exact form of the data in advance, the number of variables in the data file can vary, for example. Change the contents of the 'Test.txt' file to the following ...

```
var1=This&var2=+is&var3=+another&var4=+example%2E&count=4&
```

... and the object script associated with the target symbol to:

```
onClipEvent( data ) {

    var tmpVal = "";
    for ( var i = 1; i <= count; i++ ) {

        tmpVal += eval( "var"+i );
    }
    _root.debug += tmpVal;
}
```

Here the 'count' variable is used to break the 'for' loop once all the other variables have been used. Note the order of the variable definitions in the text file – the 'count' variable is actually defined last, even though it is used first. The order does not matter however, all the variables being loaded before the 'data' handler is triggered.

20 Encoded carriage returns can be included as parts of variable values, of course. The list file interpreter supports this functionality and the 'Dynamic Text' example movie makes use of it. See the 'The custom tag library' appendix for more details.

Configuring a movie via the movie URL

Replace the original code in the loadVars( ) method, including the initial definition of the 'uri' variable (delete the one pointing to the 'Test.txt' file). Remove the HTML generation option from the publish settings, republish the movie and run it as part of the source distribution. The variable definitions should load as before, even though the reference to the 'Test.txt' file has been replaced by a URL pointing to a server process.

The server process is evidently returning the same data as the static text file, but before looking at this mechanism in detail, it is worth asking how the request URL is constructed in the first place and in particular, where does the value of the 'app' variable which makes up the bulk of the request URL come from? This variable is declared right at the top of the root script:

```
/// Variables set from without
var app;
```

Declared, but not defined. But a glance at the debug field reveals that it is certainly getting defined somewhere:

```
The request URL is '/servlet/test?data=all'
The loaded variables are 'Hello,' and ' world!'
```

Here its value is '/servlet/test', although it will probably be different for your server configuration. It is not defined anywhere in the movie itself, so where is 'without'? To find out, view the source of the HTML page from the browser and look at the HTML that embeds the movie there. In particular, look at the 'VALUE' and 'SRC' attributes of the 'OBJECT' and 'EMBED' elements respectively. They should both be the same:

```
/movies/Test/Test.swf?app=%2Fservlet%2Ftest&
```

The reference to the movie looks just like a GET request, the definition of the 'app' variable being appended to the movie name in the same manner as a form variable. This movie reference, complete with variable definitions, is commonly known as the movie URL. Variables defined in this manner are immediately available on the root timeline of the movie.[21]

The declaration of the 'app' variable in the root script is optional. It is not necessary to declare variables defined in the movie URL any more than it is necessary to declare those defined as a result of the loadVariables( ) method being invoked. It is good practice to declare variables however, if not to avoid possible name clashes (Flash ignores variable declarations), then at least to warn of them.

21 A most convenient setup! Every movie in the source distribution makes use of this mechanism in order to retrieve certain variables without having to query the server first. In fact, it would be impossible to support different server side languages without being able to communicate the correct request URL to the movie in the first place.

Receiving data over the Internet

Returning to the static 'Test.txt' file reference for a moment, it is worth noting that such a reference will work not just on the local file system, but also over a network or even the Internet, provided the file is sitting in the right place.[22]

Consider a simple hyperlink in a web page. The fully qualified URL of its target does not have to be given – a relative URL will suffice. For example, if a website contains two pages, 'Home.html' and 'Contact.html' and both reside in the same directory, in order for a hyperlink in the former to point to the latter, a simple target of 'Contact.html' will do.

Web servers do not understand such shortened, relative URLs however, only fully qualified ones. A glance at the access log of any web server proves this. The browser therefore has to append the remainder of the URL before passing on the request. It retrieves this by inspecting the URL of the page in which the hyperlink is embedded, removing the last portion, the 'Home.html' portion in this case, and appending 'Contact.html' instead.

This behaviour is also apparent when the loadVariables( ) method is used, the reason being that the Flash player does not communicate directly with the web server but instead makes its request via the parent browser. Thus, relative or absolute request URLs are converted into fully qualified ones before being passed onto the web server. Furthermore, the browser may cache the data requested by a movie in the same way that it caches web pages, unless specific instructions are given not to do so.[23]

22 I have to admit that when running the source distribution using Resin, I was at a loss as to where to place the 'Test.txt' file so that a simple 'Test.txt' URL would pick it up. The lesson seems to be not to rely on relative URLs (the ones with no leading forward slash) in movie requests but to always use absolute ones.

23 Sometimes even an explicit instruction in the HTTP header is not enough to stop a browser caching data. Read the 'HTTPS' appendix for a sure-fire method of forcing a browser to always reload movie data.

1.4: My Method

Serving data to a movie

Not only can the first argument of the loadVariables( ) method be any valid URL, the URL itself can point to any server side process, not just a remote static file. As long as the server process generates content that conforms to the Flash data format, the movie will not be able to tell the difference.[24]

The situation is entirely analogous to that of a server process generating HTML for a browser. The following server process for example, written in pseudo code …

```
/* Print the HTTP header */
PRINT "Content-type: text/html\n\n";

/* Print the HTML */
PRINT "<HTML>";
PRINT "   <HEAD>";
PRINT "      <TITLE>";
PRINT "Hello, world!";
PRINT "      </TITLE>";
PRINT "   </HEAD>";
PRINT "   <BODY>";
PRINT "Hello, world!";
PRINT "   </BODY>";
PRINT "</HTML>";
```

… looks identical to the following static HTML file, to a browser at least:

```
<HTML>
<HEAD>
<TITLE>Hello, world!</TITLE>
</HEAD>
<BODY>
Hello, world!
</BODY>
</HTML>
```

No browser can tell the difference between HTML printed out by a server process in this manner and HTML printed out by a web server. The two data streams are simply indistinguishable. All a web server does when serving a file is to print out the required HTTP header before printing out the contents of the file, line by line, just like the server process.

Similarly, a movie cannot tell the difference between variable definitions in a text file (whether provided by the local file system or served by a web server) and variable definitions provided by a server process such as the following:

```
/* Print the HTTP header */
PRINT "Content-type: application/x-www-urlformencoded\n\n";

/* Print the variable definitions */
PRINT "var1=Hello%2C&";
PRINT "var2=+world%21&";
```

24 This should be obvious by now, since the previous chapters have alluded to it.

Furthermore, since any server process can produce a data stream that is indistinguishable from a 'statically' served file, it follows that any server process is as good as any other at providing data to a movie. It is the type and format of the data that counts, not the mode of delivery. This is a subtle but important point.

The first line printed out by both the pseudo code listings above is known as the HTTP header, which allows hidden data to be passed to the browser before the main content itself is served, the two parts (header and body) being separated a double carriage return. HTTP headers need not be included in static files – the web server itself is responsible for printing them, but server processes must explicitly print them.

Here, the HTTP header is used to specify the MIME type of the content. MIME types are made up of two parts – major and minor, the major part specifying to which group the content belongs, such as a text or binary stream; and the minor part specifying the exact nature of the content, such as HTML or form data. The MIME type of HTML for example, is 'text/html', whilst a plain text document, ending in a '.txt' extension, has a MIME type of 'text/plain'.

The MIME type of Flash data is officially the same as that of a GET request (HTTP requests have HTTP headers as well as responses), namely the rather cumbersome 'application/x-www-urlformencoded', but in fact 'text/plain' will do.[25]

25 Unlike failing to encode variables in Flash data files, replacing the 'official' MIME type of Flash data with the far more manageable 'text/plain' type does not seem to cause any problems. I doubt whether the Flash player even checks.

List files and their interpretation

It is practically impossible to maintain Flash data files of any size. The 'Test.txt' file used by the test movie is manageable, perhaps, but it contains just two variable definitions. Data files containing more than just a few variables become wholly unworkable. At the very least a mechanism is needed that allows variable definitions to be stored unencoded and on separate lines, so as to make them human-readable.

These simplified data files could be processed 'offline' to provide the necessary Flash data format files, which can then be made handy for movies to access statically. This solution becomes troublesome if the data is constantly changing over time, however. A better approach is to interpret the simplified data files with a server process in real time. If the design of the new, simplified data format is straightforward enough, the interpreter can be implemented in any server side language.[26]

Consider the contents of 'Test.txt' file again. Removing the encoding and ampersands and placing the variable definitions on individual lines gives the following:

```
var1=Hello,
var2= world!
```

This is considerably easier on the eyes than the original Flash data file. Now consider the equivalent simplified data for the amended 'Test.txt' file, the one containing the count variable:

```
var1=This
var2= is
var3= another
var4= example.
count=4
```

These two straightforward examples amply demonstrate the utility of a simplified data format. Such 'list files', as they are called, can be found in the 'data' directory of the source distribution. Some of them are quite lengthy, but all are perfectly readable.

26 I stand by this solution always. Although the overall model for the server processes used in the source distribution is perhaps not suitable for every occasion, the use of these simplified data files certainly is. Flash data files are utterly unusable and it is natural to remove the encoding and ampersands to produce a workable, alternative format. You may call list files by a different name and write your own interpreters but after several years' use, I have yet to come up with a better alternative.

The interpretation of these list files is a simple matter of re-encoding the name-value pairs and concatenating them together with the required delimiting ampersands. In pseudo code, a list file interpreter would look something like this:

```
FUNCTION template_data ( template ) {

  /* interpret and print out the list file line by line */
  WHILE ( ( line = READLINE( template ) ) != _EOF )
  {
    /* chop off the trailing carriage return */
    CHOP( line );

    /* split the line at the 'equals' sign */
    ( name, value ) = SPLIT( line, "=" );

    /* encode the name and value */
    name = ENCODE( name );
    value = ENCODE( value );

    /* print out the encoded definition and trailing ampersand */
    PRINT name + "=" + value + "&";
  }
}
```

This is hardly a difficult program to implement, in any language. Here it is written as a method called template_data( ) rather than as a stand-alone program. The list file is passed as the 'template' argument and the converted lines are printed directly to the standard output stream.[27]

27 The real list file interpreters in the source distribution are slightly more complex, allowing variable definitions to spill over from one line to the next and including support for custom tags. Custom tags are discussed in the next section or, if you must, see the 'Custom tag library' appendix.

The source distribution server model

Only a basic understanding is needed of how a server process works in order to use the examples in this book, the test server process providing a prototype on which all the other server processes are more or less based.

The test server process not only supplies data to the movie but also supplies HTML to the browser, working out which of the two clients has made the request by checking for the presence of the 'data' form variable in the request URL (a glance at the debug field of the test movie reveals that the request URL is identical to the URL of the web page in which it is embedded, except for the addition of a 'data' form variable). The actual value of this 'data' form variable is immaterial, but its presence signifies a request from the movie, its absence, a request from the browser.

In pseudo code, the test server process looks like this:

```
USE Utils;
USE Template;

{
   /* Retrieve the value of the "data" form variable */
   data = FORM( "data" );

   IF ( data != null ) {

      /* Print out the data HTTP header */
      utils_dataheader();

      /* Process and print out the list file */
      template_data( CONFIG{ "rootDir" } + "data/Test.txt" );
   }
   ELSE {

      /* Print out the HTML HTTP header */
      utils_HTMLheader();

      /* Process and print out the HTML page */
      template_HTML( CONFIG{ "rootDir" } + "template/Test.html" );
   }
}
```

The value of the 'data' form variable is retrieved first. If it is non-null, the server process responds with Flash data, otherwise it responds with HTML. Utility methods print the relevant HTTP headers whilst the data itself is printed out using the list file interpreter for the Flash data or another, similar interpreter for the HTML. Both are contained in a separate 'Template' server module. The utility methods are also to be found in a separate server module, called 'Utils'.

Because the only difference between the movie's request URL and the URL of the web page in which it is embedded is the presence of the 'data' form variable, it is possible to see exactly how the server process responds to the movie request by simply appending this variable to the URL in the browser address bar.

Before doing so however, it is necessary to change the MIME type of the Flash data to 'text/plain', many browsers not being configured to print data with a MIME type of 'application/x-www-urlformencoded' to the screen. To do this, comment out the call to the method that prints the Flash data MIME type, called utils_dataheader( ) in the pseudo-code listing above and replace it with the method to print the MIME type of plain text data. Recompile the server process if necessary and make the change to the URL in the browser address bar.[28] The result is shown in Fig. 1.12:

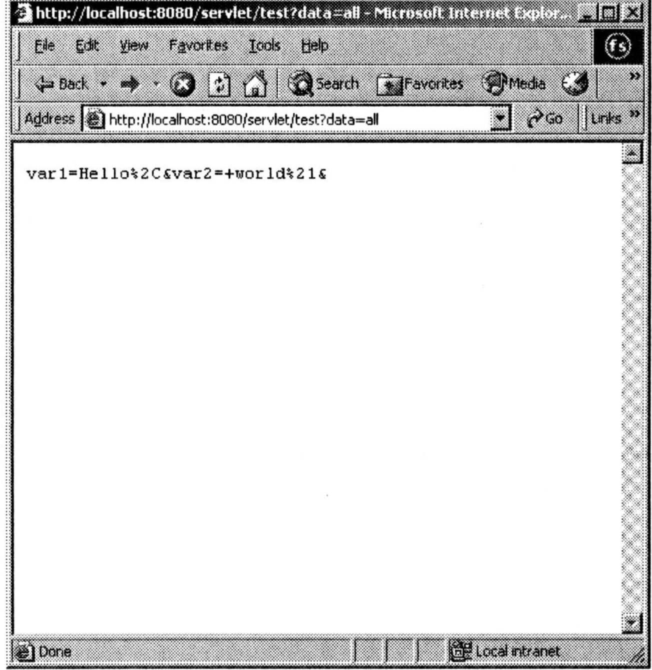

Fig. 1.12. Flash data displayed by the browser.

The data supplied by the test server process in response to a request from the test movie (which is essentially what the browser address bar now contains) is indeed identical to the contents of the 'Test.txt' file. It is the list file interpreter, invoked by the template_data( ) call in the test server process and processing the 'Test.txt' list file in the 'data' directory of the source distribution (and not the file of the same name that sits next to the test movie), that is responsible for this output. Edit this list file and change its contents then refresh the browser to see the immediate results.

Viewing the server's response to a movie request in this way can be extremely useful for debugging. The exact procedure is: change the MIME type of the response to 'text/plain', recover the request URL being used by the movie (by printing it to the debug field, say) then copy this URL to the browser address bar. This is usually enough to determine the cause of the problem and, in particular, it will discover fatal server errors which are pretty much undetectable from within the movie itself.

28 This is the only time in the book when I suggest that changes are made to the server process code, and with the exception of the appendices, the server processes are not mentioned again after this chapter. It is advisable to have some idea of their inner workings however, hence the suggestion that the simple test server process be altered and recompiled.

Adding variables to the list and template HTML files

With the 'data' form variable still appended to the URL in the browser address bar, change the 'Test.txt' list file to the following:

```
var1=Hello,
var2= world!
data=<<data>>
```

Refresh the browser – the 'data' form variable should be echoed:

```
var1=Hello%2C&var2=+world%21&data=all&
```

The list file interpreter has replaced the custom <<data>> tag with the value of the 'data' form variable.[29] Add further form variables manually to the URL in the address bar and then add the corresponding special tag to the list file. They should always be echoed. The encoded values of the source distribution configuration variables can also be printed out in this way. Try the following list file:

```
var1=Hello,
var2= world!
data=<<data>>
rootDir=<<rootDir>>
```

So the genuine list file interpreters in the source distribution do far more than just convert simple list files back into the Flash data format. They can also recognise custom tags and convert them into the appropriate form and configuration variables.

Interpreters are also used to print out the HTML so that these custom tags can be included in the HTML template files, too. Consider the 'Test.html' file in the 'template' directory of the source distribution. The appending of the 'app' variable definition to the movie name in the 'OBJECT' and 'EMBED' elements there is done using a custom tag, as is the prepending of the 'appPath' configuration variable:[30]

```
<<appPath>>movies/Test/Test.swf?<<TEST>>
```

29 See the 'Custom tag library' appendix for more information on these custom tags and the enhanced list and template HTML file interpreters that process them.
30 Mention of custom tags was avoided when discussing the test movie in the previous chapter, ostensibly to avoid putting the cart before the horse.

The latter of the two custom tags does not contain the name of either a form or a configuration variable, but instructs the HTML interpreter instead to include the contents of another list file called 'TEXT.txt', found in the root directory of the source distribution:[31]

```
app=<<appPath>><<procPath>>test<<procExt>>
```

Here, the value of the 'app' variable is built up by concatenating the values of the configuration variables, together with the name of the movie itself, as expected. In this way, the test movie can construct the request URL to query the server process, regardless of the server configuration.[32]

31 List files used to populate custom tags found in the template HTML for the purpose of constructing movie URLs are few and are kept separate from the list files used for the movie requests themselves. The former are kept in the root of the source distribution whereas the latter are kept in subdirectories of the source distribution's 'data' directory, the subdirectories being named after the 'page' form variable identifying the page in which the movie sits.

32 The use of the source distribution's configuration variables is now fully explained, albeit in a somewhat circular manner. This is as good a place as any to bring to a close a discussion of the source distribution in general terms. The purpose of going to such lengths with the server implementation was to make the movies as simple as possible, although I admit that to neophytes, the exact opposite may seem to be the case. It is worth bearing in mind however, that just about any server configuration can be supported by this model with no need to change a single line of code in the movies themselves. This can be particularly useful when porting movies or going from a development to a production environment.

Part 2
The Examples

Navigation, User Input and Dynamic Content

The movies in this section can be used as an alternative to JavaScript and dynamic HTML to provide the more advanced user interfaces on any web page. This practice does not seem to have caught on to any large extent on the Internet (at least as this book went to press) but the advantages are several. The biggest single gain is not having to resort to JavaScript when implementing graphically richer or functionally smarter interfaces.

One legitimate use for JavaScript is to provide the 'glue' which allows the various objects in a web page to communicate with one another via the browser's document object model (it would not be a good idea to make this model available directly to a movie or to any other embedded object, for that matter). Unfortunately, the 'bridging' mechanisms that are supposed to give embedded objects access to JavaScript methods constitute some of the most unreliable and poorly documented areas of Internet programming and as such, simply cannot be relied upon at all for Internet applications. So much for JavaScript.

How do the movies communicate with the browser then, if not via JavaScript? The answer is the getURL( ) method, which appears to work with every browser and on any platform, communicating directly with the browser via its embedded object interface (whatever that may be). Further proof of its universal nature can be found in the fact that a similar mechanism is available to every type of embedded object, not just to Flash movies.[33]

It only remains to point out that the size of each movie in this section is negligible, smaller, in fact, than all but the tiniest of images. Thus, the choice of a movie for interactive use over more conventional methods does not adversely affect the performance of the website – an important consideration.

---

33 Read the 'Working with browsers' appendix for more information on the getURL() method. Yet another strong case for the universal nature of this method is the fact that as this book went to press, Macromedia themselves used it (presumably) for the main navigation movie on their website.

2.1: Active Banner

Most commonly, referrals and click-thrus are registered on the target server by the inclusion in the referral URL of a unique identifier for the site from which the referral originated. This movie turns the tables by allowing the originating site to log the referral too – it notifies its own server and waits for confirmation that the referral has been logged before redirecting the browser to the target site. The movie is in the form of a banner advertisement but there is no reason why the functionality cannot be encapsulated in a simple hyperlink or icon and be embedded in another movie. Either way, its footprint is tiny.

It is the server process itself that gathers the necessary logging information such as the time of the click and the user's IP address, not the movie. All that the movie does is make a vacuous request. There is no information passed with this request and indeed, only the bare minimum is sent back. The whole mechanism is designed to execute invisibly and as fast as possible, and the resulting pause before the user is redirected is minimal.[34]

---

34 Its minimal running on a local server, anyway. Of course, the delay may increase considerably on an Internet site. However, such delays are all part of the rich Internet experience and it is unlikely that the user would even be aware that this extra step has been taken.

Defining the configuration constants

With the various elements of the movie being created dynamically at runtime rather than being placed on the stage during the design process, the movie can be configured with a few constants in the root script rather than having to be wholly redesigned should its size or appearance need to change. The various configuration constants are defined at the top of the root script:

```
/// Variables set from without
var app;

/// Background colours
var kBgColour = 0x009999;
var kBgLightshadowColour = 0x000000;
var kBgDarkshadowColour = 0x000000;

/// Constants
var kTextColour = "0xffffff";
var kTextFont = "Verdana";
var kTextSize = "17";
var kBannerOffset = 20;
var kBannerWidth = Stage.width - 2*kBannerOffset;
var kBannerHeight = 60;
var kTarget = "ffp";
var kReferralURL = "http://www.flashforprogrammers.com";
```

At the very top, the 'app' variable is defined as being '...set from without'. This is just a declaration, not a definition – the actual value of the variable is defined in the movie URL. There is little point in declaring variables in this way (whether they are defined by the movie URL or not), apart from drawing the programmer's attention to their existence - declaring a variable certainly will not protect it from being redefined at a later stage.

Each of these constants is directly available anywhere in the root script without the necessity of appending the '_root' keyword, even when referenced from within the methods.[35] The Stage object used to define the width of the banner background here is a native Flash object containing properties of the overall movie, some of which are read-only, some of which can be altered.

Next comes the definition of the 'mcCount' variable. This keeps track of which depths have been used whenever the attachMovie( ) method (or other methods that require a depth) is invoked.

[35] Its okay to omit the full paths of variables in many circumstances. Constantly prepending the '_root' keyword to every variable in the root script becomes especially tedious, for example. See the 'Scope' appendix for a complete list of the various variable scopes.

Creating the graphical elements

The creation of the various movie elements is done in the setUp( ) method and not directly in the root script. This method is invoked once only, immediately before a call to the stop( ) method, which halts execution of the root script permanently. By stopping the movie in this manner, it is essentially turned into an event-driven application – no further actions are carried out unless they are contained in event handlers attached to buttons and so forth.[36]

To continue, the first task of the setUp( ) method is to draw the banner background by calling the drawBackground( ) method:

```
function drawBackground (x,y,w,h) {

   _root.createEmptyMovieClip( "bg_mc", mcCount++ );

   _root.bg_mc._x = x;
   _root.bg_mc._y = y;

   _root.bg_mc.beginFill( kBgColour );
   _root.bg_mc.lineStyle( 1, kBgLightshadowColour );
   _root.bg_mc.moveTo(0,h);
   _root.bg_mc.lineTo(0,0);
   _root.bg_mc.lineTo(w,0);
   _root.bg_mc.lineStyle( 1, kBgDarkshadowColour );
   _root.bg_mc.lineTo(w,h);
   _root.bg_mc.lineTo(0,h);
   _root.bg_mc.endFill();
}
```

Here, an empty movie clip is created as a holder for the background graphics. Note the use of the 'mcCount' variable for the 'depth' argument, where it is immediately incremented. The empty movie clip is then repositioned and the background rectangle drawn on it. Using a parent movie clip like this makes the job of drawing and positioning the background considerably easier, cutting down on the length of the arguments for the moveTo( ) and lineTo( ) methods and allowing the background to be treated as a single element. The colour constants are used directly rather than being passed as parameters, for simplicity's sake.

The setUp( ) method then creates the remaining elements, the bounding box symbol for the hit area (more of this in a moment) being available through the inclusion of the components:

```
_root.attachMovie( "FIconSymbol", "icon_mc", mcCount++ );
_root.attachMovie( "FTextLabelSymbol", "label_mc", mcCount++ );
_root.attachMovie( "FBoundingBoxSymbol", "hitArea_mc", mcCount++ );
_root.attachMovie( "FTipTextSymbol", "label_mc", mcCount++ );
```

36 I've never managed to work out whether this call to the stop( ) method is entirely necessary. Since the movie constantly loops, one would expect the setup( ) method to be invoked repeatedly, but that doesn't appear to be the case when the stop( ) call is omitted. I always keep the call to the stop( ) method just in case, if for no other reason than to make the point that the movie is purely event-driven once it has been set up.

The icon symbol is created by encapsulating an imported image, since imported images themselves cannot have linkage identifiers and thus cannot by created with the attachMovie( ) method directly. Next, the 'TextLabel' and 'TipText' components are created.[37] Order is important here – the background is created first because it sits behind all the other elements whereas the tiptext component is created last because it must appear in front of everything else.

The icon and text label symbols are then positioned and configured. The icon symbol is straightforward – it simply needs resizing according to the size of the background. The text label needs to be configured to show the large, convincing title, so its properties are set accordingly, before its actual value is set:

```
label_mc.setStyleProperty( "textColor", kTextColour );
label_mc.setStyleProperty( "textFont", kTextFont );
label_mc.setStyleProperty( "textSize", kTextSize );
label_mc.setStyleProperty( "labelBackground", kBgColour );

label_mc.setValue( "www.flashforprogrammers.com" );
```

The tiptext component's over( ) and out( ) methods are called from mouse handlers defined on the movie's hit area, which is simply the bounding box symbol, sized to fit the background exactly and hidden by setting its '_alpha' property to zero:

```
hitArea_mc._x = hitArea_mc._y = kBannerOffset;
hitArea_mc._width = kBannerWidth;
hitArea_mc._height = kBannerHeight;
hitArea_mc._alpha = 0;
hitArea_mc.onRollOver = function () {
     TipText.over( "www.flashforprogrammers.com" );
}
hitArea_mc.onRollOut = function () {
     TipText.out();
}
```

Hiding the hit area by setting its '_visible' property to false will not work, by the way, since this will disable the mouse handlers too. Bounds also need to be set for the tiptext – it usually appears just below and to the right of the cursor but by setting its bounds it can be forced to relocate when it runs out of space. Note the use of the global 'TipText' reference to call methods on the tiptext instance here. This reference is defined by the tiptext itself on initialisation and allows its methods to be called easily from anywhere within the movie.

37 These are part of the 'Lightweight UI' and 'UI Utils' component extensions respectively. Both extensions are discussed in the 'Components' section of this book. For now, components are treated as 'black boxes'. If you can't wait to learn about them, jump to the components section. The 'UI Utils' components are actually as good a place as any to start.

Forwarding the browser to the referral page

Setting a click handler on the hit area allows the server to be polled in the usual manner using the loadVariables( ) method:

```
hitArea_mc.onRelease = function () {
    loadVariables( app + "?", target );
}
```

There is no query to append to the server request, since there is no information for the movie to provide to the server. There is no opportunity for user input – the only interaction being the decision on the part of the user to click on the banner. The addition of a variable to the request URL that is unique to each movie instance could allow the server process to keep separate lists for each particular banner or link, however. This could be set in the movie URL or hardcoded directly into the movie. On the server side, the request is logged with the IP address and time of the click, both of which are available to all server processes via one method or another.[38]

Finally, the object script on the target symbol can force the launch of a new browser window by setting the second argument of the getURL( ) method:

```
onClipEvent ( data ) {

      getURL( _root.kReferralURL, _root.kTarget );
}
```

Note that the '_root' keyword is required here – the object script sits on the same level as script within the object and not on the level of the object itself. Using the '_parent' keyword would work just as well as '_root' in this case.

[38] The server process referenced by the app variable is not the usual 'localise' server process but a process designed specifically for logging the necessary request, namely 'referrals'. It sends nothing back to the movie bar a single ampersand.

2.2: Navigation Menu

This movie is configured entirely via the movie URL – the loadVariables( ) method is not used at all. Timing considerations were the main reason for this choice (the menu should be available for use on the page as early as possible), together with the problems associated with having more than one movie requesting data from within the same web page at the same time.[39]

Bearing these limitations in mind, there is no reason why a navigation menu should not load data via the loadVariables( ) method, if it makes sense to do so. Consider a menu for navigating around a newsgroup or mailing list displayed in a web page, for example. This would typically contain hundreds of items, each of which in turn may contain dozens of sub-items. Configuring such a menu via the movie URL would be impossible. Also, there is no need to load the child items unless their parent item is actually selected, so a piecemeal approach may well be the most efficient. Such menus are suited to a web page with frames, so that changing the target page will not result in the loss of all the data the menu has already painstakingly loaded.

The only limitation to configuring a movie via the movie URL is the ceiling put on the number of characters that can be appended. When this ceiling is met, the movie completely fails to load. The amount of data appended to the navigation movie on the examples site appears to come pretty close to this limit.[40]

The movie has three graphic elements: headings, items and subitems. This hierarchy can be extended further, although the current one should be comprehensive enough for most applications. Only one section is used, in fact, for both the examples and components sites.[41]

---

39 Read the 'Working with browsers' appendix for an explanation.

40 I can't find an exact figure for this – it appears to be just under fourteen hundred characters. As far as I know, this is a limitation of the Flash player and not the browser, but I have no hard facts to back this up. If this is indeed the case (that the limitation is the Flash player's, not the browser's), at least this mechanism can be used with certainty across all browsers and platforms. Otherwise, the problem becomes yet another 'compatibility issue'. I can see no reason why this ceiling cannot be raised to several thousand characters, since the operation to parse the variables and load them into the movie only needs to be done once.

41 For an example of a dynamic menu that has several sections, see the support web site.

Retrieving the data from the movie URL

The movie URL here is constructed from a list file rather than by placing custom tags representing form and configuration variables directly into the template HTML. It is called '_Examples.txt' and can be found in the root of the source distribution. The first few lines look like this:

```
app=<<appPath>><<procPath>>localise<<procExt>>
page=<<page>>
sections=1
prefix_1=1_
```

The first and second lines set the 'app' and 'page' variables, the application in question being the 'localise' server process that prints the HTML pages;[42] and the 'page' variable holds the value of the page currently displayed in the browser. The movie uses this variable to work out which menu item needs to be disabled, the item representing the current page not needing to be active (more on this later).

The next line sets the number of sections and last, the section prefix (just the one in this case). All these variables are made available (as usual) in the root of the movie and are declared at the top of the root script as being '... set from without':

```
///    Variables set from without
var app;
var page;
var sections;
/// var prefix_XXX;
```

The 'prefix_XXX' variables are also at least mentioned, the 'XXX' here meaning 'any number'. The actual declarations are meaningless and so are commented out. The remaining possible variables are not even declared, for the sake of brevity.

[42] The 'localise' server process matches closely the functionality of the test server process, with the exception that the page it displays is specified by the 'page' form variable rather than being hardcoded as 'Test.html'. This server process is responsible for servicing movie requests too, the 'page' variable being used by the movie to specify the relevant list file, hence the need for it to be passed via the movie URL. In this case however, the 'page' form variable is only used to ascertain the currently displayed page, the movie making no further requests to the server. Only when some functionality other than the simple interpretation of a list file is required will another server process apart from this 'localise' server process be used, such as in the previous ActiveBanner movie, for example.

Drawing the menu

The menu elements (items and headings) are created by the drawMenu( ) method, its first task being to provide a parent movie clip to which all the child elements can be attached:

```
_root.createEmptyMovieClip( "menu_mc", 0 );
menu_mc._x = kMenuX;
menu_mc._y = kMenuY;
```

An entirely empty movie clip is all that is needed here, its only job being to provide a container for the child elements and thus allow their easy positioning (this is common practice, especially in components, and a similar movie clip was used to create the background in the 'Active Banner' example). The depth of this parent movie clip is explicitly set to zero. This is the only movie clip placed on the root timeline (all the other movie clips are attached directly to it), so it is excusable not to use the more common 'mcCount' variable for the depth in this instance, saving it for the menu elements themselves.

The loop that draws the menu sections, having recovered the section prefix, invokes a method to draw the header of each section header and then executes an inner loop to draw the items therein:

```
for ( var i = 0; i < eval( "sections" ); i++ ) {

    var prefix = eval( "prefix_" + (i+1) );

    drawHeading( prefix );

    for ( var j = 0; j < eval( prefix + "items" ); j++ ) {

        ...
    }
}
```

Note the (i+1) in the eval( ) method[43] here to recover the section prefix, the reason being that the numbering of both the sections and their child elements starts at unity in the list file, not zero. The drawHeading( ) method simply creates the necessary component and recovers the value of the required variable, by the way:[44]

```
function drawHeading ( i ) {

    menu_mc.attachMovie( "FHeadingSymbol", "heading_mc" + i, mc_Count++ );

    var heading = eval( "heading_" + (i+1) );

    menu_mc[ "heading_mc" + i ].setValue( heading );
}
```

43 It is my own convention to use the rather old-fashioned eval( ) method when recovering variables 'set from without' or set by means of the loadVariables( ) method, to differentiate between such variables and 'normal' ones, which are referenced using the more commonplace array syntax. The reason for the non-standard numbering in the list file is simply this: the file is automatically generated from the source XML using XSLT and I do not know enough about XSLT to fix the problem.

44 My preference is to generally grab variables set via the movie URL as late as possible and not pass them around as method parameters, which seems a little superfluous.

Next, the items themselves are drawn.[45] These are considerably more complex than the headings, which simply show the name of the sections and are not interactive. The items, on the other hand, must store the URLs to which they point (or at least store sufficient data so that these URLs can be recovered) and also allow a certain amount of user interaction.

The main items come in two flavours: those representing a page and not having children have a dot in their corresponding icon; those not representing a page but having child items instead have a plus or minus in their icons, depending on whether or not the child items are visible. Clicking on the former launches the relevant page, clicking on the latter hides or reveals its children. Child items are indented and since they always represent specific pages, they have a page-like icon.

The child items are hidden when the movie is first drawn, with one exception: if the child item represents the current page, its parent item appears expanded from the start so that the child item itself can be made visible. A grey box behind an item signifies that it represents the current page and such items are considered 'disabled' since clicking on them produces no effect.

The various combinations of whether or not a particular item is a parent, whether it is expanded or not, and so on, can all be distilled into four states – 'Empty', 'Open', 'Closed' and 'Child'. Parent items have 'Open' and 'Closed' states, other main items (those with no children) have 'Empty' states and child items have 'Child' states. Each item's initial state is set in the nested loop immediately following the retrieval of the relevant section prefix and call to the drawHeading( ) method, the main items being drawn first:

```
for ( var j = 0; j < eval( prefix + "items" ); j++ ) {

     var tmpItem = drawItem( i, j, prefix );
     var enabled = true;
     var state = "Empty";
     var items = eval( prefix + "items_" + (j+1) );

     ...

     tmpItem.setEnabled( enabled );
     tmpItem.setState( state );
}
```

45 The general rule throughout the examples and components chapters is that only those parts of a movie that demonstrate new techniques are discussed and that the actual functionality of the movie (being hopefully self-evident) usually is not. I do occasionally make exceptions however, describing the workings of a movie even when it adds little in the way of new techniques if I feel that this is necessary. This movie is a case in point, the creation and positioning of the items containing nothing new but being convoluted enough (it really is difficult to make the process any simpler) to warrant further explanation. Apart from the use of the setChangeHandler( ) method on the item components below, there are no new techniques used from now on; if you are not interested in how this menu works, you can safely move on to the next chapter.

Note that the drawItem( ) method returns a reference to the item it creates, for convenience. Once a main item has been created, its default 'enabled' and 'state' properties are stored in temporary variables. The existence and various states of its child items can affect these properties so they are applied only after the child items are themselves drawn. The drawItem( ) method itself deserves a mention:

```
function drawItem ( i, j, prefix ) {

    menu_mc.attachMovie( "FItemSymbol", "item_mc_" + i + "_" + j, mc_Count++ );
    var item = menu_mc[ "item_mc_" + i + "_" + j ];

    var value = eval( prefix + "value_" + (j+1) );
    item.setValue( value );
    item.setState("Empty");
    item.setChangeHandler( "itemPress", _root );
    item.setParams( {prefix:prefix,i:i,j:j} );

    return ( item );
}
```

The name of the created item incorporates both the number of the section to which it belongs as well as its own position. The setChangeHandler( ) method invoked here is a standard method from Flash's own FUIComponentClass class which specifies a callback method to be invoked when the item is pressed.[46] Finally, the setParams( ) method sets instance variables on the component enabling it to recall its position in the section and also to retrieve its corresponding URL, if it has one.

Returning to the list file, the next part defines these page variables for each item, as well as the values of the text that the items display. The section prefix (namely '1_') is prepended to all the variable names here and the value of the section heading is also given:

```
1_items=6
1_heading=Examples
1_value_1=Introduction
1_value_2=Navigation, User Input and Dynamic Content
1_value_3=Retrieving and Submitting Data
1_value_4=Simple Data Representation
1_value_5=3D Data Modelling
1_value_6=Interactivity and Complex Data Handling
1_page_1=examples/Introduction
1_page_2=
1_page_3=
1_page_4=
1_page_5=
1_page_6=
```

46 The item components extend this class, as do most of the components in this book. Read the chapter on the 'Lightweight' components for an explanation of the FUIComponentClass class, if you can't wait.

Note that most of the page variables are blank – these correspond to the 'parent' items. The one page variable that is not blank sets the 'Introduction' item to point to the 'examples/Introduction' page. The page variables are used to determine the initial state of the main items, in fact, the movie simply checking whether their values are non-null:

```
function isItemEmpty ( j, prefix ) {

    var itemPage = eval( prefix + "page_" + (j+1) );

    if ( ( itemPage == undefined ) || ( itemPage == "" ) ) {
        return true;
    }
    return false;
}
```

Checking whether or not an item represents the current page is also relatively straightforward:

```
function isItemActive ( j, prefix ) {

    var itemPage = eval( prefix + "page_" + (j+1) );
    var currenPage = eval( "page" );

    if ( itemPage == currenPage ) {
        return true;
    }
    return false;
}
```

Note the explicit definition of the 'currentPage' variable here, for clarity. The check for the child items is much the same, but with the 'itemPage' variable defined slightly differently. All these methods are called from within the inner loop of the drawMenu( ) method and since there is little to be gained from any further breakdown (it is well enough commented), no further explanation is given here.

The drawMenu( ) method does not position the items itself, instead is invokes the layoutMenu( ) method, which positions the elements from top to bottom by using a variable which is increased by the necessary offset each time an element is positioned:

```
function layoutMenu () {

    var y = kInitialYOffset;

    for ( var i = 0; i < eval( "sections" ); i++ ) {

        var prefix = eval( "prefix_" + (i+1) );

        menu_mc[ "heading_mc" + i ]._y = y;

        y += kTitleHeight;

        for ( var j = 0; j < eval( prefix + "items" ); j++ ) {

            menu_mc[ "item_mc_" + i + "_" + j ]._y = y;

            y += kItemHeight;

            for ( var k = 0; k < eval( prefix + "items_" + (j+1) ); k++ ) {

                if ( menu_mc[ "item_mc_" + i + "_" + j + "_" + k ]._visible ) {

                    menu_mc[ "item_mc_" + i + "_" + j + "_" + k ]._y = y;

                    y += kItemHeight;
                }
            }
        }
        y += kSpacerHeight;
    }
}
```

Note that the hidden items are not positioned here and therefore do not affect the positioning of the remaining elements underneath them. This method is also invoked from within the itemPressed( ) method, if the item in question is a parent, otherwise the browser is instructed by the itemPressed( ) method to load the relevant page.

Instructing the browser to display a page

The itemPressed( ) method is called whenever an item is pressed and is passed the 'params' object associated with the item in question:

```
function itemPress ( params ) {

     var page;
     var prefix = params.prefix, i = params.i, j = params.j, k = params.k;

     if ( k == undefined ) {
          page = eval( prefix + "page_" + (j+1) );
     } else {
          page = eval( prefix + "page_" + (j+1) + "_" + (k+1) );
     }

     if ( page == "" ) {

          var tmpItem = menu_mc[ "item_mc_" + i + "_" + j ];
          var visible;

          if ( tmpItem.getState() == "Closed" ) {
               tmpItem.setState("Open");
               visible = true;
          } else {
               tmpItem.setState("Closed");
               visible = false;
          }
          for ( var k = 0; k < eval( prefix + "items_" + (j+1) ); k++ ) {
               menu_mc[ "item_mc_" + i + "_" + j + "_" + k ]._visible = visible;
          }
          layoutMenu();
     }
     else {

          getURL( app + "?" + "page=" + escape(page), "_top" );
     }
}
```

This object is used to recover the item's related page variable. If this is null, the item is a 'parent' item, the visibility of the child items therefore being toggled and the layoutMenu( ) method being invoked accordingly. If the related page variable is non-null on the other hand, the getURL( ) method is invoked to instruct the browser to show the related page. Note that the 'page' variable is encoded before being appended to the URL and also note that the optional second argument of the getURL( ) method is set to ensure the new page is displayed in the topmost frame.

2.3: Simple Form

This movie is also configured entirely via the movie URL (like the 'Navigation Menu' example) and can be used several times on one web page if necessary.[47]
It replaces the use of HTML forms, providing a consistent and easily alterable style across the various form elements and enabling additional functionality to be included, such as checking the values of fields before submittal, without the need to clutter the HTML.
The movie is also vertically sizeable, allowing different forms with varying numbers of elements to be accommodated with no loss of space in the web page.

Components are used for the form elements and a component is also responsible for positioning them.
The button component is designed to retrieve the names and values of its siblings by default, encoding and concatenating these properties to form a query string.
This is appended to the request URL, the form information being passed to the server with the getURL( ) method.

47 Although there are practical limits on the number of movies that query the server being placed on one page (the limit is effectively just one, in fact), there are no limits on the number of movies that do not. The support website, for example, often has three or more movies on one page, all configured via the movie URL, if at all.

Sizing the movie

Although the two sets of movie dimensions (those set in the properties inspector and those set in the attributes of the HTML elements that embed the movie in a web page) should usually be the same, it is possible to work around this restriction and resize the movie, at least vertically. The height of the footprint (the area defined by the HTML attributes) can be altered so that it differs from the height of the movie stage and the movie can resize itself accordingly from within. All that is necessary is to notify the movie of the required height, via the movie URL, of course.

To demonstrate this,[48] start a new project, set the size of the stage to 100x100 pixels and add the following script to the root timeline:

```
/// Colours
var kBgColour = 0xffffff;
var kBgLightshadowColour = 0x000000;
var kBgDarkshadowColour = 0x000000;

/// We're off
drawBackground(Stage.width,Stage.height);
stop();

function drawBackground (w,h) {

     this.createEmptyMovieClip( "bg_mc", 0 );

     this.bg_mc.beginFill( kBgColour );
     this.bg_mc.lineStyle( 1, kBgLightshadowColour );
     this.bg_mc.moveTo(0,h-1);
     this.bg_mc.lineTo(0,0);
     this.bg_mc.lineTo(w-1,0);
     this.bg_mc.lineStyle( 1, kBgDarkshadowColour );
     this.bg_mc.lineTo(w-1,h-1);
     this.bg_mc.lineTo(0,h-1);
     this.bg_mc.endFill();
}
```

48 If you don't want to know how this is done, jump to the 'Positioning and configuring the form elements' section below.

Publish the movie with HTML generation enabled and launch the resultant HTML page. The movie should appear in the top left-hand corner of the page, delimited by the black border drawn by the drawBackgound( ) method. Uncheck the HTML option in the publish settings so that the HTML will not be overwritten in future and make the following changes to it: change the colour of the background from white to light grey, say; change the colour of the 'bgcolor' attributes in both the 'OBJECT' and 'EMBED' elements to blue, say; and change the 'WIDTH' attributes in both elements from 100 to 200 pixels. Place the movie in a suitably aligned table so that it appears in the middle of the page. The HTML should now look something like this (with many attributes of the 'OBJECT' and 'EMBED' elements left out for brevity):

```
<HTML>
<HEAD>
<TITLE>Sizing</TITLE>
</HEAD>
<BODY bgcolor="#eeeeee">

<table width="100%" height="100%">
<tr>
<td align="center" valign="middle">
<OBJECT WIDTH="200" HEIGHT="100">

    <PARAM NAME="movie" VALUE="Sizing.swf">
    <PARAM NAME="bgcolor" VALUE="#666699">

    <EMBED src="Sizing.swf"
           bgcolor="#666699"
           WIDTH="200" HEIGHT="100"/>
</OBJECT>
</td>
</tr>
</table>

</BODY>
</HTML>
```

Refresh the page. It should look like Fig. 2.1:

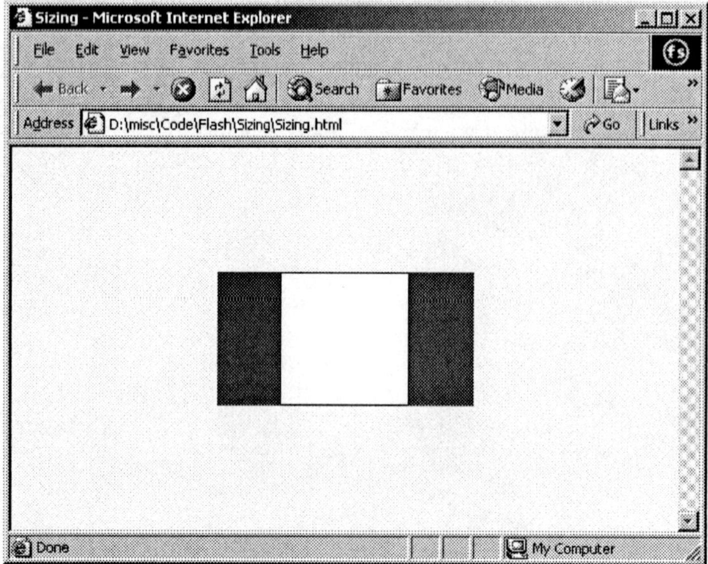

Fig. 2.1. A square movie contained in a rectangular footprint.

Apart from the obvious differences in the positioning and background colour of the movie, the major difference is the appearance of the footprint, coloured blue. The movie has not apparently been stretched to fit this footprint but retains its aspect ratio. Try different sizes for the 'WIDTH' and 'HEIGHT' attributes – the movie will expand or contract to fit the footprint as closely as possible but will maintain its aspect ratio. The blue footprint will always appear beneath it unless its own aspect ratio exactly matches that of the movie – the default behaviour.

The white background and black border, drawn by the movie itself at runtime, are set by the values of the Stage object. It certainly appears that these values are set at compile time and do not reflect the actual footprint of the movie in the web page during playback, or to put it another way, the movie does not know how 'big' it is. In particular, when the movie is resized to match the footprint as closely as possible, the 'width' and 'height' properties of the Stage object remain fixed.

What is not immediately obvious, however, is that the footprint is available to be drawn upon, provided the movie knows the correct dimensions. Set the dimensions of the footprint to, say, 100x200 pixels and call the drawBackground( ) method with these dimensions, too. Republish the movie and refresh the page. The background does indeed overlap into the footprint but unfortunately only below and not above. Clearly, the movie has been aligned centrally in the footprint by the player.

Change the height of the movie in the properties inspector to just one pixel and the parameters of the drawBackground( ) method back to the width and height of the Stage object for a moment. Republish the movie and refresh the web page (Fig. 2.2). The one pixel high movie appears exactly in the middle of the footprint, vertically, that is.

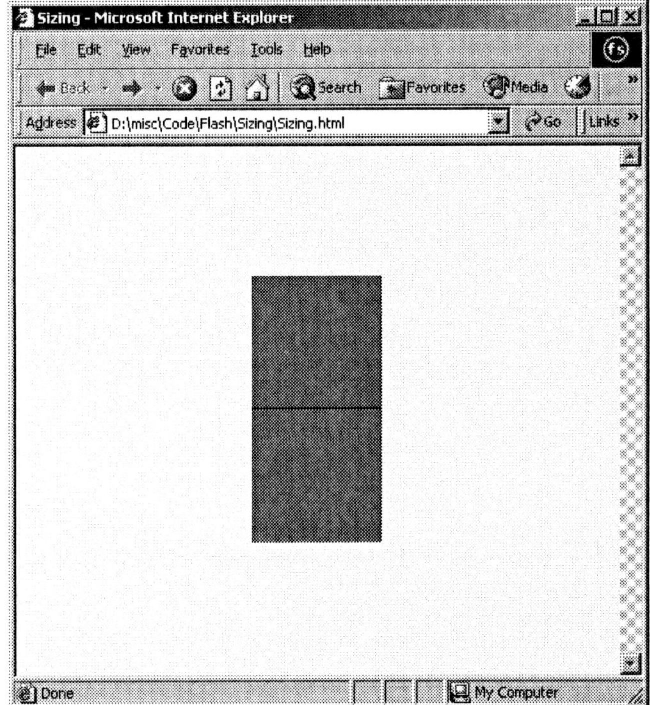

Fig. 2.2. A movie with a height of just one pixel, centred vertically by default.

If the width of the footprint and the width of the movie (as reported by the Stage object) always remain identical, and if the height of the movie is set to just one pixel in the properties inspector, the movie will never be resized, regardless of the footprint's height. To make use of the full extent of the footprint it is then only necessary to inform the movie of the footprint's height, enabling it work out the required offset itself. To do this, change the movie URL to the following:

```
Sizing.swf?height=200
```

Change the call to the drawBackground( ) method to include this 'height' variable, set from without ...

```
drawBackground( Stage.width, height );
```

... and change the drawBackground( ) method itself to reposition the background, the necessary calculation being to halve the height of the footprint and move the background upwards accordingly (adding on a pixel for good measure):

```
function drawBackground (w,h) {

     this.createEmptyMovieClip( "bg_mc", 0 );

     this.bg_mc._x = 0;
     this.bg_mc._y = -Math.floor(height/2)+1;

     ...
}
```

Try this out with different heights. Although the four occurrences of the height need to be changed each time (two in the movie URLs and two in the element attributes), there is no need to republish the movie itself.

In the source distribution, the 'height' variable is inserted in all the right places by its inclusion in the list file that generates the query part of the movie URL and by the inclusion of a custom tag for the height attribute of the HTML elements. The form height therefore becomes entirely configurable via a configuration variable with no need to either republish the movie or alter the HTML.[49]

49 The height configuration variable is actually hardcoded into the 'localise' server process to avoid being placed in the global configuration files.

Positioning and configuring the form elements

In the example movie itself, rather than the background being drawn onto an empty movie clip which is then repositioned, it is drawn directly onto the movie stage. The whole movie is then moved in relation to the footprint (it is rather surprising that this works, but it does), the necessary adjustment being made at the top of the setUp( ) method:

```
this._y = -Math.floor(height/2)+1;
```

Because the script is placed in the root timeline, the use of the 'this' keyword here references the movie as a whole. The benefit of this approach is that it effectively moves the coordinate system of the whole movie to the top left of the footprint and no further alterations are necessary when positioning movie elements. The debug field, by the way, if aligned so that its top edge is along the line of the stage, or just under it, will appear as normal.

Immediately above this line, the drawFocusRect( ) class method of the Flash's own FUIComponentClass class is undefined. This method is responsible for drawing the rectangle that appears around components when they have the input focus.[50] By undefining it here, it is undefined for every component instance that extends the FUIComponentClass class. This works firstly because classes (or anything else for that matter) defined within initialiser blocks are defined before any frame script is executed, and secondly because all definitions contained in initaliser blocks sit on the root timeline.

The focus rectangle also has to be undefined explicitly for the TickBox component, since this method overrides the drawFocusRect( ) method in the FUIComponentClass with its own method. The opportunity is also taken to simplify the behaviour of the tick box so that its value is toggled immediately upon being pressed, rather than the initial mouse click simply giving it the input focus:

```
FTickBoxClass.prototype.drawFocusRect = function () {};
FTickBoxClass.prototype.onPress = function() {
     this.toggleTick();
     Selection.setFocus(this);
}
```

Finally in this method, the various global style properties are set, mostly to constants defined at the top of the root script. The only point worth mentioning here is that the lightweight components do not stick to the predefined styles but invent a couple of their own, specifically the 'tick' and 'labelBackground' styles.

After the background has been drawn (the border is suppressed here by simply making it the same colour as the background fill), the movie creates the various form elements, based on the variables defined in the movie URL. These elements are positioned using a 'LayoutManager' component:

```
_root.attachMovie( "FLayoutManagerSymbol", "layout_mc", mcCount++ );
_root.layout_mc.setRowsAndColumns( 10,2 );
_root.layout_mc.setCellPadding( kCellPadding );
_root.layout_mc._x = kLayoutX;
_root.layout_mc._y = kLayoutY;
```

50 Components that extend FUIComponent, like the 'Lightweight' components used in this movie, exhibit this behaviour. Components and symbols that do not draw their own focus rectangles or suppress Flash's default treatment of the input focus are rewarded with a rather garish, ill-fitting yellow rectangle around them when they have the input focus.

This component is usually not visible on the stage at runtime. It simply allows the addition of 'child' elements, which it positions according to the number of columns it has been given. In many ways it behaves exactly like an HTML table. The exception to the rule of its never appearing on the stage is when the user specifies background colours for the cells in which the child elements appear.[51]

Next, a 'global' attribute object is defined for use as and when child components are added to the layout manager and finally, the components are created, one by one, then immediately hidden and redrawn at the next frame refresh. This is achieved by setting the 'onEnterFrame' handler to an anonymous method, which then resets the handler and shows the components when it is invoked:[52]

```
_root.onEnterFrame = function () {

      _root.layout_mc.refresh();

      for ( var i = 0; i < items; i++ ) {
            _root[ "input" + i ]._visible = true;
      }
      _root.onEnterFrame = undefined;
}
```

The elements are created in the drawInputElement( ) method, which retrieves the relevant variables set via the movie URL, placing them in temporary local holders and configuring the components accordingly. The correct linkage identifier is found by means of the links associative array, defined near the top of the root script:

```
var links =
{
      label:       { link: "FTextLabelSymbol"   },
      submit:      { link: "FTextButtonSymbol"  },
      checkbox:    { link: "FTickBoxSymbol"     },
      hidden:      { link: "FHiddenSymbol"      },
      text:        { link: "FTextFieldSymbol"   },
      description: { link: "FTextAreaSymbol"    }
};
```

Array initialisers are worth a mention here. Associative arrays are initialised by using curly braces and their keys do not have to be contained in quotes. The script above is equivalent to the following, for example:

```
var links = new Array();
links[ "label" ] =  { link: "FTextLabelSymbol"  };
links[ "submit" ] = { link: "FTextButtonSymbol" };
...
```

51 Read the chapter on the 'UI Utils' components for a full explanation of the layout manager's functionality.

52 It is generally a good idea to initially hide components and make them reappear at the first frame refresh, ensuring that they have the opportunity to size themselves correctly. The refresh( ) method is also called to ensure that the LayoutManager component takes the true, final sizes of the components into account.

Shorthand array initialisers have still been used on the right-hand side, for brevity. Standard, linear arrays can be initialised using square braces, as follows:

```
var names = [ "Horace", "Gregory", ... ];
```

There is an extra level of indirection in the links associative array above – the various types are not matched directly with linkage identifiers but rather to child associative arrays which in turn contain the required information. There is no particular reason for this but it does allow future revisions to associate other properties with the element types, perhaps for inclusion in individual attribute objects.

After creation, the component instance is added to the layout manager together with a reference to the 'attrObj' global attributes object defined in the setUp( ) method. This object specifies some extra properties to be associated with the component as it is positioned by the layout manager, such as row width or alignment. Here, only a minimum height is specified for each cell.

Imitating HTML form functionality

Running the movie as part of the source distribution results in a simple form being created with 'name', 'email' and 'comments' input fields as well as a 'remember me' tick box and of course, a 'SUBMIT' button. The contents of the 'comments' field are echoed each time, those of the 'email' field are always to be forgotten and the contents of the 'name' field are only remembered if the 'remember me' tick box is checked. Conversely, the 'remember me' box always returns unchecked if no name is given.

This (rather wearisome) logic comes courtesy of both the list file associated with the movie URL and also a small amount of code in the 'localise' server process. The list file is called 'SimpleForm.txt' and can be found in the 'examples/navigation' directory of the example distribution's 'data' directory.[53] The height of the movie and the number of elements are defined at the top, then the various input elements are given using indexed variables. To define a label, for example, its type and value are needed ...

```
type0=label
value0=name:
```

... whilst the 'remember me' tick box requires a label and also a 'name' property, since it represents a form variable:

```
type3=checkbox
name3=remember
label3=remember me
value3=<<remember>>
```

Note the use of a custom tag to echo the 'remember' form variable each time. The 'page' form variable is also echoed, using a hidden input element ...

```
type10=hidden
name10=page
value10=<<page>>
```

... and finally, the submit button is defined with the necessary 'action' property, used instead of the 'app' variable (omitted from the list file) since the button calls the getURL( ) method itself when its action property is non-null:

```
type13=submit
value13=SUBMIT
action13=<<appPath>><<procPath>>localise<<procExt>>
```

53 All the list files are placed in subdirectories of the 'data' directory corresponding to the value of the 'page' variable for the current page (following the convention used for HTML files in the 'template' folder). This variable is therefore commonly passed (via the movie URL) to all movies that make server requests, along with the URL of the server process itself.

Note the omission of certain indexed elements – numbers 4 and 5, for example. These omissions act as spacers, the corresponding undefined movie clip references still being added to the layout manager.

The code to alter the values of the form variables and set the height of the movie is found near the top of the 'localise' server process and needs little explanation:

```
if ( FORM{"name"} == "" ) {
     FORM{"remember"} = "false";
}
if ( FORM{"remember" != "true") ) {
     FORM{"name"} = "";
}

CONFIG{"height"} = 220;
```

2.4: Dynamic Text

This movie allows the browser to display changing text in a web page without the need for a page refresh. This can be achieved more conventionally using JavaScript, preloading the text blocks then hiding them all, bar one. Using a movie has two distinct advantages, however: firstly, the buttons can be Flash buttons (with all the advantages this entails); and secondly, no text blocks have to be preloaded, with only the text that has actually been requested being loaded by the movie. This makes for more efficient use of bandwidth.

The movie demonstrates quite clearly how with the use of fonts that match its surrounds and some careful design, a movie can blend in completely with the HTML while still providing the necessary advanced functionality.

Handling multiple data sets

Several requests to the server process can be made during the course of this movie's execution, with two being made to begin with in order to initialise it fully. Because of the limitations placed by browsers on the number of connections that can be established at any given time,[54] it is best to 'chain' these requests, the second request only being made once the server process has responded to the first, for example. Before the initial request is made however, the text field to display the text blocks needs to be created. This is done in the setUp( ) method:[55]

```
function setUp () {

     _root.createTextField( "textField_mc", mcCount++, 0,0, 1,1 );

     textField_mc._x = kTextOffset;
     textField_mc._y = kTextY + kTextOffset;
     textField_mc._width = Stage.width - kTextOffset*2;
     textField_mc._height = Stage.height - kTextT - kTextOffset*2;

     textField_mc.wordwrap = true;
     textField_mc.embedFonts = false;
     textField_mc.selectable = false;
}
```

Once the text field is created and resized, certain properties are immediately applied to it. Only the 'embedFonts' property needs further explanation here: when it is set to 'false', the operating system rather than the Flash player is forced to render the fonts.[56]

When the text field has been fully configured, the loadData( ) method is invoked to make the initial request. This method simply appends the requisite variable to the request URL to ensure that information to populate the buttons rather than information to populate the text field is returned (the correct response to the second and all subsequent requests). The target symbol specified has the instance name of 'loader', its object script calling the setUpButtons( ) and loadText( ) methods in that order.

The setupButtons( ) method draws the buttons, populating them with the necessary information retrieved from the loader target symbol as well as creating the alternative cursor to be drawn when a request is pending (more on this later). The loadText( ) method is similar to the loadData( ) method, but instead of requesting button information, it requests a text block and points the request at another target symbol, with the instance name of 'other'.

The object script of this second target symbol sets the relevant entry in the root 'texts' array (easily obtained because the server process echoes the index form variable passed in the movie request), then calls the displayText( ) method:

```
onClipEvent ( data ) {

     _root.texts[ index ] = text;
     _root.displayText( index );
}
```

54 Again, see the 'Working with browsers' appendix.

55 Creating a text field dynamically in this way is unusual – even when used as elements in components, text fields are usually drawn directly onto the stage. I've plumped for the dynamic method of creation here mainly to provide a usage example.

56 Embedded fonts are by no means a straightforward subject. The full explanation is deferred for now and taken up again in the next chapter, where the design of the graphs makes their use unavoidable. The best advice I can give on embedded fonts is to avoid their use altogether, at least until you have grasped all their subtleties and potential pitfalls.

It is important to realise that two different target symbols have been used for the two types of request here – the 'loader' symbol for the response to the initial request for button data; and the 'other' symbol for responses to requests for text blocks. The second request is made as a direct result of the response to the first, ensuring that only one request is pending at a time.

Two methods handle all the responses – the setupButtons( ) method is called from the object script of the loader target symbol and handles the response from the initial request; and the displayText( ) method is called from the object script of the other target symbol (handling the response from the second and all subsequent requests) as well as being the chosen callback method for the buttons.

As well as creating the button components, the setUpButtons( ) method creates an instance of the icon to replace the cursor while further requests are pending. This movie clip is immediately hidden upon creation and its 'onEnterFrame' handler defined so that it always appears in the same position as the cursor. It is created last of all to ensure that it is drawn above all the other elements in the movie (since it has the greater depth):

```
function setupButtons () {

    for ( var i = 0; i < kMonths; i++ ) {

        var value = eval( "loader.date" + i );

        _root.attachMovie( "FLinkSymbol","link_mc"+i,mcCount++,{ value:value,
                                                                 index:i } );
        var link = _root[ "link_mc" + i ];

        link._x = kXLinkOffset + ( i % 6 ) * kLinkWidth;
        link._y = kYLinkOffset + Math.floor( i / 6 ) * kLinkHeight;

        link.setChangeHandler( "displayText", "index" );
    }

    _root.attachMovie( "WaitingPointer", "waitingPointer", mcCount++ );
    waitingPointer._visible = false;
    waitingPointer.onEnterFrame = function () {

        this._x = _root._xmouse;
        this._y = _root._ymouse;
    }
}
```

The link buttons are created in a loop and immediately populated with their respective values by using the optional fourth parameter of the attachMovie( ) method. In this case, the 'value' and 'index' properties of each button are set to the value variable recovered by the eval( ) method and the value of the loop counter respectively. The callback method of the link buttons is specified by the setChangeHandler( ) method, which differs slightly from the standard component method of that name.[57] Here, the second parameter specifies the name of a property whose value is passed as an argument when the callback method, namely displayText( ), is invoked.

[57] The standard method is defined in the FUIComponentClass class and is hence available to any component that extends this class. A similar button component (which uses the same non-standard definition of the setChangeHandler( ) method) is discussed in the PDB molecule viewer example chapter.

Loading data on demand

When invoked as a callback method by the button components, the displayText( ) method's task is to ascertain whether the relevant text block is already loaded and, if so, to display it. If the text block is not already loaded, it checks whether a request is already pending and if not, changes the appearance of the cursor and calls the loadText( ) method with the relevant index. When called from the object script of the 'other' symbol however, its task is to update the text field with the contents of the newly arrived text block:

```
function displayText ( index ) {

    if ( index != currentIndex ) {

        if ( texts[ index ] != undefined ) {

            _root[ "link_mc" + currentIndex ].setEnabled(true);

            textField_mc.text = texts[ index ];

            var tmpFormat = new TextFormat();
            tmpFormat.color = kTextColour;
            tmpFormat.font = kTextFont;
            tmpFormat.size = kTextSize;
            tmpFormat.align = "left";
            textField_mc.setTextFormat(tmpFormat);

            currentIndex = index;

            _root[ "link_mc" + currentIndex ].setEnabled(false);

            waitingPointer._visible = false;
            Mouse.show();
        }
        else {

            if ( waitingPointer._visible == false ) {

                waitingPointer._visible = true;
                Mouse.hide();

                loadText( index );
            }
        }
    }
}
```

To achieve these various tasks, the method first checks its 'index' argument against the index of the text block that is currently visible, this value being held in the 'currentIndex' root variable, initialised to -1 at the top of the root script. If the two are the same, no further action is necessary – the user has just clicked the button corresponding to the text block that is already visible. This is unlikely to happen, since the button is immediately disabled once the corresponding text block is shown, but since the two actions of showing the text block and disabling its corresponding button cannot be done simultaneously, this check is necessary.

If the two indices differ, two cases arise: either the text block needs to be loaded or it has been loaded previously and can immediately be displayed (the value of the corresponding element in the texts array having already been set in the other target symbol's object script). In the first case, the appearance of the cursor is changed accordingly and the loadText( ) method is called with the relevant index. In the second case, the button corresponding to the currently visible text block is re-enabled, the text field is updated with the new text block, the 'currentIndex' variable is updated, the button corresponding to the new text block is disabled and finally, the mouse pointer is returned to normal.

The remaining properties of the text field must be set whenever its contents are altered, if it is not to revert to its default font metrics. These properties have to be set using a TextFormat object, and cannot be set directly since they relate to a block of text (one text field being able to hold many blocks of text with different font metrics) rather than the text field as a whole.

This is a subtle point and is well worth stressing – text fields are not limited to one set of font metrics and therefore only some of their properties can be set globally. Properties such as the current scroll position or type of the text field (whether dynamic, static or input) are good examples. Other properties (font metrics and margin settings, specifically) pertain to blocks of text and are therefore set using the TextFormat object. The colour of the text field is the one exception to this rule and can be set by either method.[58]

58 You should read the Flash documentation on the TextField and TextFormat objects carefully. In particular, note that the setTextFormat( ) method, even when applied to the text field as a whole, pertains to the contents of the text field and not the text field instance itself. Hence the need to reapply the TextFormat object each time the contents change.

Creating an alternative cursor

To construct the waiting-pointer movie clip, the required image needs to be imported onto the stage by choosing 'Import…' from the 'File' menu. The image will initially appear blurred because of anti-aliasing. In order to be used as an alternative cursor, this effect ideally needs to be turned off.

Suppressing the anti-aliasing can be done by choosing 'Modify>Trace Bitmap…' from the menu and setting the properties in the 'Trace Bitmap' dialog to the following values: 'Color Threshold' to '1'; 'Minimum Area' to '1'; 'Curve Fit' to 'Pixels'; and 'Corner Threshold' to 'Many corners'. The resultant image (Fig. 2.3) is made up of well-defined pixel areas and appears pixelated on the stage, rather than being anti-aliased.

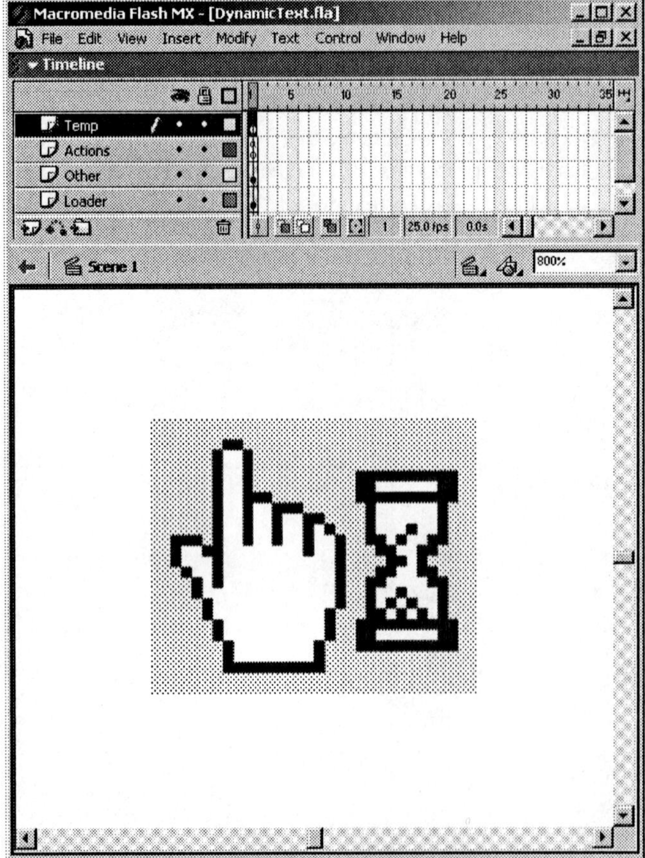

Fig. 2.3. A processed image with the background selected before deletion.

Once the background has been deleted, the image as a whole can be turned into a movie clip symbol in the normal way and used just like any other. The actual graphic symbol in the example movie has been further altered by moving the timer down several pixels to lighten the effect. It is also worth noting that by the careful positioning of this image within its parent symbol, the 'onEnterFrame' handler can be kept as simple as possible – the image can be lined up exactly with the default hand cursor simply by trial and error when testing the movie. The original image will remain in the library but can be safely removed once the required bitmap has been traced.

Retrieving and Submitting Data

These movies shift the emphasis away from the purely static representation of data to employ a more dynamic approach, allowing users to alter parts of the data on display and submit their changes for later retrieval. They amply demonstrate the ability of Flash movies to provide an enhanced user interface – consider the rather pedestrian alternative of entering data into an HTML form, for example.

Data submittal is achieved with the ubiquitous getURL( ) method – the data arrays are appended to the request URL as a series of form variables. The graphs also request the data from the supporting server process rather than receiving it via the movie URL. A unique identifier could also be passed via the movie URL to allow the graphs to request data specific to a particular user but since the examples distribution on the whole is sessionless, this functionality has not been implemented.[59]

---

59 In a real world environment, these movies would need to function on a per-user basis if they allowed the alteration and submittal of data, as well as representation. The equivalent movies on the support web site have this functionality. Read the 'Sessions' appendix for a thorough discussion of sessions and instructions on how to alter the 'Prices' movie to make use of them.

2.5: A 'Prices' Movie

This movie shows three linear data sets, two of which can be altered, within limits. These altered values can be submitted to the server and will be retrieved the next time that the movie runs. The values of the fixed prices (represented by the red horizontal bars roughly halfway up the graph), as well as the dates, are obtained from a standard list file. They are fixed and cannot be altered. The two sets of variable prices, on the other hand, are obtained from a list file in the 'submit' directory of the source distribution. These can be altered – the server process will rewrite this file upon request. Both data sets are provided by the same server process when the movie starts, which reads both list files and concatenates them into one response.

The higher and lower price values can be altered by moving their corresponding sliders. These give a rough indication of the prices, the precise values being given in figures above and below the bars. The scale of the graph is fixed. The default values fit into this scale and because the travel of the sliders is limited to the vertical extent of the graph, values that fall outside of this scale cannot be attained and thus cannot be submitted. The scale is hardcoded into the movie but this need not be the case, of course.

Embedding fonts in the movie

The setupGraph( ) method is called from the object script of the 'loader' target symbol – nothing is drawn by this movie until the data has been received. The twelve bars are then drawn in a simple loop, the necessary values to populate them being retrieved from the 'loader' symbol with the usual eval( ) calls. The initial heights of the sliders and horizontal prices bars are set here, too. An extra '.0' is added to integer price values, for appearance's sake, and only the months are added to the angled data text fields – the years are drawn separately. The algorithm to work out their positions immediately follows and is not worth further comment here (it is well commented in the movie).

The vertical scale and axes bounding the whole graph are drawn next, the axes being drawn last in order to appear in front of everything else. Note that the vertical scale is stepped by a fixed amount – there are six values, in fact. Naturally, a more universal mechanism is needed if the graph is to be scaled via the movie URL and still retain integers for the scales.[60]

The remaining movie elements are created in the setupRemaining( ) method, which creates the submit button and alternative cursor, which is displayed while the movie is waiting for confirmation of data submittal. The button, being a component, is immediately hidden on creation and made visible at the next frame refresh by setting the 'onEnterFrame' handler of the movie. The alternative cursor is also immediately hidden and its position is maintained by setting its 'onEnterFrame' handler, too.

This graph uses embedded fonts (as opposed to device fonts) for many of the text fields. Embedded fonts are rendered by the Flash player itself, whereas device fonts are rendered by the operating system. It is slightly misleading to talk of 'device fonts' and 'embedded fonts', in fact, since the actual font definition has nothing to do with it – it is the method by which the font is rendered that differentiates the two.

Persuading Flash to render a text field using an embedded font can be done in one of two ways: either by leaving the 'Use Device Fonts' tickbox in the properties inspector unchecked (embedded fonts are the default, by the way); or by giving the text field an instance name and setting the 'embedFonts' property to false directly.

If a text field is configured to use a device font, the font must be installed on the operating system (since it is the operating system that is responsible for rendering it). Using embedded fonts, on the other hand, forces the Flash player to use the font outlines embedded in the movie itself.

[60] A better scaling method is developed in the 'Volumes' movie and is also applied to a variable scale in real time.

Nothing need be done when using embedded fonts with static text fields - Flash knows exactly which font outlines to embed. With input and dynamic text fields however, Flash must be asked to include the necessary font outlines, since it cannot be expected to know beforehand which ones might be needed. A small 'Character' button appears in the properties inspector when a dynamic or input text field is selected on the stage. Pressing this button brings up the 'Character Options' dialog (Fig. 2.4). The default (and safest) option is simply to include all the font outlines in the movie every time.

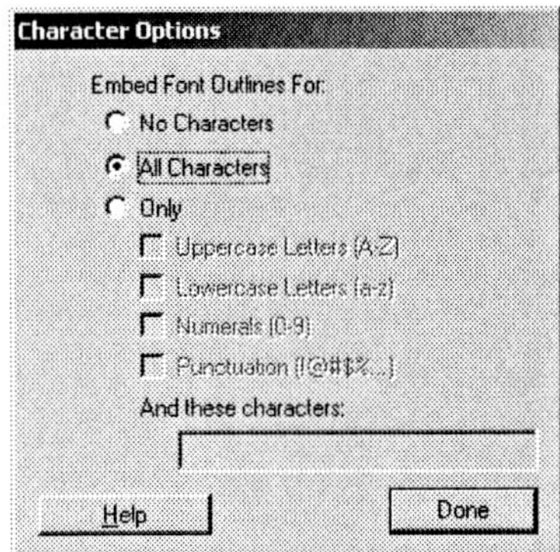

Fig 2.4. The 'Character Options' dialog box.

If text fields are to be created dynamically in a movie or it is otherwise impractical to include text fields on the stage in a movie project, there is an alternative method of embedding fonts in a movie: font objects. To add a font object to a movie, click on the small white icon near the top right of the library panel (just under the close button) and choose 'New Font...' from the popup menu. The 'Font Symbol Properties' dialog box should appear (Fig. 2.5). Choose the required font from the 'Font' dropdown list, type the identical name in the 'Name' field and click 'OK'.

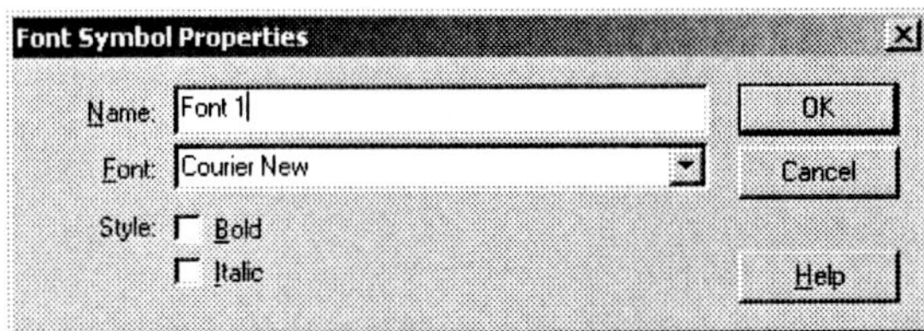

Fig 2.5. The 'Font Symbol Properties' dialog box.

The font object now appears in the library (Fig. 2.6) and will be embedded in the movie when the project is compiled. In order to use the font in the movie at runtime, it needs to be given a linkage identifier. The process is the same as specifying a linkage identifier for a movie clip – right-click on the font object, choose 'Linkage…' from the popup menu and type the required name into the 'Linkage Properties' dialog box. Keep the name of the linkage identifier the same as the font name, for convenience.

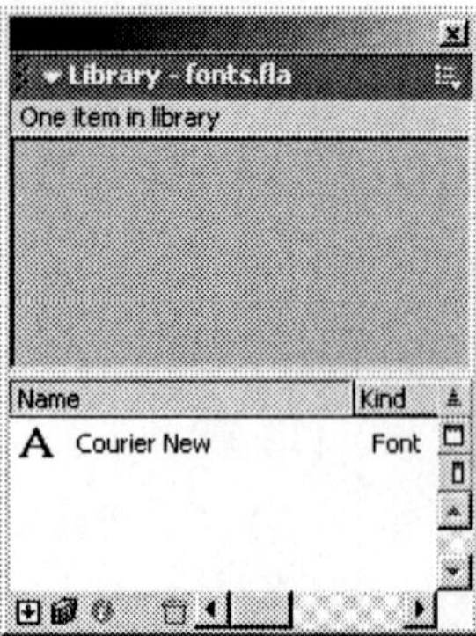

Fig. 2.6. A font object imported into the library.

If embedding a font allows the movie to use it on any platform, why not always embed fonts in movies? One reason not to do so is that it increases the movie size. Another reason is that Flash simply does not make a very good job of rendering fonts. Compare the two magnified images of the same font below, first rendered by the operating system (Fig. 2.7) and then by Flash (Fig. 2.8). Device fonts appear perfectly clearly, they are never blurred – using the desktop would quickly become unbearable if this were not the case. Flash-rendered fonts, in contrast, appear fuzzy and indistinct, regardless of point size or positioning.[61]

Device fonts should always be used where possible, then. Embedded fonts should only be used when absolutely necessary, such as when the text fields are angled (the operating system will not render fonts at an angle and the text field will simply appear blank). Embedded fonts have to be used in this movie for the angled date fields and are used throughout for the sake of continuity. Their appearance has been improved somewhat by using bold fonts and colours.

Device font

Fig. 2.7. A device font rendered by the operating system.

Embedded font

Fig. 2.8. An embedded font rendered by Flash.

[61] The appearance of embedded fonts can be slightly improved by positioning the text field precisely on a pixel. I cannot understand why Flash makes such a bad job of rendering fonts. Perhaps it uses its own line-and-fill routines to render the characters from the font outlines, rather than relying on the exact pixel renderings. This would explain the anti-aliasing, too.

Using object script

The functionality of the sliders representing the price data is defined in their object script and not in the root script. In order to draw attention to this fact, there is a suitable comment above the loop in the setUpGraph( ) method. The bar movie clip itself contains a 'README' layer to further point the programmer in the right direction[62] and all the layers containing elements with no object script are left locked.

Edit the bar movie clip and select the child instance of the 'Top' slider (actually the lower of the two sliders in the bar). Its object script should appear in the actions panel. There are two sets of handlers defined there – button handlers and frame handlers. The button handlers specify how the slider is to be dragged:

```
on ( press ) {

     this.startDrag( false, 0, 0, 0, _root.kHeight-this._height );
}

on ( release, releaseOutside ) {

     this.stopDrag();
}
```

Here, the slider is only allowed a vertical movement, the 'left' and 'right' parameters both being set to zero. Only the 'bottom' parameter is non-zero – allowing the slider to travel down to a distance of the bar height minus its own. The first parameter (set to false here) specifies whether or not the centre of the movie clip should snap to the mouse position when it is first dragged.

The 'onEnterFrame' handler is responsible for setting the value of the corresponding text field for the slider:

```
onClipEvent( enterFrame ) {

     var y;

     y = (_root.kHeight-this._y-this._height) / (_root.kHeight/_root.kScale);
     y = Math.floor( y * 10 ) / 10;

     if ( y == Math.floor( y ) ) {
          _parent.high = y + ".0";
     } else {
          _parent.high = y;
     }
}
```

An extra decimal place is added to the amount when it is an integer here, otherwise the code is pretty self-explanatory. The code for the other slider is almost identical.

62 It may seem like overkill to comment the use of object script in this manner, but it tends to become tiresome trying to keep a track of object script in a movie project otherwise. The alternative is to define the frame and button handlers on the root timeline, but since they are buried in the bar movie clip this results in code that is hardly more readable than the object script. In the case of draggable buttons in particular, I usually resort to old-fashioned object script.

Submitting data to the server

The high and low values of the text fields are retrieved by the submit( ) method in the root script and appended (suitably encoded) to a request URL:

```
function submit () {

     var uri = "";

     uri += app + "?";
     uri += "data=" + escape("set") + "&";
     uri += "page=" + escape(page) + "&";

     for ( var i = 0; i < kMonths; i++ ) {

          uri += "top"+i+"=" + escape(Number(_root[ "bar_mc"+i ].high)) + "&";
          uri += "bottom"+i+"=" + escape(Number(_root[ "bar_mc"+i ].low)) + "&";
     }

     Mouse.hide();
     _root.spinner_mc._visible = true;

     loadVariables( uri, checker );
}
```

Appending data to the request URL as GET style form variables is by far the easiest way to pass data back to the server (the same process was used by the button in the 'Simple Form' example). The escape( ) method is used to encode the values of the form variables. It should be used to encode the names of the form variables too, but since these names are known beforehand and clearly do not require it, they are not encoded. The default mouse pointer is then hidden and a 'spinning' cursor made visible instead whilst the submittal is in progress, then the loadVariables( ) method is called with the completed URL.

Note the use of the 'set' form variable to instruct the server process to save the form variables and also the use of a separate target symbol to the one used for the initial data request. The object script associated with this second target symbol simply redisplays the default mouse cursor and hides the 'spinning' cursor.

2.6: A 'Volumes' Movie

This movie is similar to the 'Prices' movie – it shows two simple, linear data sets, one of which can be altered and submitted to the server for later retrieval.

It improves slightly on the previous movie, however, by employing a variable vertical scale to cope with a wide range of data values. This scale can also be adjusted logarithmically during runtime.

Accommodating varying data ranges

The scale of the graph is not hardcoded into the movie this time but calculated once the initial data has been loaded. The object script associated with the relevant target symbol contains the code to do this, as well as the standard calls to the methods that draw the graph:

```
onClipEvent ( data ) {

    var maxvalue = 0;
    for ( var i = 0; i < _root.kMonths; i++ ) {
        maxvalue = Math.max( eval( "amount" + i ), maxvalue );
        maxvalue = Math.max( eval( "volume" + i ), maxvalue );
    }
    var scale = _root.getScale( maxvalue );

    _root.setupScaler( scale );
    _root.setupGraph( scale );
    _root.setupRemaining();
}
```

The maximum value of the all the various data elements is found and passed to the getScale( ) method. This method is used time and again in all the graph movies - it simply finds the next biggest 'suitable' number from the one provided, 'suitable' here meaning some multiple of ten, a hundred, a thousand, etc. It is well commented and no further comment is made on it here.

Next, the setupScaler( ) method is called with the initial graph scale retrieved from the getScale( ) method. This method creates and configures the scaler movie clip which provides the necessary interface to alter the vertical scale of the graph dynamically. After creating the movie clip, the height of the child pointer is calculated. Normally, the scale of the graph is derived from this height so the equation to find the pointer's height, given the initial scale, is the exact opposite:

```
var range = Math.log( kMaxScale / kMinScale ) / Math.LN10;
var size = Math.log( scale ) / Math.LN10;
var ratio = size / range;
var y = ( 1 - ratio ) * kHeight;

vertical.scale = scale;
vertical.pointer._y = y;
```

These lines calculate the ratio of the logarithms of the initial scale (the one calculated by the getScale( ) method) to the range of the scales (taken by dividing the maximum by the minimum). The resulting ratio is then easily converted into the required height for the pointer. The actual scale is also set as an instance variable in the scaler movie clip instance – it is this variable that adjusted when the pointer is moved, and retrieved when the graph is redrawn. The rest of the content of the setupScaler( ) method is concerned with defining the event handlers for the movie clip and its child pointer (more on this in a moment).

Two further methods are called from the 'loader' target symbol instance to create the graph and remaining elements: the setupGraph( ) method draws the bars, dates, scales and axes as well as defining the event handlers for the bar sliders (also dealt with in a moment); and the setupRemaining( ) method draws and configures the submit button and alternative cursor, in a similar manner to the 'Prices' movie.

Using the Flash event model

The setupScaler( ) and setupGraph( ) methods define event handlers on the vertical scaler and bar sliders respectively. Defining these event handlers in the root script hardly makes it any more readable, but using the event model is preferable in this case to using object script attached directly to the slider movie clips (the preferred solution in the 'Prices' movie).

In the case of the 'onEnterFrame' handler defined on the vertical scaler, for example, object script cannot be used since the movie clip in question is created dynamically whereas object script is always attached to instances of movie clips placed on the stage during authoring (whether as part of a parent movie clip or not). One solution would be to leave an instance of the scaler on the stage and apply the object script to it accordingly, but it is not a good idea for the very good reason that if the instance is deleted, the object script is lost forever (even though the movie clip definition remains tantalizingly in the library).

Another solution would be to embed the scaler movie clip in another parent movie clip in order to be able to attach its object script directly and protect it from accidental deletion, but this hardly seems necessary when another solution exists, namely using the 'onEnterFrame' construct.[63]

The 'onEnterFrame' handler for the vertical scaler movie clip and the two button handlers for its child pointer are defined at the end of the setupVertical( ) method. The button handlers allow the pointer to be dragged in a similar manner to the bar sliders in the 'Prices' movie. They also set a 'pressed' variable, which is used by the frame handler in the parent symbol to ascertain whether or not the pointer is being dragged. The 'onEnterFrame' handler is a little more complex:

```
scaler.onEnterFrame = function () {

    if ( this.pressed ) {

        var range = Math.log( _root.kMaxScale / _root.kMinScale ) / Math.ln10;

        var y = this.pointer._y;
        var ratio = 1 - ( y / _root.kHeight );
        var size = ratio * range;

        var scale = Math.pow( 10, size );

        var maxvalue = 0;
        for ( var i = 0; i < _root.kMonths; i++ ) {
            b = _root[ "bar" + i ];
            maxvalue = Math.max( b.amount, maxvalue );
            maxvalue = Math.max( b.volume, maxvalue );
        }

        if ( scale < ( maxvalue * 1.01 ) ) {
            this.scale = ( maxvalue * 1.01 );
        } else {
            this.scale = scale;
        }

        _root.scaleBars( this.scale );
        _root.scaleScales( this.scale );
    }
}
```

63 Object script could have been used for the button handlers on the vertical scaler's child pointer and a corresponding 'README' layer added to draw attention to its use, as in the previous 'Prices' example. It really makes no difference which method is used. My preference is to use object script for button handlers like these – the event model was used here instead in order to draw attention to the sharing of the pressed variable between the two sets of handlers and to give a usage example.

After working out the scale corresponding to the pointer's new position, the handler additionally checks whether or not this scale would accommodate the graph contents.[64] If not, the minimum allowable scale is used instead. A small adjustment is made to allow for the thickness of the bars. Also note the use of the temporary 'scale' variable, which is then applied to the main instance variable of the same name, if appropriate. The two variables do not clash because instance variables must always be qualified by the 'this' keyword in frame script.[65] Finally, the calls to the scaleBars( ) and scaleScales( ) methods will redraw the graph with the new scale whenever the pointer has been moved.

The button handlers for the sliders within the bars are along the same lines as the handlers for the sliders in the 'Prices' movie:

```
b.slider.button.onPress = function () {

     this._parent.startDrag( false, 0, 0, 0, ( _root.kHeight-2 ) );
     this._parent._parent.pressed = true;
}
b.slider.button.onRelease = function () {

     this._parent._parent.pressed = false;
     this._parent.stopDrag();
     _root.scaleBars( _root.scaler.scale );
}
```

Note the extra level of indirection here – each slider has a transparent child button symbol with a slightly larger hit area and the handlers are defined on this, rather than on the sliders themselves. The startDrag( ) and stopDrag( ) methods are thus invoked on the parent slider symbol. There is another pressed variable to notify the 'onEnterFrame' handler defined on the parent bar movie clip that the slider is being moved. Also, note the call to the scaleBars( ) method when the slider button is released – this ensures the slider is repositioned exactly according to its value and stops the sliders appearing to shift slightly when the graph is rescaled.

64 The code for calculating the height of the pointer given the initial scale of the graph should, I hope, seem a little clearer now the code to do the opposite has been given.

65 This is not the case when using object script, by the way – use of the 'this' keyword is optional.

The 'onEnterFrame' handler to adjust the value of the bar amount whenever the slider is moved is defined on the bar movie clip instance itself, rather than on the slider. This differs slightly from the similar handler in the 'Prices' movie (which is defined on the slider) but it really makes no difference. As long as the handler has access to the necessary instance variables it can be defined on any level – it could even be defined on the button itself. It simply retrieves the height of the slider if it has been moved and adjusts the corresponding bar amount accordingly:

```
b.onEnterFrame = function () {

     if ( this.pressed ) {

          var y = ( ( _root.kHeight-2 ) - this.slider._y );
          var amount = y * ( _root.scaler.scale / _root.kHeight );

          if ( amount < 1000 ) {
               amount = Math.round( 10 * amount ) / 10;
               amount = (amount == Math.round(amount)) ? amount + ".0" : amount;
          } else {
               amount = Math.round( amount );
          }
          this.amount = amount;
     }
}
```

Note the slight adjustment in the y variable to take into account the thickness of the slider. This is also present in the startDrag( ) call in the button handler. It does not affect the calculation of the amount for the bar though, which uses the full height of the graph, namely 'kHeight'.

Arranging movie elements in the library

The number of elements has increased considerably in this project and a standard method of organising them in the library is needed if it is not to become cluttered and unusable. Symbol definitions are always organised – they are never simply left in the root of library. Only if the project contains very few symbols and no components is this practice really excusable.

The standard adopted in this book is to put the elements of a project that do not belong to any particular component into a folder of their own, named after the movie itself. Movie clips that are either used directly on the stage; or that have linkage identifiers and are created dynamically at runtime, should sit in this default folder. The only elements in the root of the library should therefore be folders containing either components or significant movie clips. Components and their child elements should occupy their own folders.

One way of ensuring that the folders never split the movie clips, thus keeping the library well organised, is to prepend an 'F' to all the movie clip names. Folders will then appear either above or below the symbols as a block, as long as folder names beginning with 'F' are avoided (an easier task than trying to think up suitable names for the movie clips).

Child elements of these movie clips should occupy subfolders of the default movie folder. The standard practice is to create an 'Assets' folder and populate it with further subfolders corresponding to the child elements of each significant movie clip, wherever necessary. The contents of these subfolders can be further separated into folders containing buttons, images and so on, as in Fig. 2.9.[66]

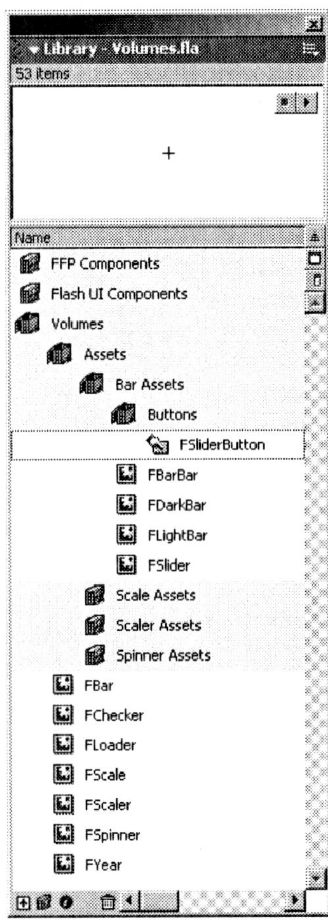

Fig. 2.9. The library window showing subfolders for assets, etc.

66 This naming convention apes components. See the next chapter for an explanation of this convention (the simple graph movie clips themselves are similar to components).

Simple Data Representation

The movies in this section appear to be more basic than the interactive ones – they display data sets statically and do not allow any interaction. They are placed after the interactive movies, however, because programmatically they take a considerable step forward.

The root scripts contain virtually nothing but the initial call to load the data and the method to create an instance or instances of the required graph once the data has been received. They look much the better for it. The code to draw the graphs is contained within the graph movie clips themselves – they have become black boxes in effect, just like components.[67]

The script in the graphs themselves takes the form of a class definition, the class itself being associated with graph movie clip using the Object.registerClass( ) method. This is the first time that object-oriented programming has been used thus far and it becomes standard practice from now on. Separating the code into logical blocks and grouping these blocks with their associated movie clips is essential if movies are to remain intelligible as their complexity increases.

67 Similarities with components abound throughout these three chapters. This section (and the one that follows) can be considered as a gentle introduction to component programming, in fact.

2.7: Bar Chart

This movie shows two sets of data interlaced in the same graph, with a legend to associate the bars with their corresponding data sets. The vertical scale is variable, allowing the graph to accommodate different data ranges.

The scale is not adjustable at runtime however, the data it represents being entirely static.

A simplified movie structure

Compared to the previous interactive graph movies, the root script is much reduced here. Apart from the loadData( ) and getScale( ) methods, the only other method is drawGraph( ), which is called from the object script in the normal manner once the scale has been calculated:

```
onClipEvent( data ) {

     var maxamount = 0;
     for ( var j = 0; j < eval( "sets" ); j++ ) {
          for ( var i = 0; i < eval( "months" ); i++ ) {
               maxamount = Math.max( eval( "amount_"+j+"_"+i  ), maxamount );
          }
     }

     var scale = _root.getScale( maxamount );

     var months = Number( months );
     var sets = Number( sets );

     _root.drawGraph( scale, months, sets, title );
}
```

The drawGraph( ) method hardly draws the graph at all – it simply creates and positions the necessary movie clip instance and calls the draw( ) method on it:

```
function drawGraph( scale, months, sets, title ) {

     _root.attachMovie( "FBarChartSymbol", "graph_mc", mcCount++ );

     _root[ "graph_mc" ]._x = kXOffset;
     _root[ "graph_mc" ]._y = kYOffset;
     _root[ "graph_mc" ].draw( scale, months, sets, title );
}
```

The graph as a complex movie clip

The graph movie clip itself contains three layers – an actions layer, a name layer and an assets layer. The actions layer is placed at the top and contains the class definition within an initialisation block. The name layer contains the name symbol. This graphic symbol has no use apart from giving the graph an appearance in the library preview window or on the stage, should it ever be dragged there rather than being created dynamically.

The assets layer contains instances of movie clips that are dynamically created by the graph. Like the name symbol, assets play no part in the actual appearance of the movie during runtime; in fact, they are made as small as possible on the stage and removed by the graph during initialisation. The assets layer is commonly hidden and turned into a guide layer by double-clicking on its icon and choosing 'Guide' from the 'Type' group of the resulting 'Layer Properties' dialog.[68]

It is most important to ensure that a movie clip contains as assets all the elements that it may create at runtime, otherwise the definitions will not be available if the movie clip is copied to another project. To see the assets easily, either hide all the other layers and magnify the movie clip as much as possible, or look at them in the movie explorer. An instance of the parent movie clip must be present on stage in order to view its contents in this way, however. If the movie clip is only ever dynamically created (and thus, no instances are present on the stage), simply drag one onto an empty layer and delete it again when the contents of the assets layer have been verified.

The frame script in the actions layer consists of a constructor, the class definition, some class constants and one public method, namely draw( ). The remainder of the initialisation script contains private methods to draw the various graph elements, mostly called from the draw( ) method. The constructor basically takes care of any housekeeping to be done before the graph is actually drawn:

```
/// Constructor
function FBarChartClass()
{
    this.deadPreview._width = this.deadPreview._height = 0;
    this.deadPreview._visible = false;

    this.keyAsset.unloadMovie();
    this.yearAsset.unloadMovie();
    this.monthAsset.unloadMovie();
    this.scaleAsset.unloadMovie();
    this.titleAsset.unloadMovie();
    this.dividerAsset.unloadMovie();

    this._xscale = this._yscale = 100;

    this.height = this.kDefaultHeight;
    this.width = this.kDefaultWidth;

    this.mcCount = 0;
}
```

68 The graph movie clip's use of the actions, name and assets layer together with the name and assets symbols closely apes the structure of components.

Firstly, the name symbol that represents the graph is hidden – the graph has no use for it during runtime. Next, the assets are removed and the graph is scaled to its full size.[69] This step is rarely necessary – only if the graph were dragged onto the stage and distorted somehow (by being a child element of another movie clip, for example) would these lines make any difference. Next, the 'width' and 'height' instance variables are defined. These values have nothing to do with the '_width' and '_height' properties of the associated movie clip (at least, not directly) although the two sets will often coincide. The syntax highlighter picks them out however, since they are so ubiquitous. Finally, an 'mcCount' instance variable is initialised and is used in the same manner as the one defined in the root scripts of previous movies.

The class definition, the definitions of the class constants and the public draw( ) method all follow the constructor and are not worth further comment. The drawAxes( ) method is responsible for drawing most of the graph, apart from the bars themselves. It closely follows similar methods called from the object scripts of the 'loader' target symbols in the interactive movies, the only big difference being that the various dynamically created graph elements are attached to the graph movie clip, rather than to the root of the movie itself.

In fact, an empty container movie clip called 'axes_mc' is created, which is used as a holder for the various graph elements created by this method. Its presence is not so important in this case but if the graph were to be redrawn, in response to a change in the data, say, the easiest way to remove the child elements would be simply to remove the parent movie clip to which they were all attached. The axes themselves are drawn onto the 'axes_mc' movie clip, as are the scale movie clips:

```
var depth = 0;
for ( i = 0; i <= this.kNumScales; i++ ) {

    this.axes_mc.attachMovie( "FScaleSymbol", "scale_mc" + i, depth++ );
    this.axes_mc[ "scale_mc"+i ].label.text = scale * i/this.kNumScales;
    this.axes_mc[ "scale_mc"+i ]._x = 0;
    this.axes_mc[ "scale_mc"+i ]._y = this.height * ( 1 - i/this.kNumScales );
    this.axes_mc[ "scale_mc"+i ].line._width = this.width;
}
```

The 'kNumScales' class variable is used here, even though it was never explicitly set in the constructor. It is available directly by use of the 'this' keyword however, anything defined on a class as a whole using the 'prototype' method (whether method or variable) being available to any particular instance of that class. A local 'depth' variable is used here, too – the 'mcCount' variable is reserved for the empty movie clips attached to the graph, which contain the child elements.

69 More functionality common to components. The unloadMovie( ) method is used here to remove instances of the assets – the removeMovieClip( ) method only works on movie clip instances that are created dynamically. In contrast, the name symbol is only minimised and hidden. This is the preferred method in the FUIComponentClass constructor and since these graphs borrow much from the FUIComponent movie clip, this practice is maintained. Exactly why this method is preferred is a mystery to me.

Array syntax must be used to reference the dynamically created scales - the second argument in the attachMovie( ) method merely specifies the name of the 'scale' movie clip relative to the 'axes_mc' movie clip to which it is attached. There is a way of obtaining a shortened reference to dynamically created movie clips however – the attachMovie( ) method itself returns a reference to the movie clip that it creates. This method is used in the script to create the month labels in the next loop:

```
var month = substring( eval( "_root.loader.date" + i ), 0, 3 );
var tmpMnth = this.axes_mc.attachMovie( "FMonthSymbol","month_mc"+i,depth++ );

tmpMnth._x = ( i + 1/2 ) * ( this.width / months );
tmpMnth._y = this.height;
tmpMnth.label.text = month;
```

Note that although the same 'tmpMnth' variable is used repeatedly, it points to a different movie clip instance each time. It also has the benefit of not being an instance variable – it is merely temporary and can be discarded when the loop terminates. The remainder of the drawAxes( ) method creates and positions the year labels in a similar manner to the interactive movies.

The drawBars( ) method is called next, retrieving the necessary data directly from the 'loader' target symbol. The data is not provided by any argument to the draw( ) method and does not become associated with the graph movie clip at all. Instead the standard eval( ) methods are used:

```
this.createEmptyMovieClip( "bars_mc", this.mcCount++ );
this.bars_mc.lineStyle( 1, 0x333333 );
for ( var j = 0; j < sets; j++ ) {
     for ( var i = 0; i < months; i++ ) {

          var amount = eval( "_root.loader.amount_"+j+"_"+i );
          this.drawBar( this.bars_mc, i, j, amount, scale, months, sets );
     }
}
```

Another empty movie clip is created as a container for the bars, ensuring they sit above all the other elements drawn so far. The movie clip's line style is set here, too, and inherited by the bars themselves. The amount for each bar is recovered and passed to the drawBar( ) method, together with a reference to the 'bars_mc' container and other variables besides. This method is straightforward enough and no more mention of it is made here.

The last method called is drawLegend( ). This draws and positions the legend in the top right-hand corner of the graph. Again, an empty container movie clip is created and the legend contents drawn on it. Normally, dynamically created movie clips sit at the top left-hand corner of the parent movie clip's coordinate system but this time the container movie clip is positioned explicitly, based on the size of its contents.

2.8: Line Chart

This movie shows two sets of data by drawing two separate graphs altogether. The data values are made up of coordinates rather than indexed amounts, with the date information consisting of an end date and quarterly values. The variable, vertical scale remains the same as the previous 'Bar Chart' example, however.

Instantiating multiple graph movie clips

The data set for these graphs is considerably larger than any other data set so far – the total number of items runs to well over a hundred and although this still only constitutes a few kilobytes, it is best to split it up and load the data for each graph separately. This keeps the mechanics of the movie as simple as possible, the second set of data being loaded over the top of the first, once the first graph has been drawn.

Only one target symbol is used, the drawGraph( ) method checking to see which data set has been loaded and after drawing the corresponding graph, calling the loadData( ) method a second time if necessary. The initial call to the loadData( ) method is made directly from the root script:

```
/// We're off!
loadData( 1 );
stop();

function drawGraph ( date, days, count, scale, title, num ) {

     _root.attachMovie( "FLineChartSymbol", "graph_mc" + num, mcCount++ );

     _root[ "graph_mc" +num ]._x = kXOffset + kWidth * (num-1);
     _root[ "graph_mc" +num ]._y = kYOffset;
     _root[ "graph_mc" +num ].draw( date, days, count, scale, num, title );

     if ( num == 1 ) {
          loadData( 2 );
     }
}
```

Note that the loadData( ) method has an argument this time, which it passes on to the server process, enabling it to respond with the required data set. This number is then echoed with the data so that it is available again to the target symbol, which passes it to the drawGraph( ) method.

Labelling the axes

Although drawing the actual graph remains straightforward, populating the x-axis is a more difficult task, the movie working out the values and positions of the quarterly values itself since the server process only provides the end date and number of days.[70]

This is done in the drawAxes( ) method, which creates the standard, empty 'axes_mc' movie clip before drawing the axes outline and attaching the scales. The end date symbol is then attached and positioned in at the rightmost extent of the x-axis:

```
var tmpDate = this.axes_mc.attachMovie( "FDateSymbol", "endDate", depth++ );
this.axes_mc.attachMovie( "FDividerSymbol", "endDivider", depth++ );

tmpDate._x = this.width;
tmpDate._y = this.height;
tmpDate.label.text = enddate;

this.axes_mc[ "endDivider" ]._x = this.width;
this.axes_mc[ "endDivider" ]._y = this.height;
```

Note the use of a temporary variable and the array syntax here, to reference the date and divider movie clips respectively.[71] The positioning of the date is made as simple as possible by editing the movie clip itself and positioning the child text field on the stage by hand. This rule applies to most of the graph labels, in fact.[72]

In order to retrieve the remaining values for the x-axis, the first task is to convert the end date string into days, months and years. This is done by splitting it up and converting the months into their corresponding numbers using an associative array as a lookup table:

```
var tmpArray = enddate.split( " " );
var dddd = tmpArray[0],
    mmm = tmpArray[1],
    yyyy = tmpArray[2];

var monthLookup = { jan:0, feb:1,  mar:2,
                    apr:3, may:4,  jun:5,
                    jul:6, aug:7,  sep:8,
                    oct:9, nov:10, dec:11 };

var day = Number(dddd.substr( 0, dddd.length-2 ));
var month = Number(monthLookup[mmm]);
var year = Number(yyyy);
```

70 Again, the remainder of this chapter is an exception to the rule that I only comment on those parts of the example movies that demonstrate new techniques. The process of working out the quarterly values and positions is convoluted enough to warrant further explanation, however. If you are not interested in this subject, you can move on to the next chapter.

71 I tend to use the two methods interchangeably and have no hard and fast rule for which to apply and when.

72 Usually the opposite is true – child elements are aligned so that their top left corners and coordinate centres coincide. Although this means that the script to position them will be more complicated, it allows them to be used confidently in more than one situation. Since the labels for the simple graphs are used only once however, in the vast majority of cases fine positional adjustments are made quickly and easily by editing the movie clips. See the next section on advanced movies for a more standard approach to positioning child elements.

The next task is to work out how many days separate the end date from the start of the quarter to which it belongs, storing the result in the offset variable. Calculations are approximate, by the way – the number of days in each month is a constant (and not even an integer), held in the class variable 'kMonthDays'. To continue, the 'offset' variable is used to enable a loop to count from the day corresponding to the start of the last quarter back to zero, in steps corresponding to the approximate number of days in a quarter:

```
var qtr = Math.floor(month/3);
var offset = (month-3*qtr) * this.kMonthDays + day;

...

for ( i = (days-offset); i >= 0; i -= this.kQtrYear ) {

     ...
}
```

Each step in this loop corresponds to the beginning of a quarter and so dividers are drawn at the equivalent positions on the x-axis, with the proviso that no divider is drawn too close to the end date:

```
var x = i * ( this.width / days );
if ( x < this.width - this.kRightAxisMask ) {

     this.axes_mc.attachMovie( "FDividerSymbol", "divider" + count, depth++ );
     this.axes_mc[ "divider" + count ]._x = x;
     this.axes_mc[ "divider" + count ]._y = this.height;
     count++;

     x -= ( this.kQtrYear/2) * ( this.width / days );

     if ( x > 0 ) {

          ...
     }
}
```

The dividers are easily positioned by rescaling the loop counter. This coordinate is then offset by an amount equivalent to half the width of a quarter and a further test is made to see whether it still falls within the limits of the graph (that is, if it is greater than zero). If this is the case, a label is created and positioned, its value being set to the relevant quarter using the quarters associative array:

```
tmpX = x;

this.axes_mc.attachMovie( "FQuarterSymbol", "quarter" + count, depth++ );

this.axes_mc[ "quarter" + count ]._x = x;
this.axes_mc[ "quarter" + count ]._y = this.height;
this.axes_mc[ "quarter" + count ].label.text = quarters[ qtr ];
count++;

...

qtr--; qtr = ( qtr == -1 ) ? 3 : qtr;
```

The ‘count’ variable is then incremented (it was defined just before the start of the loop) and the ‘qtr’ variable decremented and reset if necessary.

The final task is to draw the year labels. The position of the first one (the movie assumes that the data spans no more than two years) is calculated by saving the index of the first quarter to be drawn in the ‘rightQtr’ variable and using it to calculate the necessary offset when the quarter at the start of the year is encountered:

```
if ( rightQtr == undefined ) {
    rightQtr = qtr;
}
if ( qtr == 0 ) {

    x += rightQtr * (this.kQtrYear/2) * ( this.width / days )

    this.axes_mc.attachMovie( "FYearSymbol", "year" + count, depth++ );

    this.axes_mc[ "year" + count ]._x = x;
    this.axes_mc[ "year" + count ]._y = this.height + this.kYearOffset;
    this.axes_mc[ "year" + count ].label.text = year;
    count++;

    year--;
    rightQtr = 3;
}
```

The year offset clearly needs to be the half the number of quarters displayed for the particular year, multiplied by the width of a quarter. Once this label is positioned, the ‘year’ variable is decremented and the ‘rightQtr’ variable reset. When the loop finishes, a further check is made to see whether or not another year label has to be drawn. The ‘qtr’ variable is first reset to its real value (being decremented at the end of each loop, it ends up one less than its true value) and if it is non-zero, another year label needs to be drawn:

```
qtr++; qtr = ( qtr == 4 ) ? 0 : qtr;
if ( qtr > 0 ) {

    x = tmpX + ( rightQtr - qtr ) * (this.kQtrYear/2) * ( this.width / days
);

    ...

}
```

Note the use of the ‘tmpX’ variable – the ‘x’ variable itself is corrupted by being used to position the quarter labels so the real value is saved just before the quarter labels are drawn. The remainder of the drawAxes( ) method simply draws and positions the graph title and needs no further comment here.

2.9: Pie Chart

This movie shows a single data set, allowing different colours for each slice or even pre-defined patterns.

The slices themselves are named, the name labels appearing along each side of the chart, with jointed lines connecting them to their corresponding slice.

Preprocessing the data

This movie differs from the previous two in the way it handles the graph data, which is processed before being made available to the graph. The processed data is held in arrays on the root of the movie, and the graph movie clip looks there to retrieve it rather than to the 'loader' target symbol. Patterns for the slices are also created, and again these are left in the root of the movie and picked up by the graph movie clip as and when they are needed (more on this in a moment).

The data retrieved from the server process is processed in the drawGraph( ) method before the pie chart is created and its draw( ) method invoked:

```
function drawGraph ( count, sort ) {

     for ( var i = 0; i < count; i++ ) {
          items[ i ] = { value:Number( eval( "loader.value" + i ) ),
                         offset:Number( eval( "loader.offset" + i ) ),
                         name:eval( "loader.name" + i ),
                         pattern:eval( "loader.pattern" + i )     };
     }
     if ( sort == "true" ) {
          items.sort( function (a,b) {

               if ( a.value > b.value ) { return +1; }
               if ( a.value < b.value ) { return -1; }
               return 0;
          } );
     }

     ...
}
```

The various properties for each slice are added to an associative array which is then added to the items array. This array is then sorted, if necessary, using the native sort( ) method with an anonymous comparator method. This comparator ensures that the array is sorted by the value keys of each item.

The optional patterns for the slices are created with the drawPatterns( ) method, which has two child methods at its disposal: the createPatternFromGraphic( ) method (the preferred method) and the createPatternLines( ) method. Both create a movie clip containing a pattern and an empty movie clip to use as a mask; and both return the reference to the newly created pattern movie clip. The former also takes an argument specifying the linkage identifier of the pattern to be incorporated:

```
function createPatternFromGraphic ( name ) {

     var depth = 0;

     _root.createEmptyMovieClip( name, mcCount++ );
     _root[ name ]._x = kXOffset;
     _root[ name ]._y = kYOffset;

     _root[ name ].attachMovie( name, "graphic_mc", depth++ )
     _root[ name ].createEmptyMovieClip( "mask_mc", depth++ );
     _root[ name ].setMask( _root[ name ].mask_mc );

     return _root[ name ];
}
```

The resultant movie clip is centred in the same place as the graph so that it covers the full extent of the pie chart. It is then hidden completely by applying an empty movie clip as a mask. Masking a movie clip means that the only parts made visible are those that lie beneath non-empty parts of the mask. In this case, a reference to the masking movie clip is retrieved by the graph (being a child of the pattern movie clip itself, it is easily retrieved) and if necessary, the filling of the slice is added to the mask, allowing the pattern to show through the relevant slices.

The graph elements as movie clips

The two previous movies drew the graph elements directly using the moveTo( ) and lineTo( ) methods. In this movie however, the graph elements (namely, the slices are their respective labels) are movie clips in their own right, their structure closely mirroring that of the parent graph movie clip, in fact. The slice movie clip has its own name symbol and assets layer, for example, as well as its own associated class. The graph draws each slice by creating a slice movie clip and invoking the necessary methods on it:

```
FPieChartClass.prototype.drawSlice = function ( sideX, sideY, i ) {

     this.attachMovie( "FSliceSymbol", "slice_mc" + i, i, { controller:this,
                                                            index:i,
                                                            side:sideX} );

     this[ "slice_mc" + i ].drawSlice();
     this.adjustYCoords( sideX, sideY );
     this[ "slice_mc" + i ].drawLabel();
}
```

Here, the fourth argument is used to set instance variables on the newly created slice. The 'controller' variable is particularly important, giving the slice a reference to its parent movie clip, which it uses to access the graph's instance variables directly.[73]

The contents of the graph's FPieChartClass class are considerably simplified by the abstraction of much of the calculation involved in drawing the slices to the class of the slice movie clip itself. The remaining complexity is mainly due to having to work out the order in which the slices are drawn, so as to enable their associated text labels to be positioned correctly.

As well as the usual lines to hide the name symbol and ensure that the graph is sized correctly, the constructor contains definitions of instance variables that are used both across the methods of the class and also by the child slice movie clips (by way of the 'controller' variable). These are used to position both the slices and their corresponding text labels:

```
function FPieChartClass()
{
     this.deadPreview._width = this.deadPreview._height = 0;
     this.deadPreview._visible = false;

     this._xscale = this._yscale = 100;
     this._x = this._y = 0;

     this.angles = new Array();

     this.tmpCoord = undefined;
     this.textCoord = undefined;
     this.middleCoord = undefined;

     this.savedY = undefined;
}
```

73 This is component speak again – the controller variable forms an important part of components, giving child elements access to the properties and methods of the parent or 'host' component.

The 'angles' array stores the angles that divide the slices, easily calculated by the draw( ) method from the cumulative totals of the data 'items' provided in the items array:

```
var totals = new Array();
var total = 0;
totals[ 0 ] = 0;
for ( i = 0; i < this.count; i++ ) {
     totals[ i + 1 ] = totals[ i ] + _root.items[ i ].value;
     total += _root.items[ i ].value;
}
for ( i = 0; i <= this.count; i++ ) {
     this.angles[ i ] = 2*Math.PI * totals[ i ] / total;
}
```

The '_root' keyword prepended to the items array is not necessary here but is left in to draw attention to the origin of the array. The remainder of the draw( ) method splits the graph into four 'quarters' along both axes to enable the slices to be drawn upwards and downwards from the horizontal on each side of the graph. This enables the text labels to be positioned so as not to overlap, the lines linking them to their corresponding slices being jointed if necessary. The nearest part of the line to the slice may also itself be displaced slightly so as not to appear to 'stick' to its neighbour.

All these various positions are maintained in the 'tmpCoord', 'textCoord' and 'middleCoord' instance variables defined in the constructor and are altered both by methods in the graph and in the case of the 'tmpCoord' variable, by the slices, too.[74]

The constructor for the slice class copies the required values from the root items array to instance variables, for the convenience of the other class methods:

```
function FSliceClass()
{
     this.deadPreview._width = this.deadPreview._height = 0;
     this.deadPreview._visible = false;

     this._xscale = this._yscale = 100;
     this._x = this._y = 0;

     this.name = _root.items[ this.index ].name;
     this.value = _root.items[ this.index ].value;
     this.offset = _root.items[ this.index ].offset;
     this.pattern = _root.items[ this.index ].pattern;

     this.angle1 = this.controller.angles[ this.index ];
     this.angle2 = this.controller.angles[ this.index + 1 ];

     this.middle = ( this.angle1 + this.angle2 ) / 2;

     this.xOffset = Math.sin( this.middle ) * this.offset;
     this.yOffset = -Math.cos( this.middle ) * this.offset;
}
```

74 Unlike the mechanism to populate the x-axis in the previous movie, I am not going to give this one any further explanation. It is rather depressing to note how straightforward this movie would be without the need to space the text labels in this manner, a task that at first sight appears much simpler that it actually is.

The angles that delimit the slice are also retrieved from the parent movie clip here by using the 'controller' variable. This is the advantage of using the optional fourth array of the attachMovie( ) method – the properties of the argument are immediately applied to the resultant movie clip and are thus available as instance variables in the constructor.

The drawSlice( ) method either draws the slice directly with the requisite fill colour or, if a pattern is required, creates an empty movie clip to attach to the pattern's masking movie clip and draws on that. It then draws just the rim, 'on top'. It also sets the 'tmpCoord' variable of its parent movie clip to the coordinate of the end of the line that joins it to its text label. The remaining private methods are self-explanatory.

3D Data Modelling

These three movies take another step up from the simple and interactive graphs, in terms of both appearance and programming complexity. Common tasks have been abstracted to a superclass and data is held in the graphs themselves.

In particular, the eval( ) method is not used to retrieve the data from the 'loader' target symbol. Instead, the graphs store their own data internally using a data provider object.

2.10: The 'Fake' 3D Graphs

Both movies[75] here use a less than realistic perspective to render the graphs, although it is arguable whether a 'true' perspective would, in fact, do a better job. The use of perspectives without the foreshortening usually associated with increased distances from the eye actually suits the relatively limited extent of the graphs and the uniform nature of the data.

The bar chart uses what is commonly called an isometric view – each of the coordinate axes (the graph axes corresponding exactly to the coordinate axes in both cases) is at sixty degrees to the other two. The viewpoint thus appears to be someway in front of and above the scene – the user looks down on a scene that does not appear to diminish with distance in any direction.

The line chart uses a view where the x and y axes appear at right angles to one another, in the same manner as a standard, two-dimensional Cartesian view. The z axis then trails off at forty-five degrees between them, giving an illusion of depth. The viewpoint thus appears to be in front of the scene but also some way above and to the right of it.

75 This chapter discusses the first two of the 3D graph movies together, since there is so little to choose between them.

Creating the data object

Because the data to draw the graphs is stored in the graphs themselves, the 'loader' target symbol can be safely unloaded once the graphs have been drawn. This is done by the object script itself, as soon as the requisite root methods have been invoked:[76]

```
onClipEvent( data ) {

     _root.drawGraph( sets, items, title );
     _root.drawLegend( sets );

     this.unloadMovie();
}
```

Here, the drawGraph( ) and drawLegend( ) methods are called, the former with some (but not all) of the loader's associated data passed as parameters, for convenience. The drawGraph( ) method now immediately retrieves the data from the 'loader' symbol and stores it in a temporary object:

```
function drawGraph( sets, items, title ) {

     var i,j;
     var dataObj = new Object;

     dataObj.sets = sets;
     dataObj.items = items;
     dataObj.title = title;
     dataObj.amount = new Array();
     for ( j = 0; j < sets; j++ ) {
          for ( i = 0; i < items; i++ ) {
               dataObj.amount[i+j*items]=eval("_root.loader.amount"+"_"+j+"_"+i );
          }
     }
     dataObj.date = new Array();
     for ( i = 0; i < items; i += 1 ) {
          dataObj.date[i] = eval( "_root.loader.date" + i );
     }
     dataObj.label = new Array();
     for ( j = 0; j < sets; j += 1 ) {
          dataObj.label[j] = eval( "_root.loader.label" + j );
     }

     var link = "F3DBarChartSymbol";
     _root.attachMovie( link, "graph_mc", mcCount++, {dataProvider:dataObj} );

     delete dataObj;

     _root[ "graph_mc" ]._x = kXOffset;
     _root[ "graph_mc" ]._y = kYOffset;
     _root[ "graph_mc" ].draw();
}
```

76 Of course, the loader symbols could have been removed in the previous movies as well.

The graph movie clip is then created in the usual manner, but with the addition of an optional fourth argument to the attachMovie( ) method to pass the data object to the graph. The graph movie clip thus has access to all the data it requires from the start and never once uses the eval( ) method to retrieve data directly from the 'loader' target symbol. Instead, it keeps a copy of the data object with an instance name of dataProvider (hence the original can be safely deleted) and refers to this whenever necessary.[77]

77 Choice of the name 'dataProvider' here follows component convention, where component data is stored in an instance of a data provider class. This class has methods to change the data in real time and also allows several components to access the same data set. Here, a more basic mechanism is used – the data provider object simply providing a convenient place-holder in order to keep the data separate from the graph's other instance variables.

Abstracting common functionality

Because the graph data is passed via the attachMovie( ) method, it is immediately available to the graph class constructor, which stores some of it as instance variables after the usual initialisation. In fact, the constructor calls an init( ) method, rather than performing these tasks itself:[78]

```
#initclip 1

/// Constructor
function F3DBarChartClass()
{
     this.init();
}

/// Class definition
F3DBarChartClass.prototype = new F3DGraphClass();
Object.registerClass("F3DBarChartSymbol", F3DBarChartClass);

/// Initialiser
F3DBarChartClass.prototype.init = function () {

     super.init();

     this.yearAsset.unloadMovie();
     this.monthAsset.unloadMovie();
     this.scaleAsset.unloadMovie();

     /// Set these data provider properties for convenience.
     ///
     this.sets = this.dataProvider.sets;
     this.items = this.dataProvider.items;
}

...

#endinitclip
```

The init( ) method contains the usual calls to unload the graph's assets, as well as copying the sets and items variables of the data provider into instance variables. It also contains a call to the init( ) method of its superclass, defined in the 'class definition' lines above as being the F3DgraphClass class. This class is defined in the F3DGraph movie clip, a copy of which is kept as a child of the graph movie clip itself, in order to ensure that its definition is available should the graph be copied to another movie entirely. This mirrors the practice of including assets in a movie clip, the movie clip containing the superclass definition being kept in its own 'SuperClass' layer, however, rather than in the assets layer.

When one movie clip class extends another in this manner, the definition of the latter must already be available. For this reason, a number is added to the #initclip instruction so that the initialiser blocks (those lines of code delimited by the #initclip and #endinitclip instructions) are executed in a definite order. The number trailing the #initclip instruction in the definition of the F3DGraphClass class is zero for example, ensuring it is defined before either graph class.

78 Again, this practice mirrors component convention, where the body of the constructor simply contains a call to the class initialiser, or may contain an additional check to see whether the initialiser needs to be invoked at all. Cases when the initialiser needn't be called include occasions when it is a child asset of another component; or if the class is nameless, being instantiated because of the inclusion of the new keyword in a class definition. See the 'The trouble with Flash class inheritance' appendix for more details.

There is a subtle but important difference between the order of initialisation and the order of execution. All initialisation blocks will be executed before any frame script in a movie, with class definitions and such like therefore available immediately at runtime. There is no need, for example, to set the order of the initialisation of the title movie clip class, since it is only referenced at runtime when an instance is dynamically created. Only when one class is dependent on another is it necessary to make explicitly clear to Flash which should be defined first.

To continue, the graph superclass itself contains much of the functionality that is common to all three graphs. The superclass init( ) method, for example, includes the usual code to hide the name symbol, position and scale the graph correctly and so on:

```
#initclip 0

/// Constructor
function F3DGraphClass()
{
}

/// Class definition
F3DGraphClass.prototype = new MovieClip();
///Object.registerClass("F3DGraphSymbol", F3DGraphClass);

/// Initialiser
F3DGraphClass.prototype.init = function () {

     this.deadPreview._width = this.deadPreview._height = 0;
     this.deadPreview._visible = false;

     this._x = Math.floor(this._x);
     this._y = Math.floor(this._y);
     this._xscale = this._yscale = 100;

     this.mcCount = 0;

     this.titleAsset.unloadMovie();

     this.title = this.dataProvider.title;
}

#endinitclip
```

There is no need to associate this class with its corresponding movie clip, by the way, which does nothing apart from provide a container for the frame script containing the class definition. Hence, the usual line to do this is commented out. It is necessary that this class extend the MovieClip class, however. This is most important – the final superclass of any set of class definitions must extend this class if the topmost subclass (the one corresponding to the visible movie clip) is to have access to the usual movie clip properties.[79]

Variables and properties are shared transparently between the two classes when one extends the other. The 'deadPreview' references here point to child elements of the parent graph movie clip, for example, and the 'dataProvider' reference is just as valid here. Going the other way, the 'mcCount' instance variable is available to the graph class. Finally, note that there is no call to the init( ) method in the constructor but if it did contain such a call, the init( ) method of the graph class would be invoked (if it was defined) and not the init( ) method here.

79 Flash's own FUIComponentClass class extends MovieClip, for example.

The remainder of the F3DGraph class definition contains methods common to the graphs – the getScale( ) method, for example, previously left on the root script of many of the movies, now becomes a class method, as does the getYearPositions( ) method, which calculates the positions of the two year labels for graphs spanning one year. Neither needs further comment here. The remaining drawTitle( ) method is called from the draw( ) method of the F3DGraph class which, like the initialiser, is called from the graph class using the 'super' keyword.

A comprehensive library structure

Both the title and F3DGraph movie clips are common to all three graph movies and hence their definitions are contained in the libraries of each. There is no straightforward way to keep such shared assets synchronised other than by constantly dragging revised elements into all the other projects that use them. Keeping shared elements in appropriately named folders at least makes this process a little more manageable.[80]

The easiest way to explain the various folders is to have a look at the fully expanded library of one of the movies. In Fig. 2.10 the movie clips already present on the stage or dynamically created in the root script at runtime are kept in the root '3DGraphs' folder, named after the group of movies to which the graph movie belongs, rather than the graph movie itself. The remaining movie elements are divided between various child folders of the 'Core Assets – Developer Only' folder. This folder includes a 'Global Assets' folder to hold assets common to all the movies and, in particular, the F3DGraph movie clip.

Fig. 2.10. The library window with the project folder fully expanded.

The FKey movie clip is included in root '3DGraphs' folder, by the way, because although it is shared amongst all the three movies, it is referenced from the root script and does not form part of the graph movie clips themselves. The reason for this is that the creation of the legend (of which the FKey movie clip is a part) is not a task that is devolved to the actual graph movie clips, since the legend only needs to be drawn once per movie and not once per graph. The drawLegend( ) method therefore sits in the root script and is copied from one movie to another.

80 In fact, Flash is pretty bad at getting the folder right when movie elements are dragged from one project to another. The folders that hold a particular symbol definition usually aren't duplicated or, if they are, they are placed in the wrong folder themselves. A symbol definition will therefore often have to be repositioned in the library once it has been imported in this manner.

Building the graphs

The remaining functionality in the graph classes simply finds a suitable scale for the graphs (a task previously done in the 'loader' target symbol's object script) and then draws the graph axes and bars accordingly. The sets and items instance variables, initially passed (amongst others) directly to the drawGraph( ) method in the root script are again passed to the child methods that draw the graph proper:

```
F3DBarChartClass.prototype.draw = function() {

     var maxAmount = 0;
     for ( var j = 0; j < this.sets; j++ ) {
          for ( var i = 0; i < this.items; i++ ) {
               var tmpAmount = this.dataProvider.amount[i+j*this.items];
               maxAmount = Math.max( tmpAmount, maxAmount );
          }
     }

     this.getScale( maxAmount );

     this.drawAxes( this.sets, this.items );
     this.drawGraph( this.sets, this.items );

     super.draw();
}
```

Note the use of the 'dataProvider' object here and also that, because there is no support for multi-dimensional arrays, the various items of each data set have to be referenced linearly.

The drawAxes( ) methods draw and label the axes, according to the differing perspectives of each graph. There is little to note here apart from a slight difference in positioning between them – the month and year labels of the bar chart are shifted along by one sixth of the width of a bar, since the base of the graph has a border of this size around the bars, whereas the labels of the line chart are moved back by half the width of the line (the distance between two points, effectively), since they sit underneath each point rather than halfway between them (which the getYearPositions( ) method assumes).

The labels for the graph axes themselves, although common to both (and sharing the same names in both, too) have separate definitions in each movie and are placed in a child folder of the core assets folder that reflects the movie name, rather than in the 'Global Assets' folder. It is simply easier to define them individually in this way rather than have to position them using script in the drawAxes( ) method.

The drawGraph( ) methods similarly require little further comment, apart from noting that in order to achieve the effect of certain graph elements appearing in front of others, all that is necessary is that they are drawn in the correct order, the furthest ones being drawn first. Specifically, there is no need to attach each individual graph element to its own empty, container movie clip – each new primitive is drawn in front of the previously drawn ones, as required.

2.11: A 'True' 3D Graph

This movie employs a more realistic perspective than the previous two graph movies, using a true perspective geometry to render the graph. The pie chart is defined using three-dimensional world coordinates which are then projected onto an imaginary, invisible 'screen' placed immediately in front of the viewer. The resulting set of two-dimensional coordinates are then used to position the required lines, fills and text.

Although the calculations for projecting world coordinates onto a viewing plane are relatively easy (intuitive, even), the fact that the scene is made up of curve segments rather than straightforward points and lines means that there are some complex calculations to do. Whether the end justifies the means remains debatable, though the end result is certainly pleasing to the eye.

Explicitly typing the data

This movie makes two requests to the server, one for each of the graphs displayed, chaining them so that only one request is made at a time. When both graphs have been drawn the 'loader' target symbol calls the method to draw the legend before unloading itself in a similar manner to the previous two graph movies.

The root drawGraph( ) method similarly populates a data object and passes it to the graph movie clips that it creates via the fourth parameter of the attachMovie( ) method. The only slight difference is that the values of the amount array in the data object are explicitly cast to number data types using the Number( ) method, rather than their types being left as indeterminate:

```
dataObj.amount = new Array();
for ( j = 0; j < sets; j += 1 ) {
    dataObj.amount[j] = Number( eval( "_root.loader.amount" + j ) );
}
dataObj.offset = new Array();
for ( j = 0; j < sets; j += 1 ) {
    dataObj.offset[j] = Number( eval( "_root.loader.offset" + j ) );
}
dataObj.adjust = new Array();
for ( j = 0; j < sets; j += 1 ) {
    dataObj.adjust[j] = Number( eval( "_root.loader.adjust" + j ) );
}
```

This was not necessary for the previous two graphs (or any of the previous movies, for that matter) for one reason or another, but it is necessary here.[81]

81 In fact, the default type for variables loaded via the getURL( ) method and then referenced using the eval( ) method is String. Most mathematical operations on strings will give a result of data type Number, provided both strings represent numbers in the first place, of course. Explicitly typing movie data is usually unnecessary and I've avoided doing so until now for the sake of brevity.

Defining the graph in 3-space

The pie chart itself is defined in terms of its position in 3-space, the points on its rim and centre being projected as required. A separate class, FCoord, is defined to hold both the three-dimensional and two-dimensional projected coordinates of each point as well as holding the method to translate the former into the latter:

```
#initclip

/// Constructor
function FCoord ( x,y,z ) {

     this.x = x;
     this.y = y;
     this.z = z;

     this.px = 0;
     this.py = 0;
}

/// PUBLIC methods
FCoord.prototype.project = function ( scale ) {

     this.px = scale * ( this.x / this.z );
     this.py = - scale * ( this.y / this.z );
}

#endinitclip
```

Projecting the 3D coordinates is a simply matter of dividing the x or y coordinate by the distance (namely the z coordinate) and multiplying by the required scale factor. Note that the constructor here has arguments (a first) and also note the lack of an integer trailing the #initclip instruction – the FCoord class has no dependency relationships with any other classes so the order of its initialisation is irrelevant.

The FCoord class differs from every class so far in that it neither extends the MovieClip class (directly or otherwise), nor associates itself with any movie clip. It simply stands alone as a helper class for the other classes in the movie. It does not even have its own movie clip holder but instead has a layer all to itself in the F3DPieChart movie clip.[82]

82 Defining classes like this is perfectly legitimate, it just seems a little odd. With the exception of the F3DGraphClass class, all the classes so far have been associated with movie clip definitions. Stand-alone classes are perfectly legitimate however, and are used extensively both in this movie and in the PDB molecule viewer.

Drawing the graph elements

Default values pertaining to the shape and position of the pie chart in 3-space are defined as class variables of the pie chart class itself and translated into instance variables at the top of the drawGraph( ) method:

```
F3DPieChartClass.prototype.drawGraph = function ( sets, scale ) {

     this.scale = scale;

     this.size = this.kDefaultSize;
     this.depth = this.kDefaultDepth;

     this.x = 0;
     this.y = this.kDefaultY;
     this.z = this.kDefaultZ;

   ...
}
```

Variables that correspond to the final size and position of the graph movie clip on stage, on the other hand, are defined in the root script as usual and are either applied directly to the movie clip (in the case of the position) or passed as arguments to the graph's public draw( ) method. The pie chart's position in 3-space is in front of and somewhat below the viewer (to achieve the desired effect) and thus its projected position appears considerably below the horizontal. For this reason, the root 'kYOffset' variable needs to be a correspondingly large negative number in order to 'lift' the projected image back onto the stage.[83]

The drawGraph( ) method calculates the cumulative totals of the amounts in order to work out the angles that divide the various slices and then calculates the angle of the point on the rim that corresponds to the rightmost projected point. A naïve guess would put this angle at ninety degrees to the vertical but because of foreshortening, it is in fact a little greater. It is calculated in the getAngle( ) method, which projects the required point on the imaginary viewing screen back onto the pie and calculates the angle between this point, the centre of the pie and the farthest point on the rim.

Like its two-dimensional counterpart, the pie is then split up into sections in order to facilitate its drawing but here, the sections are simply the two halves. Each side is then drawn from front to back, ensuring that the nearest slices have the greater depth and thus appear in front of the farthest ones. Note that this time, it is the depths of the various slice movie clips (the slices are themselves movie clips with their own associated classes) that ensures the nearest ones appear in front of the farthest ones, rather than the order in which they are drawn.

83 This is not the least difficult aspect of the rendering process to visualise. Like the mechanism to populate the x-axis of the graphs in the 'Line Chart' example, the necessary calculations to draw the pie chart contain nothing in the way of new techniques. I would suggest that you read no further unless you specifically want to know how this kind of perspective is implemented.

Each slice is passed a 'controller' variable pointing to the parent graph movie clip as well as the values that define it. These values take the form of the distance around the rim ranging from zero to the graph resolution. The 'angle' value is divided by the 'step' variable (essentially dividing it by two times Pi and multiplying it by the graph resolution) before being passed as an argument so that the various values can be compared directly. The index of the slice is also passed to enable it to recover its amount, colour and so forth:

```
var link = "FSliceSymbol";
for ( i = 0; i < j; i++ ) {

    var begin = this.resolution * ( this[ "total" + i ] / total );
    var end = this.resolution * ( this[ "total" + ( i + 1 ) ] / total );

    this.pie_mc.attachMovie( link, "slice"+i, depth++, {controller:this} );
    this.pie_mc["slice"+i].draw( begin, end, angle/this.step, i );
}
```

The slice itself retrieves much information directly from its controller, storing it as instance variables in the constructor for convenience. Its draw( ) method then invokes the necessary child methods to create the various constituent parts of the slice, making sure to get the order correct to guarantee the nearest parts appear foremost:

```
var left = this.res - angle,
    right = angle,
    middle = this.res/2;

if ( ( end > right ) && ( begin < left ) ) {
    if ( begin < right ) {
        if ( end < left ) {
            this.drawRim( right, end, count );
        }
        else {
            this.drawRim( right, left, count );
        }
    } else {
        if ( end > left ) {
            this.drawRim( begin, left, count );
        }
        else {
            this.drawRim( begin, end, count );
        }
    }
}
if ( end < middle ) {

    this.drawCut( end, count );
}
if ( begin > middle ) {

    this.drawCut( begin, count );
}
this.drawTop( begin, end, count );
```

Firstly, the rim around the outer edge of each slice is drawn. Only the visible part needs to be shown, so its beginning and ending are checked against the angle variable specifying where the rim turns back on itself at the rightmost and leftmost edges. Next the 'cut' from the centre to the rim is drawn (again, only if needed) and lastly, the 'top' is drawn.

The child methods called from the draw( ) method rely heavily to the FCoord class to create the necessary coordinates on the rim and translate these positions into two-dimensional coordinates with which to draw the lines and fills. A helper method, getCoord( ), is used to recover the coordinate in 3-space corresponding to any particular point on the rim. The remainder of the draw( ) method retrieves the amount and offset of the slice, creating and positioning the necessary text field and finally positioning the slice as a whole.

Complex Data Handling

These two 'advanced' movies push Flash to something close to its limits, both in terms of the processing needed at runtime and the complexity of the projects themselves. Despite this, the size of the compiled movies remains relatively small, around 50K for the server explorer and 25K for the molecule viewer, so there is no appreciable performance hit for the web pages that display them.

Both of these movies admit a pretty continuous interaction with the server, with the advantage that the only the minimum of information needs to be exchanged – there is no need for a page refresh when new molecules are loaded or additional directory information is supplied, for example.[84]

[84] The 'Active Banner' and interactive graph example movies also had this property of exchanging data with the server at the user's request without forcing a page refresh, but now the process is continuous. Both movies store the data they receive, of course, so server requests are kept to a minimum.

2.12: PDB Molecule Viewer

This movie renders PDB molecule definition files[85] using a similar perspective to the 3D pie chart movie.[86] The molecules can be rotated and scaled at will – the movie gives a true three-dimensional representation of the molecule, not an imported animation but a real real-time scene.

The amount of processing power Flash requires to run this movie is staggering, considering the scenes are made up of no more than a dozen or so elements. Contrast this with modern arcade-style games that often show scenes with hundreds of elements, including texture mapping and even lighting. It is not simply the final rendering of the scene by the Flash player that takes the time either (although this is hardly impressive by modern standards); even the basic operations involved in calculating the coordinates of the elements seem to take forever. With this in mind, only the most simple of molecules can be shown.

---

85 PDB stands for 'Protein Data Bank', a publicly available database of thousands of protein molecules. The format adopted here is quite well suited to small molecules aswell, however, and is widely used on the Internet. PDB format files cannot be used directly by Flash, of course, and need to be converted. This can be done by a server process but I've chosen to do it offline. The PDB folder in the source ditribution contains the original PDB files and the converted filed (these are simply list files) aswell as the conversion script, written in Perl. A commercial version of this program which can read PDB files directly with only a small amendment is also available. See www.flashmol.com for more details.

86 There is a difference between the perspective used in these two movies. This one projects onto a unit sphere rather than a flat viewing plane, meaning that the projections of the 'balls' always remain as circles, regardless of their position. Projecting spheres onto a plane on the other hand, results in ellipses in all cases bar the one when the sphere is directly in front of the viewer. Projecting onto a sphere makes much more sense in this scenario then, and in particular makes the drawing of the 'sticks' (itself only an approximate process) a much simpler task.

Advanced program structure

The relative complexity of this movie means that it is more important than ever to sort out its various operations into logical blocks, so classes are used throughout. Apart from declaring the usual 'app' variable and a few other global variables, the root script does nothing but create an instance of the application class and define a global pointer to it:

```
/// The global application object
_global.theApp = undefined;

///::: MAIN
{
	theApp = attachMovie( "FApplicationSymbol", "app_mc", 0 );
}
```

The application class is instantiated in the normal manner, by creating an instance of the movie clip with which it is associated. Not all the classes in the movie are associated with movie clips however, only those which require movie-clip functionality. The application class defines an 'onEnterFrame' handler on its associated movie clip instance, as well as having a 'data' handler and attaching child movie clips, so it needs movie-clip functionality.[87]

Other classes that associate themselves with their container movie clips include the molecule class, which needs to attach child movie clips; the 'camera' class, which uses a child hit area movie clip; and the molecule loader class, which uses the 'onData' construct.

The remaining classes do not need access to movie clip functionality – most are placed in their own movie clips merely for convenience. Some classes are grouped together into one movie clip and in this case, each class has its own layer. The FClasses movie clip contains three classes, for example: FCoord, FMatrix and FAtom. The constructor of the FCoord class deserves further mention, since it makes some effort to provide a means of method overloading:

```
function FCoord ( x, y, z ) {

	if ( arguments.length == 0 ) {
		this.x = this.y = this.z = 0;
		return;
	} else {
		if ( arguments[0] instanceof FCoord ) {
			this.copyFrom( arguments[0] );
			return;
		}
	}

	this.x = Number(x);
	this.y = Number(y);
	this.z = Number(z);
}
```

87 It is possible to define the application class without recourse to its associated movie clip symbol but for simplicity's sake, I've avoided doing so. Although the child movie clips can be attached to the root rather than to the application movie clip and the onEnterFrame handler can similarly be defined on the root movie object, it would be stretching credibility a little too far to create another symbol just to handle the data event.

Here, the constructor has three optional arguments. If none are passed, the class is instantiated with zero-valued instance variables. If the first argument is another FCoord class on the other hand, its values are inherited. Only if both these cases are not met are the actual values of the arguments inspected directly. An equivalent Java listing would look something like the following ...

```
public class Coord {

    /// Constructors
    public Coord () {

        this.x = this.y = this.z = 0;
    }
    public Coord ( Coord c ) {

        this.x = c.x;
        this.y = c.y;
        this.z = c.z;
    }
    public Coord ( double x, double y, double z ) {

        this.x = x;
        this.y = y;
        this.z = z;
    }

    double x;
    double y;
    double z;
}
```

... where three constructors are provided, all with the same name but with different sets of arguments (hence the term 'method overloading'). ActionScript does not support this useful mechanism so the FCoord class does its best to mimic it.

The FAtom class has three child FCoord classes and these represent the coordinates of the atoms at the various stages of the rendering pipeline. The first set of coordinates represents the position of the atom, relative to the coordinate axes of the molecule itself. The next set represents the coordinates of the atom, rotated around the centre of the molecule (calculated separately and not the same as the centre of its coordinate system, by the way). The third set represents the 'world' coordinates of the atom, relative to the viewing centre, obtained by simply adding on the distance between the molecule and the camera to the value of the z coordinate.

The Coord class is contained in the FMacros movie clip and defines helper methods on the FCoord class. These methods do not make it into the FCoord class for two reasons: firstly, they are usually applied to two coordinates, not just one; and secondly, by placing them in an alternate utility class, the FCoord class is kept as small as possible. The Coord class itself is instantiated just once and a reference to it is made available throughout the movie as a global variable:

```
#initclip

_global.Coord = new Object();

Coord.plus = function ( r, a, b ) {
     r.x = a.x + b.x;
     r.y = a.y + b.y;
     r.z = a.z + b.z;
}

...

#endinitclip
```

Note that this class is both instantiated and defined at the same time, and that this all takes place inside the initialiser block, before any frame or object script is executed. It is perfectly legitimate to instantiate classes at this stage.[88] Strictly speaking, this is hardly a class definition, with the Coord global variable simply pointing to a newly created instance of the native Object class. Methods are then added to this particular instance, rather than being defined on a class using the prototype keyword. This shortcut is ideal if the resultant 'class' is only going to be instantiated once – there is nothing wrong with neglecting to use the 'prototype' keyword in this case.

Similarly, the FQuickSort class is instantiated only once, again inside the initialisation block. In this case however, the class is defined in the normal manner and the creation of the one instance is done by calling the class constructor, rather than the constructor of the built-in Object class:[89]

```
#initclip

_global.QuickSort = new FQuickSort();

/// Constructor
function FQuickSort() {}

/// Constants
FQuickSort.prototype.STACKSIZE = 50;
FQuickSort.prototype.MINSIZE = 7;

QuickSort.istack = new Array ( QuickSort.STACKSIZE );

/// PUBLIC methods
FQuickSort.prototype.Qsort = function ( arr, index ) {
     this.sort( arr.length - 1, arr, index );
};

...

#endinitclip
```

88 The inspiration for this came from the (apparently unnecessary) instantiation of classes when they are extended. See the 'The trouble with Flash class inheritance' appendix for more details.

89 This QuickSort algorithm outperforms the native sort algorithm by a considerable margin. The whole movie was optimised, in fact, and the Profiler component used to gather timing information has been left on the stage, albeit disabled. Read the 'Profiling' appendix for more information on profiling.

Two class constants are defined here, along with an array for internal use. The array is defined on the one instance of the class, in fact, but it makes no difference either way.

Note that none of these class definitions are contained within ordered initialiser blocks. It is tempting to impose an order based on which classes are used and where (for example, the FCoord class is used in the FCameraClass class, so it should be defined first; the FCameraClass class is used in the FApplicationClass class, so it should be defined before the latter; and so on, ad nauseam). This is simply not necessary, however - only if one class actually extends another does the order of initialisation become important.

There are no asset layers in any of the movie clips (this movie is certainly not designed to be converted into a component), yet many of the container movie clips are neither present on the stage nor created at runtime. In order for their initialiser scripts to be executed therefore, each movie clip is explicitly exported at runtime. This is done by setting the 'Export in first frame' checkbox of the 'Linkage Properties' dialog (Fig. 2.11):

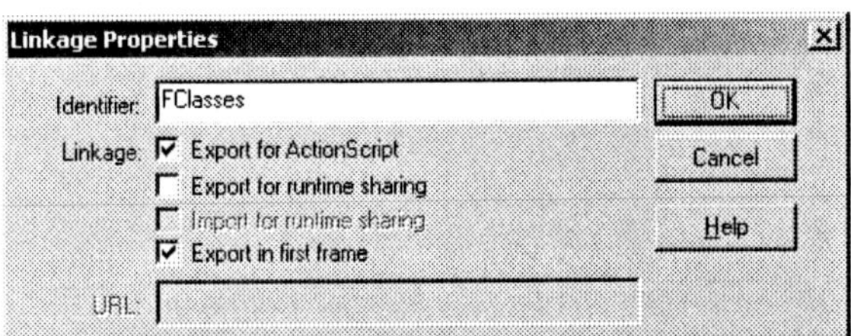

Fig. 2.11. The 'Linkage Properties' dialog box again.

Every relevant movie clip must be given a linkage identifier if it is exported in this way, even though the identifier is never used at runtime nor required to associate the movie clips with the class definitions they contain.

Movie clips that act as containers for class definitions should always be exported in the first frame in this manner. It is never enough simply to include them in the assets layers of movie clips that are created at runtime. Although being contained in an assets layer will guarantee that a movie clip definition is brought along when its parent movie clip is dragged into the target movie, this does not guarantee that its initialisation block will be executed. Exporting it in the first frame will guarantee this, however.[90]

90 The reason why the initialiser blocks of movie clips in assets layers do not automatically get executed at runtime is that assets layers are usually turned into guide layers (I can't think of any reason for this apart from aesthetics, but I've kept up the practice myself) and the contents of guide layers are ignored at runtime. If guide layers were not treated in this way, there would be no need to export assets in this manner. Notice how the container symbols for many of the superclass of the Flash components, such as DataProvider, SelectableList and so on, all have linkage identifiers and are exported in the first frame of the movie for this very reason (presumably).

Handling user input

When the application class is initialisation, it creates empty movie clips to hold both the molecules and their corresponding bonds, as well as a 'camera' movie clip that handles the keyboard and mouse input, providing the necessary information the application needs to enable it to scale and rotate the molecule. The camera's mouse and keyboard handling is set up in the FCameraClass class constructor:

```
function FCameraClass()
{
    this.attachMovie( "FHitAreaSymbol", "hitArea_mc", 0 );

    this.hitArea_mc._width = Stage.width;
    this.hitArea_mc._height = Stage.height - 50;
    this.hitArea_mc._x = 0;
    this.hitArea_mc._y = 50;
    this.hitArea_mc._visible = false;
    this.hitArea = this.hitArea_mc;

    this.onRelease = function () {};

    this.hitarea_mc.onMouseDown = function () {
        if ( this._ymouse > 0 ) {
            this._mouseDown = true;
        }
    }
    this.hitarea_mc.onMouseUp = function () {
        this._mouseDown = false;
    }

    this.keyListener = new Object();
    this.keyListener.controller = this;
    this.keyListener.onKeyDown = function() {
        if ( Key.getCode() == Key.SHIFT ) {
      this.controller._shiftDown = true;
        }
    }
    this.keyListener.onKeyUp = function() {
        if ( !Key.isDown(Key.SHIFT) ) {
            this.controller._shiftDown = false;
        }
    }
    Key.addListener(this.keyListener);

    this._mouseDown = false;
    this._shiftDown = false;

    this.mouseButtonDown = false;
    this.shiftKeyDown = false;
    this.prevMouseButtonDown = this.mouseButtonDown;
    this.prevShiftKeyDown = this.shiftKeyDown;
}
```

Firstly, a child movie clip is created, set to the required dimensions, hidden and designated as the camera's hit area. This is not strictly necessary – only if the 'onPress' and 'onRelease' handlers are defined on a movie clip is a hit area actually used. Here the 'onMouseUp' and 'onMouseDown' handlers are preferred and these work in much the same way as keyboard event handlers in that they correspond to global input events rather than being specific to a particular movie clip extent. Using a hit area has two advantages, however: firstly, it enables the hand cursor to be shown, rather than the normal arrow, enabling the user to differentiate between the drawing area and the area occupied by the links; and secondly, it allows the movie to keep the mouse focus even when the cursor is dragged away from the full extent of the movie altogether – a useful feature.[91]

Next, the 'onMouseDown' and 'onMouseUp' handlers are defined on the hit area movie clip. As already mentioned, it does not matter on which movie clip these handlers are defined – the extent of the movie clip has nothing to do with their operation. The reason for choosing the hit area rather than its parent movie clip is simply to make the calculation of whether or not the mouse is over the hit area a little easier, a gap of fifty pixels having been left in the hit area at the top of the stage in order to accommodate the link components. The '_ymouse' property is used for this, being a property of any movie clip.

Keyboard events are handled by creating a dedicated 'keyListener' object on which the 'onKeyUp' and 'onKeyDown' handlers are defined. The bodies of these handlers use the controller variable of the object to set the '_shiftDown' instance variable of the parent movie clip. Note that although there is an easy way to determine which key has been pressed (a corresponding property exists on the Key object if the required key does not have an obvious ASCII value), working out when a key has been released is a little more troublesome. Keyboard handlers are global in the sense that they are called whenever the state of any key changes, rather than being defined for one particular value. A good compromise is to allow the release of any key to reset the value of the '_shiftDown' variable, provided it is set in the first place.[92] The 'keyListener' object is then added to the list of keyboard listeners (those objects on which the 'onKeyUp' and 'onKeyDown' handlers are called when the keyboard state changes) and finally in this method, the default values for those parent instance variables effected by the mouse and keyboard handlers are set.[93]

91 Hand cursors are the default for buttons, arrows for movie clips. In order to force Flash to treat the hit area as a button, a (vacuous) button handler needs to be defined on the owner movie clip. Here, an onRelease( ) method is defined immediately below the definition of the hit area for this purpose. There is a method called useHandCursor( ) defined on the MovieClip class which can be used to turn the hand cursor on and off but this only works if the movie clip in question is already being treated as a button.

92 In fact, I don't think you can do any better than this.

93 The remainder of the camera class definition gets no further comment here, as it contains nothing in the way of new techniques. The class is fully commented though, should you wish to learn how mouse and keyboard events can be translated into the necessary positional shifts and rotations.

Creating the link components

Having created the virtual camera, the application then goes on to request the data necessary to create the link components for each molecule. It does this by using a slightly different version of the loadVariables( ) method with only one argument, the target being specified by the object on which the method itself is invoked. In this case, the target is the application object itself:

```
this.loadVariables( _root.app + "?data=list" );
```

The 'data' event is handled directly with an 'onData' handler defined as a class method on the application class – there is no target symbol with its associated object script involved here:

```
FApplicationClass.prototype.onData = function () {

     var link = "FLinkSymbol";
     var xGap = Stage.width / this.kColumns, yGap = 20;
     for ( var i = 0; i < this.count; i++ ) {

          this.links_mc.attachMovie( link, "link"+i, i, {value:this["file"+i]} );
          this.links_mc[ "link" + i ]._x = ( i%this.kColumns + 0.5 ) * xGap - 10;
          this.links_mc[ "link" + i ]._y = Math.floor( i/this.kColumns ) * yGap;
          this.links_mc[ "link" + i ].setChangeHandler( "load",theApp,"value" );
     }

     this.links_mc[ "link" + 0 ].onPress();
}
```

This method creates and positions the link components then calls the 'onPress' handler on the first link, thus forcing the loading of the first molecule. Calling button handlers directly in this way (or clip event handlers for that matter) is perfectly legitimate. The 'onData' handler is just another class method and is called by Flash in the normal manner, for example.

The link component consists of a child label and the small amount of functionality required to set its text style and allow it to handle button events. Because the 'onPress' handler is defined as a method on its associated class, the component itself acts as a button. The constructor sets the text style of the label as well as configuring the input focus handling:

```
function FLinkClass()
{
     this._focusrect = false;
     this.tabEnabled  = false;
     this.focusEnabled = false;

     this._x = Math.floor( this._x );
     this._y = Math.floor( this._y );
/// this.attachMovie("FMultiLabelSymbol", "fLabel_mc", 2);

     if (this.textStyle==undefined) {
          this.textStyle= new TextFormat();
     }
     this.textStyle.font = "Verdana";
     this.textStyle.size = "10";
}
```

Here, the usual ability of buttons to grab the input focus is explicitly turned off by setting the 'tabEnabled' and 'focusEnabled' movie clip properties to false. The focus rectangle usually drawn around movie elements when they have the focus is also turned off for this component by setting the '_focusrect' property to false, just to be safe, although if the component is forbidden from grabbing the input focus in the first place, this situation should never arise.[94]

Next, the coordinates of the component are set to their nearest integer values. This is most useful when components are dragged onto the stage and is especially important when they use embedded fonts (which tend to look better when placed precisely in this way). Usually at this point the child elements of the component are dynamically created but, to keep things as simple as possible here, the label field element is used directly, rather than being named as an asset and removed in the constructor. The normal attachMovie( ) call is left in place but commented out, for emphasis.[95]

A TextFormat object is created to hold the text style of the component and two of its properties are immediately set. This can be used by all the child elements (actually only one in this case) of a component, which apply it to their own child text fields to achieve a uniform and easily configurable text style across the component as a whole. Child elements may often create this object on behalf of their host component if they find that it is missing when they themselves are created, and since they may set some of its properties immediately, it is always best to check whether the 'textStyle' instance variable has already defined, to avoid the risk of overwriting existing text styles.[96]

The only two public methods this component implements are the setEnabled( ) and setChangeHandler( ) methods. The former method sets the underline style of the child label component as well as setting its position and colour:

```
FLinkClass.prototype.setEnabled = function(enabled)
{
    this.enabled = ( enabled == false ) ? false : true;

    this.textStyle.underline = this.enabled;

    this.fLabel_mc.setColour(this.kDefaultColour);
    this.fLabel_mc.setLabel(this.value);

    this.width = this.fLabel_mc.labelField.textWidth + 4;
    this.height = this.fLabel_mc.labelField.textHeight;

    this.fLabel_mc._x = -Math.floor(this.width/2);
}
```

94 The subject of input focus and how components can take advantage of it is covered in the chapter on the 'Lightweight' components. For now it is enough to know how to turn this functionality off.

95 Have a look back at the simple and advanced graphs for examples of including assets in movie clips and then removing them in the associated class constructor. The one disadvantage of using child elements directly is that you cannot call class methods on them from the parent component's constructor. The setting of the child label's text and position is thus deferred to the setEnabled( ) method here. I have no idea why this should be the case. I think it is a bug.

96 Again, using the child label component directly on the stage here rather than creating it dynamically in the constructor has led to some confusion. It appears that the label's associated class constructor is not called before the component's (although it certainly gets called eventually) and thus the check for the presence of the 'textSyle' object isn't strictly necessary. The root of this problem probably has some bearing on the inability of the component to call class methods on the label, too. The child label component is an instance of the FMultiLabel component, by the way, which improves and enhances Flash's own FLabel component.

The colour comes courtesy of a default class variable whereas the value is defined as an instance variable using the fourth parameter of the attachMovie( ) method when the component is created. Simply changing the values of the component's 'textStyle' object will not cause the child label component to update itself, by the way. The usual method to force it to look afresh at the text styles that it inherits from its host component is to call its setLabel( ) method. Once updated, the child label component's dimensions are recovered, applied to the 'width' and 'height' instance variables of the parent component and used to position the child label component itself.

The setChangeHandler( ) method works together with the executeCallBack( ) private method and 'onPress' handler to provide the necessary button functionality:

```
FLinkClass.prototype.setChangeHandler = function(chng,param,obj)
{
	this.changeHandler = chng;
	this.changeParam = param;
	this.handlerObj = (obj==undefined) ? this._parent : obj;
}

FLinkClass.prototype.executeCallBack = function()
{
	this.handlerObj[this.changeHandler](this[this.changeParam]);
}

FLinkClass.prototype.onPress = function () {

	this.executeCallBack();
}
```

The setChangeHandler( ) method takes three parameters, two of them optional: the name of the callback method to invoke; the name of the instance variable to pass when this method is invoked; and the object on which to call the method. These values are saved to local instance variables and used in the executeCallBack( ) method. Note how a method can be called on an object by simply by appending a set of parentheses. In this case, the named instance variable is passed to the method in question by way of the array syntax. By the way, the component assumes the method is to be called in its parent if no target object is passed to the setChangeHandler( ) method.[97]

97 An easier way of specifying which method to call would be to pass a reference to the method itself. The only reason I can see to choose the method name is that this allows the method to be specified in the component definition as a string and thus be set in the properties inspector when the component is selected on stage. I have kept to this way of doing things when I override the setChangeHandler( ) method in my components, for the sake of compatibility, but revert to function objects for other methods on my components that specify callback methods or something similar.

Drawing the molecules

The definition of each molecule is held in a separate instance of the FMoleculeClass class and the molecule itself is drawn directly on to the associated movie clip using the draw( ) method, called from the 'onEnterFrame' handler of the application object every time the molecule is moved. The draw( ) method calculates the world and projected coordinates of the molecule's constituent atoms and orders them according to their distances from the camera by calling the setupOrder( ) method:

```
FMoleculeClass.prototype.setupOrder = function () {

     for ( i = 0; i < this.balls; i++ ) {

          this.distance[i+kArrayAdjust]=this[ "atom" + i ].distance;
          this.order[i+kArrayAdjust]=i;
     }

     QuickSort.sort( this.balls, this.distance, this.order );

     for ( i = 0; i < this.balls; i++ ) {

          this.retrieve[ this.order[i+kArrayAdjust] - kArrayAdjust ] = i;
     }
}
```

This method sorts an array of integers called 'order' whose indices correspond to the positions of the atoms in the original atom list, and whose element values correspond to their relative distances from the camera.[98] The indices and elements are then swapped around in the 'retrieve' array for convenience.[99]

The atoms are drawn by sizing, positioning and colouring the appropriate ball movie clips. These are attached to the molecule movie clip when the molecule definition is first loaded and are repositioned and coloured each time the molecule is redrawn. There are the same number of ball movie clips as atoms; each has a fixed depth though, so different balls will correspond to different atoms as the molecule is moved around and different atoms come to the foreground. It is the 'retrieve' array that pairs the atoms with the ball movie clips each time ...

```
for ( i = 0; i < this.balls; i++ ) {

     var atom = this[ "atom" + i ];
     var ball = this[ "ball" + "_" + this.retrieve[ i ] ]

     this.drawBall( ball, atom );
}
```

98 In fact, the 'kArrayAdjust' global constant is used to number both the indices and elements of the array from unity, rather than zero. This is necessary due to a shortcoming in the QuickSort algorithm, which orders arrays from their second element and not their first, zero-indexed one. If you want to revert to the native sort method, set this global constant (defined in the root script) to zero. Read the 'Profiling' appendix for more information on the various pros and cons of the QuickSort algorithm.

99 Which also gives the opportunity to remove the adjustment to the order array, leaving the elements of the retrieve array conventionally numbered from zero.

… and the drawBall( ) method, taking an atom-ball pair, that configures the ball movie clip to represent the corresponding atom:

```
FMoleculeClass.prototype.drawBall = function ( ball, atom ) {

     var size = kMoleculeSize * atom.scale;

     ball._x = atom.px;
     ball._y = atom.py;

     ball._width =
     ball._height = kMoleculeSize * atom.scale;
     ball.colour.setRGB( colours[ atom.colour ] );
}
```

Note the use of the setRGB( ) method on the colour parts of the balls here. These are instances of the built-in Color object, created when the balls were first attached to the molecule movie clip. The thickness of the border around the balls remains constant regardless of their scaling by the way, so long as the size of the ball never exceeds that of the original movie clip. The ball movie clip definition is therefore appropriately large (several hundred pixels) to ensure this situation never arises.

Drawing the sticks requires a little more ingenuity. The stick shapes themselves are drawn onto empty movie clips – there is no 'stick' movie clip as such. Sticks fit in between the molecules so the depths of the ball movie clips are spaced out to allow several (nine, in fact) empty movie clips between each ball. The reason for this is that several sticks can be connected to one ball and all must appear behind it whilst remaining in front of all the other balls (or at least in front of all the other balls that are behind the ball in question). The sticks are drawn onto these empty movie clips using the drawStick( ) method:

```
FMoleculeClass.prototype.drawStick = function ( p, q, i, j ) {

     ...

     var tmpWidth = this.q.scale * kStickSize;

     var s = this[ "stick" + "_" + i + "_" + j ];

     s._x = this.p.px
     s._y = this.p.py;
     s.lineStyle( tmpWidth, "0x000000" );
     s.moveTo( 0, 0 );
     s.lineTo( this.q.px - this.p.px, this.q.py - this.p.py );
     s.lineStyle( tmpWidth - 2, "0x999999" );
     s.lineTo( 0, 0 );
}
```

The desired border effect is created here by drawing one line directly on top of another but with a slightly smaller width. A record is kept of which of these 'stick' movie clips have been used in the 'visibleSticks' array so that they can be 'wiped clean' before the next batch of sticks is redrawn when the molecule is moved again:

```
FMoleculeClass.prototype.eraseSticks = function () {

     var v;
     while ( v = this.visibleSticks.pop() ) {
          this[ "stick" + "_" + v.i + "_" + v.j ].clear();
     }
}
```

The clear( ) method invoked here will remove all the graphics primitives drawn onto a movie clip using methods such as lineTo( ).[100]

100 Discussion of the drawing of the molecule has been kept to a minimum here – only those places where new techniques are used have been included. Read the comments in the molecule class if you really want to find out exactly how it is done. The important thing to note is that the movie clips themselves, for both the balls and sticks, are created only once and then reused each time a molecule is redrawn.

2.13: Server Side Explorer

This movie allows constant interaction with the server, retrieving file and directory information when requested and displaying it in a classic 'file explorer' style window.[101] The left pane contains a tree component showing the directory structure whilst the right pane contains a list box showing the contents of the currently selected folder. Below these two panes is another pane containing a list box for messages. Dividers exist to allow the panes to be resized both horizontally and vertically.

With the exception of the initial server request to populate the root node of the directory tree, requests are made when the user clicks on a folder for which the data has yet to be loaded. To communicate with the server process, a text based proprietary protocol has been used. This is preferred to XML, say, which would increase the length of the request and response streams but add little in the way of readability.[102]

Such functionality as this movie provides[103] can be provided with actively generated HTML, so why use a movie? One reason, apart from appearances, is that it puts considerably less load on the server. The size of the movie is relatively small, but efficiency really comes from the fact that the page in which it is contained does not have to be refreshed every time new directory information is requested. Each request requires just one brief connection and even the most basic HTML page will likely contain more bytes in its header than the total length of a response needed to list the contents of an entire directory here.

---

101 It does little else, in fact. Files cannot be previewed, renamed or their permissions changed (to list three possible uses for this movie). All this functionality can be added, of course. The main reason for not doing so was to keep the size of an already complex project down but also, I simply ran out of steam.

102 I have shied away from XML for the sake of simplicity on the server side, mainly. There is nothing difficult about parsing XML in a movie (or generating it, for that matter).

103 And much of the interactivity that it currently lacks.

Creating a user interface using components

The whole of the movie's user interface is created using components. Four are used altogether – Flash's FTree component for the directory tree; two instances of the MultiListBox component: one for the 'files' pane on the right and one for the 'messages' pane at the bottom; and an extended SizeableFrame component which resizes the tree component directly and the two list box components by means of a callback method (more on this in a moment).

Once the visual elements of the movie have been created, the various global styles are set, as well as specific styles for the 'messages' list box. These include 'multi-styles', which are used to change the colour of the items to reflect their origin: blue for messages from the server, red for error messages and so on:

```
messages.setMultiStyleProperty( "error", "textColor", "0x990000" );
messages.setMultiStyleProperty( "command", "textColor", "0x009900" );
messages.setMultiStyleProperty( "remote", "textColor", "0x000099" );
messages.setMultiStyleProperty( "local", "textColor", "0x0000ff" );
```

As well as having a name and a value, these styles also have an identifier, the first argument of the setMultiStyleProperty( ) method, which enables several styles of the same name to be applied to the same component. The child elements can then recall a particular style by means of this identifier.[104]

Next, a linkage identifier for the item component belonging to the 'files' list box is specified. The default item component contains only a label component (with support for multi-styles, however) whereas the one for the 'files' list box explicitly set here shows an icon, too.[105]

The sizeable frame needs to adjust the whole of the user interface whenever it is resized. This is achieved by setting the tree component as its child with an additional callback method which resizes both of the list boxes so that they completely fill the space remaining once the tree component has been resized. The sizeable frame's setCallback( ) method takes a function pointer as an argument, rather than a method name, so the callback method can be defined anonymously:

```
sizeableFrame.setCallback( function (t,b,l,r) {

     files._x = r;
     files._y = 0;
     messages._x = 0;
     messages._y = b;
     files.setSize(Stage.width-1 - r, b);
     messages.setSize(Stage.width-1,Stage.height-1-b);
     this.vDivider_mc._height = this.hDivider_mc._y;
} );
```

Resizing the two list boxes is a relatively straightforward task since the sizeable frame passes its adjusted dimensions as arguments. Note that the two divider symbols are also adjusted at this stage. These are used in preference to the default border of the sizeable frame, which is hidden by invoking the component's showBorder( ) method in the extended sizeable frame's constructor (more on this in a moment).

104 The multi-styles of each list box item are specified as an optional parameter of the addItem( ) method. Multi-styles are implemented courtesy of the FMultiLabel component and discussed in the 'Implementing multiple text styles' appendix.

105 The design of the item symbols for the MultiListBox component differs considerably from that of Flash's own ListBox items and is discussed in the chapter that deals with this component.

An anonymous method is also defined to check the height of the sizeable frame whilst it is being resized:

```
sizeableFrame.setCheckHeight ( function ( h ) {

     var scrollBarHgt = this.child_mc.scrollBarHgt;
     var itmHgt = this.child_mc.itmHgt;
     var numDisplayed = Math.floor((h-scrollBarHgt-2+_DRAG_ADJUST)/itmHgt);
     numDisplayed = ( numDisplayed < _MIN_ROWS ) ? _MIN_ROWS : numDisplayed;
     numDisplayed = ( numDisplayed > _MAX_ROWS ) ? _MAX_ROWS : numDisplayed;
     var height = 2+numDisplayed * itmHgt + scrollBarHgt;

     return height;
} );
```

The sizeable frame passes its assumed height to this method (if it has been defined) whilst it is being resized and adjusts itself again if the return value differs. In this case, the callback method works out the various allowable heights for the tree component (multiples of its item height plus offsets for its horizontal scrollbar and borders) and returns the nearest one. This has the pleasing effect of causing the lower edge of the sizeable frame to snap to the allowable heights as it is dragged.

A parting call in the root script to the sizeable frame's refresh( ) method forces its callback method to be invoked and thus ensures that all the components appear correctly sized when the movie is first drawn.

Altering component functionality at runtime

The allowable heights of the directory tree and 'files' list box components are made to coincide by fixing their item heights. In the case of the list box, this can be done by calling the setFixedItemHeight( ) method but no such method exists on the tree component. To force the tree component to comply then, both its setSize( ) and measureItmHgt( ) methods must be redefined.

These and other redefinitions are placed in a 'REDEFINES' layer on the root movie timeline. Being topmost, the frame script in this layer gets executed first and in particular, before the script in the standard actions layer immediately below. In this way the necessary changes can be made to the class methods of the components before they are created.

This approach works well because there are no instances of the components initially on the stage – they are all created dynamically at runtime. Hence the redefinitions contained in the topmost layer do indeed get implemented before the classes which they affect are instantiated[106] and since the original method definitions exist on the root timeline, as do all the contents of initialiser blocks in fact, they will be overwritten by the redefined ones.

To continue, the measureItmHgt( ) method of the FTreeClass class is redefined to set the tree component's 'itmHgt' instance variable to the same global '_ITEM_HEIGHT' constant that was used to fix the item heights of the list boxes:

```
FTreeClass.prototype.measureItmHgt = function () {

     this.itmHgt = _ITEM_HEIGHT;
}
```

This is not enough however, and the tree component's setSize( ) method must also be redefined to take the same approach to resizing as the MultiListBox component:

```
FTreeClass.prototype.setSize = function(w, h) {

     this.measureItmHgt();

     this.scrollBarHgt = this.hsb_mc._height;
     this.numDisplayed = Math.floor((h-this.scrollBarHgt-2)/this.itmHgt);

     this.width = w;
     this.height = 2 + this.numDisplayed*this.itmHgt + this.scrollBarHgt;

     if ( this.mask_mc == undefined ) {
          this.attachMovie( "FBoundingBoxSymbol", "mask_mc", this.mcCount-2 );
     }
     if(this.container_mc != undefined) {
          this.container_mc.removeMovieClip();
     }

     this.createEmptyMovieClip("container_mc"+this.mcCount, this.mcCount-2);
     this.container_mc = this["container_mc"+this.mcCount];

     super.setSize(this.width,this.height);
}
```

106 With the exception of the 'nameless' classes instantiated by inheritance. Read the 'The trouble with Flash class inheritance' appendix for more information. This approach fails when the components are placed on the stage, in which case they will be created (and their associated classes instantiated) before any frame script on the root timeline is executed. See the 'Profiling' appendix for an in-depth look at what script gets run and when. An alternative solution in this case is to create an empty movie clip and place the redefined method in an initialiser block of sufficiently high order within it. A movie clip is needed because initialiser code cannot be placed directly in frame script on the root timeline.

Here, the number of visible items is calculated based on the space available once the scrollbar and border heights have been taken into account. This number is then used to calculate the real height of the tree component.[107]

The one remaining redefinition relating specifically to the tree component is that of the item's layoutContent( ) method, which normally forces the use of embedded fonts. This fix is not necessary however, and so the method is redefined accordingly, with the offending line simply commented out.[108] The remaining redefinitions simply turn off the mouse handling for the list boxes and the highlighting for all the component items.[109]

107 This seems to be a more intuitive way of working out the component's height. I have to admit that the default setSize( ) method remains something of a mystery to me. The method above also relies on a redefinition of the setSize( ) method on the FSelectableListClass class, which is discussed in the MultiListBox chapter.

108 The original justification for forcing the use of embedded fonts seems to have been that masking did not work with device fonts. This bug has been fixed with later versions of the Flash player however, so the fix can be discarded. There is also an attempt to force the issue in the tree component's class constructor but since this is ineffective, it can be safely be ignored and saves us the trouble of redefining this method too.

109 Redefining methods in this manner may seem like fudging but I wanted to make the point that it is perfectly legitimate to do so and often the simplest course of to take.

Extending components

Two of the methods on the SizeableFrame component also need to be changed – the getOver( ) method that tests whether or not the cursor is over the component's border; and the drawBorder( ) method that draws the border during resizing. The former method is redefined so that only bottom and right edges of the sizeable frame can be dragged; and the latter method is redefined to position the added horizontal and vertical dividers whenever the border is redrawn.

Rather than redefining these methods however, a more conventional approach is to extend the existing component, subclassing its associated class to provide the additional functionality. The extended component is created by dragging an instance of the sizeable frame component onto the stage and encapsulating it in a new movie clip. This new parent movie clip can then be safely removed from the stage, with its definition given the requisite linkage identifier and moved to the 'ServerExplorer' folder in the library.

There is actually no need to include the old component as an asset in this way unless the new, extended component is going to be used in another movie altogether but it is still good practice to do so. The layer in which the old component resides can also be turned into a guide layer (for appearance's sake) and renamed 'SuperClass'. The two dividers can be included as assets, too. The child sizeable frame component can be given an instance name of 'scAsset' and a final touch is to explicitly unload it from the extended component in the constructor:[110]

```
#initclip 1

/// Constructor
function FSizeableFrameExClass()
{
     scAsset.unloadMovie();

     super();

     this.attachMovie("FHorizontalDividerSymbol","hDivider_mc",this.mcCount++
);
     this.attachMovie("FVerticalDividerSymbol","vDivider_mc",this.mcCount++
);

     this.showBorder(false);
}

/// Class definition
FSizeableFrameExClass.prototype = new FSizeableFrameClass();
Object.registerClass("FSizeableFrameExSymbol", FSizeableFrameExClass);

...

#endinitclip
```

Note the increased initialisation order and that the FSizeableFrameExClass class extends the original component's class, rather than MovieClip. The 'super' keyword is used on its own here to call the superclass constructor, then the two dividers are created and the border movie clip hidden.

110 A couple of steps have been left out in turning this new component into a full functional one: firstly, the new component has no appearance on the stage since it has no bounding box or name symbol; and secondly, the original component definition is not inherited and therefore is not available in the properties inspector. Both these omissions only affect the functionality when the component is used on stage however and can easily be rectified if need be.

The overridden getOver( ) method simply apes the original method but with two of the four tests (for the top and left side of the frame, to be specific) missed out. The new drawBorder( ) method is responsible for positioning the dividers attached in the constructor:

```
FSizeableFrameExClass.prototype.drawBorder = function () {

    super.drawBorder();

    _root.hDivider_mc._y = this.bottom;
    _root.vDivider_mc._x = this.right;
}
```

Here, the drawBorder( ) method of the superclass is invoked and the new functionality simply added on to the end of the method. Utilising the existing method in this way is one reason to override methods, rather than redefining them.[111]

111 This approach would not work with the setSize( ) method of the tree component however, where the method must be redefined rather than being overridden. The call to the original setSize( ) method by means of the 'super' keyword must be made so that the setSize( ) methods of the tree component's own superclasses are invoked but it is impossible to skip the setSize( ) method of the tree component itself. All the good work of the overridden method would thus be undone and although it is possible to redefine the setSize( ) method on the tree component to a vacuous one that merely passes control onto the superclass, this somewhat defeats the objective of the override in the first place.

Implementing the movie functionality

Two handlers are set on the tree component so that its contents and those of the 'files' list box can be updated whenever its state changes. The expansion handler is called whenever the expanded state of a branch node is altered and the change handler is called whenever the selected item changes. This latter method is also invoked directly from the root script to force the request of the initial, root directory data once this node has been configured and assigned to the tree component:

```
/// Set up the root node for the directory tree
var rootNode = new FTreeNode( "root", {path:"/",complete:false} );
rootNode.setIsBranch();
rootNode.setIconSymbolName("FRootStandardSymbol");
dirs.setRootNode( rootNode );

/// We're off!
_local("Getting root directory information...");
dirs.setSelectedNode(rootNode);
changeHandler(dirs);
stop();
```

Note the optional argument of the FTreeNode constructor here – an associative array whose elements are used to store the path of the remote directory to which the node corresponds and a flag to specify if the directory information has been loaded. This optional argument can be recovered or reapplied by means of the getData( ) and setData( ) methods, respectively and the expansion handler uses the former to work out what action to take when it is invoked. If the directory information is already present when the node is expanded, no action is necessary whereas if it is missing, it must be loaded immediately. This is done by selecting the node and calling the change handler directly (again).

The expansion handler is also invoked when the node is contracted, in which case it must check whether or not the currently selected node is a child. The convention is that the selected node (represented by an open folder) must be visible and hence if it is a child of a node that is about to be contracted, this node is selected instead. The checkNodeIsParent( ) method is used to ascertain whether or not one node is the child of another:

```
function checkNodeIsParent(pNode,cNode) {
     var nodes = pNode.getChildNodes();
     for ( var i = 0; i < pNode.getNumChildren(); i++ ) {
          if ( nodes[i]==cNode ) {
               return true;
          } else {
               if ( checkNodeIsParent(nodes[i],cNode) ) {
                    return true;
               }
          }
     }
     return false;
}
```

This method is recursive, calling itself in order to navigate through the child branches of the parent node until a match is found or all the avenues have been exhausted.

The contents of the currently selected node are placed in the 'files' list box by the setFiles( ) method, which first clears the existing contents of the list box before retrieving the names of child nodes by looking at their labels directly. The remaining contents of the corresponding directory are recovered by means of a linear array called 'nonDFiles' that is populated when the directory information is first recovered (more on this in a moment). The two sets of data are kept separate in this manner so that the directories can be added to the 'files' list box first.

Having updated the contents of the 'files' list box, the setFiles( ) method resets the icon of the selected node, which would have been set to the appropriate 'waiting' icon if its directory information was being loaded. None of the nodes are left to use the default icon at any time, by the way – custom icons are always used. These contain just one frame, as opposed to the default icon. This has three labelled frames: 'leaf', 'branchClosed' and 'branchOpen', but cannot be used directly because of the difference in usage for the open folders and the need to show 'waiting' icons whilst data is being loaded. The custom icons consist of the required graphic plus a 'sizer' movie clip to ensure that they all have the same size and are thus positioned correctly by the tree component. This is hidden by setting its alpha value to zero on the stage using the properties inspector, but will still contribute to the parent movie clip's dimensions.

The changeHandler( ) method also checks to see whether or not the relevant node has loaded its directory information and if so, simply calls the setFiles( ) method. Otherwise, it saves the directory path and selected node, sets the node's icon to the appropriate 'waiting' movie clip and makes the request to the server process. Note the use of the 'undocumented' updateControl( ) method to force the tree component to update its view immediately.[112]

The request for directory information is handled by a standard target symbol whose object script calls the root listFiles( ) method. This method retrieves the directory information from the response string by splitting it into an array and unencoding its elements:

```
var fileArray = new Array;
if ( ( fileData != "" ) && ( fileData!=undefined ) ){
     fileArray=fileData.split( " " );
}
for ( var i = 0; i < fileArray.length; i++ ) {
     fileArray[ i ] = unescape( fileArray[ i ] );
}

var remoteString = "LIST ";
for ( var i = 0; i < fileArray.length - 1; i++ ) {
     remoteString += "\""+fileArray[ i ] + "\", ";
}
remoteString += "\""+fileArray[ i ] + "\"";
_remote( remoteString );
```

112 I'm not sure that this actually makes any difference. The waiting pointer can sometimes not appear when the request returns quickly (as it should do on a local server) but a better fix seems to be increasing the frame rate. There is no reason why movies, even 'complex' UI ones such as this, should not run at faster than the default 12fps to improve responsiveness.

A more readable version of the response is also created here and added to the 'messages' list box. Next, so long as the 'path' value returned by the server process and the 'path' element of the 'pendingRequest' object agree, the new child nodes are added and the 'nonDFiles' array created:

```
var requestNode = pendingRequest.node;

var nonDFiles = new Array()
for ( i = 0; i < fileArray.length; i++ ) {
     var file = fileArray[ i ];
     if ( file.substr(file.length-1)=="/" ){
          var fileNode = new FTreeNode( file, {path:path+file} );
          fileNode.setIconSymbolName( "FFolderStandardSymbol" );
          fileNode.setIsBranch();
          requestNode.addNode( fileNode );
     }
     else {
          nonDFiles.push(file);
     }
}
requestNode.setIsOpen( true );
requestNode.setData({path:path,complete:true,nonDFiles:nonDFiles});
```

Note how the 'nonDFiles' array is added to the data associated with the node and the value of the complete element is also updated.

Part 3
The Components

3.1: Writing Components

The design of the components that accompany this book closely apes that of the Flash components, which provide a kind of unofficial API, topmost component classes giving examples of how to export the necessary functionality and superclasses underneath providing the mechanisms to implement most of it.

When writing components to be packaged into an extension, as opposed to creating 'local' components for use in a single project, a dedicated project must be used.[113] It is the component project and not the resultant movie that goes into making up an extension, together with the requisite documentation and description XML files. This project can also be used for demonstration purposes, the movie being used to showcase the components whilst the project itself provides the necessary usage examples.

113 Read the 'Packaging extensions' appendix for more information.

Turning a movie clip into a fully fledged component

The hard and fast definition of a component is simply a movie clip, some of whose variables can be set using the properties inspector when it is placed on the stage. Precisely which variables can be set, plus a few other properties such as whether or not it should appear in the components panel, are specified in the 'Component Definition' dialog box (Fig. 3.1), which can be brought up by right-clicking on the movie clip definition in the library and choosing 'Component Definition...' from the popup menu.

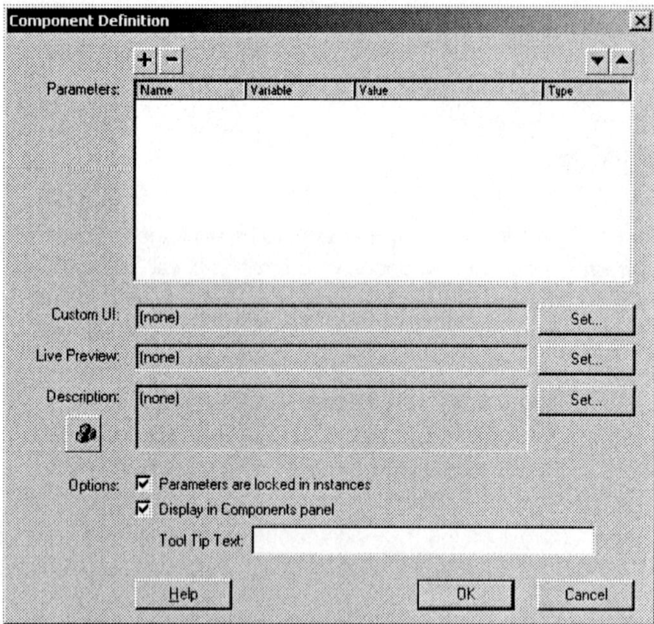

Fig. 3.1. The 'Component Definition' dialog box.

Adding variables is done by pressing the plus button above the 'Parameters' list box and filling in the fields as required. The 'Variable' field allows a different name to be used for the associated variable to the one that appears in the properties inspector.[114] Types include both linear and associative arrays (objects), in which case a small 'Values' dialog can be brought up to input their elements by clicking on the magnifying-glass button that appears in the 'Value' field when either of these types is selected.

Any movie clip that has variables defined in the 'Parameters' list box will appear as a component in the library, regardless of whether or not the 'Display in Components Panel' tick box is left checked or not.[115] It will also automatically appear in the components panel (should the project be packaged into an extension and installed) unless this tick box is explicitly left unchecked. The PopUp and Dialog components in the PopUp extension, for example, are not meant to be used directly and therefore are prevented from appearing in the components panel by this means.

---

114 I have never found a use for this feature and always leave this field blank to avoid confusion.

115 This feature is used to turn many movie clips into 'imitation' components, their definitions in the library having the default component icon rather than the standard movie clip one. Component superclasses typically get this treatment, for example. The exact procedure is to leave the 'Display in Components panel' tick box unchecked but to add one variable to the 'Parameters' list box, leaving all the fields blank except for the 'Type' field, which is set to 'Default'.

Components typically have custom icons. These are simply imported image files and should be around 25x18 pixels in size. They are automatically assigned in preference to the default icon if they are given the exact same name as the component and placed in a folder called 'FCustomIcons' on the same level in the library. When imported, an icon will inherit the name of the image file but this can easily be altered to match the component name exactly. Because Flash keeps a reference to the original image file, it can be updated at will if need be, although Flash needs to be restarted before the icon is reapplied to the component. The icon movie clip itself must be dragged into the assets layer of the component so that it is available when the component is used in another project.

Utilizing the variables set in the properties inspector

Variables set in the properties inspector are applied to the component instance and are immediately available as instance variables. They can be used in the constructor of the associated component class, for example. In fact, the component cannot tell the difference between instance variables set in this manner and ones set using the ubiquitous fourth parameter of the attachMovie( ) method. Furthermore, variables set via the properties inspector are always defined, even if their corresponding value field is left empty. In this case, the variable values will be the appropriate null value for the variable type, an empty string, for example, or the number zero.

Constructors for component classes should always check the values of instance variables set via the properties inspector or fourth argument of the attachMovie( ) method and in the latter case, it is good programming practice to ensure that the elements of the associative array passed at least form a subset of the variables that can be set via the properties inspector. Components must not rely on these variables being present. The easiest approach is to check whether or not a particular instance variable remains undefined and use a default value instead, should this be the case.

For example, consider a component that implements the standard setSize( ) method. This method usually contains the code necessary to draw the component and must therefore be called at least once during initialisation. The component definition should therefore contain a 'size' object with 'height' and 'width' elements and this should be looked for when the component is initialised:

```
FMultiListBoxClass.prototype.init = function() {

     ...

     if ( this.size != undefined ) {

          this.setSize( this.size.width, this.size.height );
     }
     else {

          this.setSize( this.kDefaultWidth, this.kDefaultHeight );
     }
}

...

FMultiListBoxClass.prototype.setSize = function(w,h) {

     w = Math.max(w,this.kDefaultMinWidth);
     h = Math.max(h,this.kDefaultMinHeight);

     ...
}
```

The init( ) method here uses the default class values if the 'size' object is not defined, otherwise it blindly uses those values supplied by the 'size' object but checks the values against the minimum permitted ones in the setSize( ) method. In this way, it can always size itself correctly, regardless of how it is configured.[116]

116 I usually get a component working first without troubling over the added instance variables and always supply default values where appropriate. Only when a component appears to work fully is it worth adding the necessary functionality to deal with additional instance variables. If the component fails to work properly at a later stage or needs further revision, I comment out this functionality and return to the default values.

3.2: The 'UI Utils' Components

These components are basic user interface utilities. Their associated classes do not inherit from the FUIComponentClass class and therefore they have no access to style properties or the other mechanisms defined therein. They are fully functioning components however, having all the necessary functionality such as assets, name symbols and the like.[117]

117 It is very difficult to divorce the subject of components from that of well-designed movies in general, and consequently many of the techniques associated with components have been dealt with already in the preceding chapters. Both the simple and 3D graph movie clips have a basic component architecture, for example. To avoid repetition, I have not added similar discussions to this section and you should look back at these movies and also to the component discussions in the PDB molecule viewer and server explorer chapters if you get lost.

TipText

This component shows a tiptext style label just under and to the right of the mouse pointer whenever it hovers over graphical elements in a movie. Ideally, it can simply be dragged onto the topmost layer of the stage (to ensure that it appears above everything else) and left there, or it can be created dynamically with a suitably large depth. It creates a global reference to itself when instantiated, so that its over( ) and out( ) controller methods can be invoked without difficulty from anywhere in a movie.

Apart from the standard setEnabled( ) method, it implements only one other method, setBounds( ), which defines the available drawing area and thus ensures that the tiptext is repositioned should the mouse pointer approach the right or bottom of the area. These bounds are usually set to the size of the stage, although this is not the default and the setBounds( ) method is called from the constructor with no arguments to create the bounds object but leave its elements zeroed.

The tiptext itself is made up of an FMultiLabel component and a background drawn onto an empty container movie clip. The text style properties of the label are set directly by means of the standard 'textStyle' object created in the constructor and there is no functionality to allow these styles to be altered.[118] The remaining body of the constructor sets up the internal variables to handle the timing of the tiptext as well as defining the global 'TipText' reference to the component.

To get the component to actually show a tiptext, its over( ) method must be called with the required text as a parameter and after the requisite pause, the tiptext duly appears. To hide the tiptext again, the out( ) method can be called, otherwise it will hide itself after a couple of seconds. These two methods are best placed in mouse handlers for movie clips, the former called when the mouse hovers over a movie clip, the latter for when it moves away. In the components project, these method calls are to be found in the mouse handlers for the FText component:

```
FTextClass.prototype.rollOver = function () {
    if ( this.tiptext != undefined ) {
        TipText.over( this.tiptext );
    }
}

FTextClass.prototype.rollOut = function () {
    if ( this.tiptext != undefined ) {
        TipText.out();
    }
}
```

118 This approach to text styles was used in the FLink component and was discussed (together with the basics of component architecture) in the chapter on the PDB molecule viewer.

As well as the normal assets, name and actions layers, the component also has a 'Bounding Box' layer that contains a simple box movie clip. This forms part of the component's appearance when it is placed on the stage and is sized to fit around the name symbol accordingly. It has no other use apart from this, and the constructor contains code to remove it (or hide it, at least), just beneath the usual code to hide the name symbol.[119]

Exactly when the tiptext appears, and for how long, is controlled by the 'state' instance variable, set by the five private methods between the layout( ) method and the 'onEnterFrame' handler. These are called directly by the few public methods or else from the 'onEnterFrame' handler itself, which takes care of the necessary timing whenever the component is 'active' (its state is non-null):

```
FTipTextClass.prototype.onEnterFrame = function() {

     if ( this.state != "" ) {

          this.end = getTimer() / 1000;

          if ( this.state != this.previous ) {
               this.begin = this.end;
          }

          ...

          this.previous = this.state;

          if ( ( this.end - this.begin ) > this.delay ) {

               ...
          }
     }
     else {

          this.previous = "";
     }
}
```

The current time is retrieved with a call to getTimer( ), which returns the time since the movie started playing in milliseconds. This is used to work out the various stages in the 'life' of the tiptext, from the initial pause before it is shown to the amount of time it is visible before it disappears again.

119 This bounding box forms part of all the components in this section, for the sake of convention – it is used in all the Flash components and remains in the 'Flash UI Components' folder in the library. Although often doing nothing more than adding to the appearance of the component on the stage, it is sometimes left visible and resized to form a border around the component at runtime. It also provides a useful definition of a rectangular movie clip should one be needed for masking, say, and thus has a linkage identifier so that it can be created dynamically, if needed.

SizeableFrame

This component can be used to resize a graphical element by drawing a border around it whose edges can be dragged to adjust its size on the stage. Two sets of default cursors are also included, as well as functionality to specify custom ones, these cursors being shown whenever the edges of the border are dragged.

The constructor follows the (now familiar) pattern of hiding the child elements and unloading the assets. Assets take on the function of containers for the component's child elements (skins) from now on and do not have linkage identifiers themselves.[120] Usually assets contain just the one child element but this is not strictly necessary - all the cursors are bundled into one asset, for example.

The asset movie clips are placed in the 'FFPComponents>Core Assets – Developer Only>Other Assets>FSizeableFrame Assets' folder. The skins that they contain are placed in the 'FFP Components>Component Skins>FSizeableFrame Skins' folder and it is these movie clips that have the linkage identifiers and are attached to the parent component.[121]

The component skins themselves can contain child movie clips (skin elements), the border skin uses two sets of skin elements, for example, although the cursor skins contain only bitmap tracings. These skin elements are held in the 'Skin Elements' child folder of the component's assets folder, and being buried deep in the 'Core Assets – Developer Only' folder hierarchy in this manner ensures that they do not to get in the way of the more important component skins (their parents).[122]

The main functionality of the component (its handling of mouse input to enable the user to drag the edges of border) is realised using three methods: inactive( ), waiting( ) and active( ), each being assigned as the component's 'onEnterFrame' handler as the need arises. The inactive( ) method is the first to be used and is set in the constructor. Note that no parentheses are present here – the function object is being assigned, not invoked:

```
this.onEnterFrame = this.inactive;
```

The same approach is used by the two methods that define the component callbacks, namely setCallback( ) and setCheckHeight( ). References to function objects, not function names, must be passed to these methods:

```
FSizeableFrameClass.prototype.setCallback = function ( callback ) {
     this.callback = callback;
}

FSizeableFrameClass.prototype.setCheckHeight = function ( checkHeight ) {
     this.checkHeight = checkHeight;
}
```

120 I take a slightly different approach to the Flash components, which do give linkage identifiers to assets. I feel this is unnecessary – assets should simply enable their child elements, the component skins, to be included in the component and then be unloaded with the minimum of fuss.

121 Although the border and all the cursor movie clips are denoted as component skins, they are not fully functional ones in that they do not inherit style properties from their parent component. These are first used by the lightweight components and a full explanation is given in the relevant chapter.

122 At least I assume this is the reason. Of the three sets of elements here – assets, component skins and skin elements, the component skins are arguably the ones that should be the most readily available for inspection in the library. They have the linkage identifiers, for example, and also contain the code to associate the skin's own elements with the component's style properties. More on this in the next chapter.

The callback methods are then invoked by appending parentheses to the function pointers and in this way, parameters can also be specified. The checkHeight( ) method is invoked from within the active( ) method, for example, when the top or bottom edges of the border are being dragged, whereas the callback method is invoked from within the resizeChild( ) method:

```
FSizeableFrameClass.prototype.resizeChild = function () {

    this.child_mc._x = this.left + this._x;
    this.child_mc._y = this.top + this._y;
    if ( this.child_mc.setSize == undefined ){
        this.child_mc._width = this.width;
        this.child_mc._height = this.height;
    } else {
        this.child_mc.setSize(this.width,this.height);
        if ( this.child_mc.height > 0 ) {
            this.height = this.child_mc.height;
            this.bottom = this.top + this.height;
        }
    }
    this.drawBorder();
    this.callback(this.top,this.bottom,this.left,this.right);
}
```

It is also possible to check for the presence of a method using function pointers in the same way as the value of a movie clip property or instance variable can be checked, the presence of the setSize( ) method on the child movie clip being looked for in the method above, for example.

LayoutManager

This component allows a group of graphical elements to be ordered into rows and columns in a similar manner to cells in an HTML table. It also supports background colours, fixed dimensions for the cells and even horizontal and vertical alignment. Just like the sizeable frame, child elements (those affected by the component) do not have to be child movie clips; indeed they should not be. The child movie clips in the component project are created alongside the component on the root timeline, for example.[123]

In the component project, each child graphical element is an instance of the simple FText component (created specifically for demonstration purposes). It is used for the usage hint on the stage as well as the four child elements of the layout manager. It is added to this component together with an optional attributes object, formed by inspecting the properties of each entry in the elements array:

```
var elements =
[
	{	link:"FTextSymbol",
		text:"Some text, right aligned.",
		tiptext:"www.flashforprogrammers.com",
		width:"200",
		align:"right",
		bgColour:"0x993366" },

	...
]
```

The first three properties of each element are used to create and configure the component to be added to the layout manager (always an FText component in this case) with the remaining properties (if there are any) added to a temporary attributes object:

```
for ( var i = 0; i < elements.length; i++ ) {

	var tmpElement = elements[ i ];
	var tmpElement_mc = attachMovie(tmpElement.link,"element_mc"+i,mcCount++);

	tmpElement_mc.setText( tmpElement.text );
	tmpElement_mc.setTipText( tmpElement.tiptext );

	if ( hasAttributes( tmpElement ) ) {
		var tmpAttrObj = new Object();
		for ( prop in tmpElement ) {
			if ( isAttribute( prop ) ) {
				tmpAttrObj[prop] = tmpElement[ prop ];
			}
		}

		layout_mc.addElement( tmpElement_mc, tmpAttrObj );
	}
	else {

		layout_mc.addElement( tmpElement_mc );
	}
}
```

123 It's worth pointing out (again) that the component project can also be used for demonstration purposes. All this book's component projects contain a fair amount of root script and component instances on the main stage to provide definitive usage examples. With this in mind (and because there is little else to write about) I take a close look at the root script here.

Note the use of the 'in' keyword to retrieve each of the properties of the elements in turn. This is also used in the hasAttributes( ) method.

Any one of several methods called on the layout manager can force it to redraw itself (specifically, to reposition its child elements), not least the addElement( ) method. Since several of these methods may be called one after another, and because the redrawing process is a moderately complex and therefore a time-consuming one, it is important to find a way of ensuring that the component does not needlessly redraw itself when it could instead wait until all the methods have been called on it in one go.

To facilitate this, the component invalidates[124] itself when any of these methods are called, making a note of the fact that it needs to be updated without actually doing so immediately, instead waiting for the next available opportunity. This is done by setting the 'onEnterFrame" handler to a suitable intermediary method which, when invoked, resets the 'onEnterFrame' handler before calling the redraw( ) method to actually redraw the component:

```
FLayoutManagerClass.prototype.addElement = function( mcRef, attrObj ) {

     var tmpRef = new Object();
     tmpRef.ref = mcRef;
     tmpRef.attr = attrObj;
     this.layoutElements.push( tmpRef );
     this.invalidate();
}

FLayoutManagerClass.prototype.invalidate = function() {
     this.onEnterFrame = this.update;
}

FLayoutManagerClass.prototype.update = function() {
     this.onEnterFrame = undefined;
     this.redraw();
}
```

It does not matter how many times the invalidate( ) method is called in the space of one movie refresh, the redraw( ) method will only be called once, when the 'onEnterFrame' handler is triggered, and then will not be called again until another function requires it.

124 This is a standard concept borrowed from many modern runtimes and, not least, from the Flash components themselves. It is the Flash event model and function objects that make this mechanism possible.

3.3: The 'Lightweight' Components

These components are simple user-interface elements such as buttons, text fields and so on. They can be used instead of HTML form elements and with this in mind, they include a 'hidden'[125] component and have support for names as well as values.

The button component mimics a standard HTML form button, gathering the required information from its sibling components by default. Each component's associated class inherits from Flash's FUIComponentClass class, the components therefore having full support for style properties.[126]

125 This component has no user interface and is just used to hold hidden variables. Because it is so simple and the techniques employed in what little code it contains have already been discussed, it does not have a dedicated section here.

126 Indeed, most of this chapter is concerned with leveraging the functionality of the FUIComponentClass class. All the remaining components extend this class but the association is closest here.

TextLabel

This component shows a text label with a background, the colour of which can be changed with a call to the setStyleProperty( ) method using the 'labelBackground' custom style property.[127] The font metrics of the label can also be altered with a call to this method, of course.

The init( ) method contains the usual code to attach both the label (an instance of the FMultiLabel component) and the background label component skin, as well as turning off the input focus handling and setting the 'controller' variable to point to the component instance. Because the background skin is used by several components (the TickBox component also uses it, for example), it is kept in the 'Global Skins' child folder of 'FFP Components >Component Skins' folder and has a name to reflect this global usage.

The skin itself comprises a skin element movie clip (stored in the 'Skin Elements' child folder of the 'Global Assets' folder) which is given an instance name and two lines of frame script to associate the skin element with the required style property. These lines are executed immediately the skin is created:

```
var component = _parent.controller;

component.registerSkinElement(Background_mc, "labelbackground");
```

It is worth noting here that the skin element movie clip contains nothing more than a rectangle graphic. The only difference between most skin elements, in fact, is that they start off with differing colours to roughly reflect their intended use. They are resized (or rather, their parent skin components are resized) and precisely positioned by their parent components to build up the necessary scrollbars, bevelled edges, buttons and so on. Some skin elements may contain more realistic graphic elements such as an arrow for the scrollbar buttons, for example, but the vast majority are simply plain rectangles.

To continue, the 'component' variable is set here to point to the skin's host component.[128] This is usually the component that created the skin but not always. Buttons are a good example – their skins often inherit the styles of the button's own parent component because the 'controller' variable is set to the parent component instance rather than the button instances themselves.

---

127 I use the phrase 'custom style property' for those style properties whose names have not been reserved by the Flash components. There is no need at all to stick to these reserved names and the lightweight components make up a couple of their own.

128 There are two major departures in my treatment of component skins from Flash's own treatment. Firstly, the skins themselves are attached to the components and not their assets (this has already been mentioned). Secondly, I use '_parent.controller' in the first line in a component skin's frame script rather than Flash's '_parent._parent' or even '_parent._parent._parent.' This is both clearer and allows skins to be attached at differing levels, making them much more versatile. The only (slight) drawback is that the 'controller' variable must be defined by the skin's parent, but this should be standard practice in well designed components.

The registerSkinElement( ) method is then invoked on the host component. This method is defined in the FUIComponentClass class and is responsible for registering the skin's interest in a particular style property, essentially just storing the two arguments it is passed (a reference to the skin element and the name of the style property in question) in an object stored in the component:

```
FUIComponentClass.prototype.registerSkinElement = function(skinMCRef, propName)
{
     if (this.styleTable[propName]==undefined) {
          this.styleTable[propName] = new Object();
          this.styleTable[propName].useGlobal = true;
     }
     if (this.styleTable[propName].coloredMCs==undefined) {
          this.styleTable[propName].coloredMCs = new Object();
     }
     this.styleTable[propName].coloredMCs[skinMCRef]=skinMCRef;
     if (this.styleTable[propName].value!=undefined) {
          var myColor = new Color(skinMCRef);
          myColor.setRGB(this.styleTable[propName].value);
     }
}
```

The 'styleTable' here is an associative array defined in the init( ) method of the FUIComponentClass class. When a new style is registered with a component, a new element is added to this array, using the name of the style property as a key.[129]

The element itself is an instance of the native Object class and contains several variables[130] including the actual value of the style (which is always just a colour) together with a child 'coloredMCs' object which holds references to the child elements of all the skins that 'listen' to the style in question. If the value of the style has already been set, it is immediately applied to the skin element using a Color object and its setRGB( ) method.

To continue, the public methods implemented by this component include the setValue( ) and getValue( ) methods, which set and recover the value of the child label component; setEnabled( ), which enables or disables the component but has little effect here since the component admits no direct interaction; and the setSize( ) method, which takes parameters for both height and width but ignores the former and only uses the latter if it is greater than the width of the child label.

129 The names of property styles are no more than keys in an associative array, so any name can be used. This also explains why style properties are not case sensitive.

130 The 'useGlobal' variable is quietly overlooked here, as is the implementation of global styles in general, partly because mention of global styles would only complicate the discussion here, but mainly because I don't quite understand their implementation.

Measuring the 'height' and 'width' of the component entails attaching a temporary label, setting its value to the value of the component (or some nonsense text if the component value is yet to be defined), retrieving the resulting dimensions and then making a necessary small adjustment:[131]

```
FTextLabelClass.prototype.measureItmHgtAndWdth = function(text) {
     this.attachMovie("FMultiLabelSymbol", "tmpText_mc", 1000);
     this.tmpText_mc.setLabel( (text==undefined)?"Sizer: PjtTopg":text );
     this.itmHgt = this.tmpText_mc.labelField.textHeight;
     this.itmWdth = this.tmpText_mc.labelField.textWidth;
     this.tmpText_mc.removeMovieClip();
     this.itmHgt += 4;
     this.itmWdth += 5;
}
```

The resultant 'itmHgt' and 'itmWdth' instance variables are then applied to the 'height' and 'width' instance variables for the component as a whole and finally, the private layout( ) method is invoked, which positions and sizes the various child elements.

131 The method most commonly used by the components is the meaureItmHgt( ) method, which takes no parameters and only measures the height of a temporary text field containing the requisite nonsense text. My use of the itmHgt instance variable differs from the Flash components in that the adjustments are made inside this method, rather than being made whenever the 'itmHgt' variable is used.

TextField

This component shows an input text box, comprising an editable text field and a surrounding bevelled edge. The bevelled edge is created using three component skins stacked one on top of another, which listen to three different style properties, namely 'lightShadow', 'darkShadow' and 'background'. Unlike the TextLabel component, it does admit some user interaction and therefore must be able to handle the input focus gracefully.

The input focus is passed around various elements of a movie using the tab key, with the movie element that has the input focus duly responding to keyboard events. For example, characters can be entered into a text field or a button can be pressed using the space bar. By default, the movie element that has the input focus is designated by a rather garish yellow surrounding box. This can be turned off by setting its '_focusRect' property to false. The init( ) method of the FUIComponentClass class (wisely) does this and a much more appealing black and white box is usually drawn around the component instead.

Since it is the child label component (or rather its own child text field) that actually admits interaction with the user and not the component itself, the correct approach is to explicitly disable input focus handling for the component and enable it for the text field instead. The 'focusEnabled' and 'tabEnabled' properties[132] of the component are therefore set to false, whereas the 'tabChildren' property is set to true, to allow the text field to receive the input focus as required.

The responsibility of handling the input focus thus being passed to the child text field, its own relevant properties must be set accordingly. This is done in the setEnabled( ) method, since the values of the properties will change depending on whether or not the component is enabled:

```
FTextFieldClass.prototype.setEnabled = function(enabledFlag) {
     this.enable = (arguments.length>0) ? enabledFlag : true;
     this.fLabel_mc.labelfield.type = this.enable ? "input":"dynamic";
     this.fLabel_mc.labelfield.tabEnabled =
     this.fLabel_mc.labelfield.focusEnabled =
     this.fLabel_mc.labelfield.selectable = this.enable
     this.fLabel_mc.setEnabled(this.enable);
     if (!this.enable && this.focused) {
          Selection.setFocus(undefined);
     }
}
```

Note the use of the 'enable' instance variable here, used in preference to the 'enabled' variable, which is reserved by Flash and used to set the enabled state of buttons, disabling their 'on', 'over' and 'down' frames when set to false.

To continue, the type of the child label's text field is set explicitly here and the two properties pertaining to the input focus, namely 'tabEnabled' and 'focusEnabled' are set to the same value as the enable state of the component. Next, the setEnabled( ) method is invoked on the child label (which does nothing apart from setting the text colour, by the way) and finally, if the component currently has the input focus and is being disabled, the setFocus( ) method of the native Selection object is called with an undefined parameter.

The Selection object used here is native to Flash, an instance of it existing in every movie (there being no need to instantiate it, therefore). Calling its setFocus( ) method and passing a reference to a movie element gives that element the input focus (if it is capable of handling it) and takes it away from the movie element that currently has it. Thus, calling the setFocus( ) method here with undefined as the parameter takes the input focus away from the component (since it currently owns it) but does not pass it on to any other movie element.

---

132 I am not quite sure exactly what effect these properties have individually but according to the Flash documentation, the 'focusEnabled' property specifies whether or not a movie element can receive the input focus (buttons and text fields do so by default, movie clips do not) whereas the 'tabEnabled' property specifies whether or not a movie element does (as opposed to can) receive the input focus. It seems to me that one property would suffice where two have been used. The safest bet is to follow the example of the init( ) method in the FUICompnentClass class and always set the two properties in tandem.

As well as allowing the input focus to be explicitly set in this manner, the Selection object also allows listener objects to be specified, calling their onSetFocus( ) methods whenever the input focus changes, passing as parameters references to instances of both the movie element that has acquired the input focus and the one that has just relinquished it. The init( ) method of the FUIComponentClass class defines one (and only one) such object globally, adding it as a listener to selection events. When the onSetFocus( ) method is called on this global object, it in turn invokes the myOnSetFocus( ) and myOnKillFocus( ) methods on these two references respectively:

```
_global._focusControl = new Object();
_global._focusControl.onSetFocus = function(oldFocus, newFocus)
{
     oldFocus.myOnKillFocus();
     newFocus.myOnSetFocus();
}
Selection.addListener(_global._focusControl);
```

Two such methods are defined on the text field of the component's child label field (remember, it is the text field that receives the input focus and not the parent component) and they in turn invoke identically named methods on the component itself:

```
FTextFieldClass.prototype.myOnSetFocus = function() {
     if ( this.enable ) {
          this.focused = true;
          this.drawFocusRect();
     }
}

FTextFieldClass.prototype.myOnKillFocus = function() {
     this.focused = false;
     this.focusRect.removeMovieClip();
}
```

Note the setting of the 'focused' instance variable here to keep a track of whether the component has the input focus or not. This variable is used in the setEnabled( ) method above to ascertain whether or not the input focus should be forcibly removed if the component is being disabled.

These methods allow a custom focus rectangle to be drawn around the component when it receives the input focus, the drawFocusRect( ) method itself being defined on the FUIComponentClass class although the movie clip that it creates each time is explicitly removed here.[133]

133 This is covered in more depth in the next section.

TickBox

This component shows a simple tick box and an associated text label, and responds to keyboard events when it has the input focus, changing its value when the space bar is pressed.[134] When it first receives the input focus by way of a mouse click, its value is not toggled; only when it retains the input focus will further mouse clicks affect its value.[135] When enabled, the tick and background skins listen to the 'arrow' and 'background' style properties respectively and when disabled, the 'foregroundDisabled' and 'backgroundDisabled' styles are used. The label always listens to the 'textColor' style and remains enabled when the component is disabled. Both Boolean and string values are supported, the component staying with whichever type is specified by the setValue( ) method.

Unlike both the TextLabel and TextField components, the default input focus properties defined in the init( ) method of the FUIComponentClass class are the correct ones and therefore they are not redefined in the component's own init( ) method. They are set in the setEnabled( ) method however, matching the enabled state of the component, since disabled components should not receive the input focus. The enabled state of the label is set once, and once only, in the constructor, since only the tick box itself should change appearance when the enabled state of the component is altered.

The tick box part is made up of four skins: three skins for the background (complete with bevelled edges) and one skin for the tick. The tick skin also contains a 'sizer' movie clip in its own layer, which is immediately hidden when the skin is created by setting its alpha value to zero in the skin's frame script. This allows the tick graphic to be slightly smaller than the background box whilst the tick movie clip as a whole retains the same dimensions as the background, making resizing much easier.

Both the background and tick skins have two labelled frames that correspond to the enabled and disabled states of the component.[136] Their frame script contains an additional stop( ) call after the first of the two skin elements has been registered and also note that there is no need to redefine the 'component' variable in the second frame – the definition is carried over from the first. Precisely which frame is shown at any one time is controlled by the component's setEnabled( ) method ...

```
FTickBoxClass.prototype.setEnabled = function(enabledFlag) {
     this.enable = (arguments.length>0) ? enabledFlag : true;
     var frame = this.enable ? "enabled":"disabled";
     this.Background_mc.gotoAndStop( frame );
     this.Tick_mc.gotoAndStop( frame );
     if (!this.enable && this.focused) {
          Selection.setFocus(undefined);
     }
}
```

... the 'frame' variable being set according to the component's enabled state and passed to the gotoAndStop( ) method invoked on both the background and tick instances.

134 Holding the space bar down will cause the tick box to check and uncheck itself continuously. I don't know why this happens and since I can't turn it off, consider it a feature.

135 Turning off this behaviour is easily done by removing the check for the value of the 'focused' instance variable in the 'onPress' handler.

136 I have fallen into the habit of naming skins with multiple frames somewhat differently from normal ones. The usual practice of prepending an acronym representing the component and an underscore to the skin's description and keeping the whole name lower case is dropped in favour of a more natural name, comprising the name of the component followed by the skin's description, both halves being proper names. The corresponding asset and skin element names use the existing naming conventions, however.

The size of the tick box is controlled by the 'height' parameter of the setSize( ) method with no notice being taken of the method's 'width' parameter. Both the tick box and the label are sized and positioned in the private layout( ) method, which positions the child label in a similar way to the TextLabel component and adjusts the vertical position of the tick box to match the label, rather than the other way around. The offset used to position the tick box is also saved as an instance variable and used in the overridden drawFocusRect( ) method to ensure that the focus rectangle is drawn correctly around the tick box:

```
FTickBoxClass.prototype.drawFocusRect = function()
{
    this.drawRect(-2, -2+this.offset, this.height+4, this.height+4);
}
```

This method is defined in the FUIComponentClass class and provides an extra level of indirection so that the longwinded drawRect( ) method does not have to be rewritten should the focus rectangle only require repositioning and not redesigning. Note the use of the 'height' instance variable for both the width and height of the focus rectangle here, as well as the 'offset' variable to adjust the vertical position.

Each time it is invoked, the drawRect( ) method itself creates an empty movie clip with an arbitrarily high depth, on which the two rectangles that comprise the input focus rectangle are drawn:

```
FUIComponentClass.prototype.drawRect = function(x, y, w, h)
{
    var inner = this.styleTable.focusRectInner.value;
    var outer = this.styleTable.focusRectOuter.value;
    if (inner==undefined) {
        inner = "0xffffff";
    }
    if (outer==undefined) {
        outer = "0x000000";
    }

    this.createEmptyMovieClip( "focusRect", 1000 );

    ...
}
```

Note the retrieval of the two style properties here, done by querying the 'value' properties of the 'focusRectInner' and 'focusRectOuter' elements of the 'styleTable' array directly.

TextButton

This component is a button with a child text label. If its 'action' property is set, either through the properties inspector or by means of the setAction( ) method, it will attempt to find all the other sibling lightweight components on its level, retrieving their names and values to form a query string which it appends to the value of the 'action' property and passes to the server process using the getURL( ) method.[137]

The component can respond to both mouse and keyboard events. Mouse events are processed by handlers defined directly on the component's associated class:[138]

```
FTextButtonClass.prototype.onPress = function( ) {
     this.pressed = true;
     this.layout();
     if ( !this.focused ) {
          if ( this.enable ) {
               this.selected = true;
               Selection.setFocus(this);
          }
     }
}

FTextButtonClass.prototype.onRelease = function( ) {
     this.pressed = false;
     this.layout();
     if ( this.action == undefined ) {
          this.executeCallBack();
     } else {
          this.executeAction();
     }
}
```

The 'onPress' handler must force the input focus onto the component here if the component is enabled – it is not automatically given to buttons when they are the recipients of mouse events (or movie clips with button behaviour, for that matter).[139] The 'onRelease' handler calls the appropriate method depending on whether or not the 'action' property has been set, the executeCallBack( ) method being defined on the FUIComponentClass class and invoking a named callback method set with the standard setChangeHandler( ) method.

137 Adding this functionality makes the lightweight components eminently suitable for replacing form elements with little (if any) further configuration. Each component (with the exception of the TextLabel and TextButton components) 'registers' itself when its 'name' property is set by adding its reference to an inputElements array which it defines on its parent movie clip (if this hasn't be done already). Using the parent movie clip in this way is a little underhand but a relatively safe option nonetheless.

138 The selected instance variable here is needed because the 'onDragOut' handler is invoked when the input focus is forced in the 'onPress' handler (I think this is a bug). Since the button should be returned to the 'up' state when the 'onDragOut' handler is invoked only if it has been invoked for the right reason (namely the user dragging the mouse away from the button), it must be notified that it has been wrongly invoked as a result of the button being pressed. This is done by setting the selected instance variable to true in the 'onPress' handler and testing its value in the onDragOut handler.

139 This is not the case for text fields incidentally, which do receive input focus automatically when clicked on.

Handling the input focus is a little more involved. Keyboard events can be passed to any object that has registered itself with the Key object, an instance of which is available in every movie, like the Selection object. Rather than creating a single, global object to handle selection events however, the init( ) method of the FUIComponentClass class creates a 'keyListener' object for each component:

```
this.keyListener = new Object();
this.keyListener.controller = this;
this.keyListener.onKeyDown = function()
{
     this.controller.myOnKeyDown();
}
this.keyListener.onKeyUp = function()
{
     this.controller.myOnKeyUp();
}
```

Setting the 'controller' instance variable of this object to point to the object's parent component allows it to invoke the myOnKeyUp( ) and myOnKeyDown( ) methods on the component whenever the relevant keyboard event is triggered. The object itself is added and removed from the list of keyboard listeners whenever the input state of the component changes:

```
FTextButtonClass.prototype.myOnSetFocus = function() {
     this.focused = true;
     this.drawFocusRect();
     Key.addListener(this.keyListener);
}

FTextButtonClass.prototype.myOnKillFocus = function() {
     this.focused = false;
     this.focusRect.removeMovieClip();
     Key.removeListener(this.keyListener);
}
```

The methods invoked by the key listener object, namely myOnKeyDown( ) and myOnKeyUp( ) now simply have to change the state of the button and invoke the callback methods if necessary.

TextArea

This component is similar to the TextField component but admits a child label with multiple lines rather than just a single-lined label. Otherwise, the functionality is pretty much identical, with the component using the same background skin as the TextLabel component and thus listening to the 'labelbackground' as well as the 'lightshadow' and 'darkshadow' style properties.

The 'height' of the component cannot be specified exactly by the height parameter of the setSize( ) method. Instead, this parameter is divided by the item height and the largest whole number smaller than the result, the number of rows in effect, is multiplied by the item height and a small offset is then added to give the exact height:

```
FTextAreaClass.prototype.setSize = function(w, h) {
     this.measureItmHgt();
     this.fLabel_mc.setLabel(this.fLabel_mc.getLabel());
     var numItems = Math.max(Math.floor(h/this.itmHgt),1);
     this.width = w;
     this.height = numItems*this.itmHgt+4;
     this.layout();
}
```

The item height is specified in the measureItmHgt( ) method as being the text height of the child text field of the temporary label, plus one pixel. This is less than the item height of the TextField, for example, which has to include the necessary 'padding'. Here, the extra padding is added once the item height has been multiplied by the requisite number of rows.[140]

The component's 'height' and 'width' instance variables are also set here, this being the case with all the components, in fact. In particular, the setSize( ) method of the FUIComponentClass class (which is usually responsible for setting these variables) is not invoked by way of the 'super' keyword here.[141]

The component's style properties are set by calling the setStyleProperty( ) method,[142] defined in the FUIComponentClass class and taking two parameters, specifically the name and value of the style property. Three courses of action can be taken by this method depending on the type of the style property in question.

If the style name is 'embedFonts', the component is invalidated and no further action is taken. This style is essentially a text style, although it is not included as a property of the TextFormat object. It is applied by label components directly to their child text fields whenever their setLabel( ) method is invoked.

140 In order to size a multiple-line text field correctly, the item height requires this small adjustment, which seems to work for a wide variety of fonts and sizes.

141 Although this is another departure from convention, I just find it easier to work this way, setting these properties in the topmost class so that they are available to the setSize( ) methods further down the class hierarchy. The only other use of the setSize( ) method in the FUIComponentClass class is removing the input focus rectangle but I cannot see the point of this and therefore do not invoke the method at all.

142 A major feature of the lightweight components is that they rely heavily on the FUIComponentClass class for much of their functionality (hence the name). This class is responsible for implementing both the style property and invalidation mechanisms. A discussion of both these mechanisms seems appropriate here, not least because there would be little else to discuss in this section otherwise.

If the style is a text style, it is added in abbreviated form to an instance of the TextFormat object (which the method creates if it is not already defined), before the component is invalidated:

```
if (propName.subString(0,4)=="text") {
     if (this.textStyle==undefined) {
          this.textStyle = new TextFormat();
     }
     var textProp = propName.subString(4, propName.length);
     this.textStyle[textProp] = value;
     this.invalidate("setSize");
}
```

If the style is a colour, it is immediately applied to the elements of all the skins in the component that have registered an interest in it:

```
for (var j in this.styleTable[propName].coloredMCs) {
     var myColor = new Color(this.styleTable[propName].coloredMCs[j]);
     if (this.styleTable[propName].value==undefined) {
          ...
     } else {
          myColor.setRGB(value);
     }
}
```

Thus, style properties effectively fall into two categories: text styles (including the 'embedFonts' style), which are updated indirectly by invalidating the component; and colour styles, changes to which are affected immediately by calling the setRGB( ) method on Color objects defined on the component's skin elements.

Components are invalidated by adding a method name to their method tables and then setting the 'onEnterFrame' handler:

```
FUIComponentClass.prototype.invalidate = function(methodName)
{
     this.methodTable[methodName] = true;
     this.onEnterFrame = this.cleanUI;
}
```

The 'methodTable' instance here is an instance of the Object class (an associative array would do just as well and array syntax is used, in fact), method names being added as properties (keys) and their corresponding values simply being set to true. It is the cleanUI( ) method that is actually responsible for invoking the methods, resetting the component's 'onEnterFrame' handler when it has finished:

```
FUIComponentClass.prototype.cleanUI = function()
{
     if (this.methodTable.setSize) {
          this.setSize(this.width, this.height);
     } else {
          this.cleanUINotSize();
     }
     this.methodTable = new Object();
     delete this.onEnterFrame;
}
```

Note that the setSize( ) method overrides all other methods here, the cleanUINotSize( ) method being called only if this method has not been invoked:

```
FUIComponentClass.prototype.cleanUINotSize = function()
{
     for (var funct in this.methodTable) {
          this[funct]();
     }
}
```

Invalidating a component and adding the setSize( ) method to the method table therefore ensures that the component's text styles are updated, providing the setLabel( ) methods of the component's child labels are invoked, of course. The use of the otherwise superfluous call to the setLabel( ) method in the component's setSize( ) method should now be apparent, since although the value of the child text field will not change, the component's text styles will be reapplied to it.[143]

143 You can see the difference between the two methods of updating a component most clearly when changing the styles of the PopUp components dynamically. The colour changes happen immediately while the text styles take effect after a short pause.

3.4: The 'PopUp' Components

These components consist of 'PopUp' or 'Dialog' style user interfaces, containing various child components such as menu items, buttons, labels and so on.
Two out of the five components are not meant to be used directly, instead being subclassed by the remaining three components and implementing much of their common functionality.

The classes of all five components inherit from the FUIComponentClass class (directly or by means of extending components that do) and also make use of multiple text styles.[144]

144 Multiple styles add an extra level of indirection to standard style properties, allowing style names to be associated with more than one value. They are implemented in the FMultiLabel component and form an integral part of the components in this extension, as well as the MultiListBox component.

PopUp

This component is the base component for all the others in the extension, implementing their common functionality as well as forming the basic 'PopUp' style user interface, consisting of a simple rectangular face with a bevelled edge which can be dragged around the stage and will invoke a callback method when it is first moved.

The constructor contains an additional check to see whether the class is named and only proceeds with calling the init( ) method if this is the case (named classes having non-null '_name' properties because they are associated with instances of movie clips):

```
function FPopUpClass()
{
     if ( this._name != undefined ) {
          this.init();
     }
}
```

Since classes are also instantiated when other classes are defined that extend them, this added check stops the init( ) method being called for a class that has no associated movie clip instance.[145]

The init( ) method contains the usual code to set to input focus properties, attach the component skins and set the 'controller' variable. It does not contain calls to either the setEnabled( ) or setSize( ) methods, however, a call to the former being omitted because it may well in turn invoke the latter and repeatedly calling setSize( ) in the constructor (albeit indirectly) is both wasteful and can make the components almost impossible to debug. Similarly, there is no direct invocation of the setSize( ) method and the component consequently has no default 'width' and 'height' class variables.[146]

The setSize( ) method itself contains just one call to the private layout( ) method, which sizes and positions the component skins and hit area. This call may seem innocuous but it is quite important. When the setSize( ) method is invoked on a component that extends this one, it in turn invokes the setSize( ) method here (and in fact, there may be other components that sit in-between) and only then is the layout( ) method invoked, again on the topmost component. Thus, all the setSize( ) methods in the class hierarchy are called first, in order, followed by all the layout( ) methods. This allows topmost components a second opportunity to position their child elements.[147]

Note also that the setSize( ) method does not set the width and height instance variables, a job which is always done in the topmost components. The reason for this is that this component has no idea of the finished component's size, only drawing the required panel 'underneath' once the dimensions have been determined by the topmost component.

145 This is because of the presence of the 'new' keyword in the class definition syntax. Read the 'The trouble with Flash inheritance' appendix for more details.

146 It is up to components that extend this one to call these methods. This component also has no component definitions. These are the only differences between this 'base' component and a standard component. There is no reason why you cannot use this component in the normal manner by adding the required default height and width class variables, adding the requisite setSize( ) call to the constructor plus any necessary component definitions.

147 The Toolbar component, for example, repositions the child title element, originally positioned in the Dialog component's setSize( ) method, in its own layout method.

The common functionality implemented by this component includes a redefinition of the executeCallBack( ) method, the new method providing the index of the item that has initiated the callback together with a reference to the instance of the component itself:[148]

```
FPopUpClass.prototype.executeCallBack = function(index)
{
    this.handlerObj[this.changeHandler](this,index);
}
```

A clearItems( ) method is also provided which removes all the items currently held in the component and reinitialises the items array. The measureItmHgt( ) and measureItmWdths( ) methods, being common to most of the topmost components in the extension, are also defined here, as is a refresh( ) method to invalidate the component and thus refresh its user interface.

148 Items are used by the PopUpMenu, MessageBox and ToolBox components.

PopUpMenu

This component extends the PopUp component and adds support for clickable items and separators. It sizes itself precisely around the item list and also disables the dragging functionality implemented by the base component. Each item's enabled state and icon can be set dynamically by supplying the relevant item index to a method invoked on the component. Callback methods are set on the component as a whole and supply the index of the item that initiated the callback as well as a reference to the component itself.

The init( ) method contains none of the usual code to attach child elements, set the 'controller' variable and so on since all of this functionality is implemented in the base FPopUpClass class (which the FPopUpMenuClass class extends). It does contain the setSize( ) calls, however, (which are absent from the superclass) as well as disabling the dragging functionality and setting the default linkage identifiers for the child item and separator components. A call to the clearItems( ) method sets up an items array to hold the item details and finally, the 'containerCount' instance variable is defined for the depth of the empty movie clip to which the various child elements are attached.

Items and separators are not created immediately when added to the component; instead their details are held in the items array and the component is then invalidated. The addItem( ) method creates an object to hold the item's details, pushes it onto the items array and duly calls the invalidate( ) method. Other methods that change the appearance of the component by acting on the elements of the items array also use this mechanism. This is standard practice for many complex components, item details usually being held in such data arrays and only when the component's setSize( ) method is invoked (by way of invalidating the component) are the changes realised. This is generally the most efficient mechanism for updating components as it is particularly suited to list boxes and the like.[149]

The setSize( ) method here begins by creating a new instance of the container movie clip to which the child elements are attached, removing the previous ones in the process. It then calculates various values used to position the items and separators, such as the maximum icon size or item width. The component's width is calculated immediately from these values whereas the height is calculated by counting the items and separators and multiplying them by the required values. The setSize( ) method of the base component is then invoked using the super keyword and is passed the new width and height instance variables. The separators and items themselves are actually created in the private layout( ) method.

Both the item and separator components are held as assets and stored in the 'Core Assets>FUIComponent SubClasses' folder in the library. They have only one public method, namely draw( ), which configures the components directly. They also have access to the parent component's instance variables by means of the 'controller' variable, set in the normal way via the fourth parameter of the attachMovie( ) method.

The separator component, FPopUpMenuSeparator, uses its 'controller' variable to ascertain the parent component's width in order to calculate its own, passing this information on to its setSize( ) method:

```
FPopUpMenuSeparatorClass.prototype.draw = function()
{
    this.setSize(this.controller.width-2);
}
```

149 This is an important point. Similar mechanisms are used in just about all the components from now on, and most of the built-in Flash components. Item details are usually stored in an instance of the DataProvider class, but I've opted to keep them inside the components themselves (in the items array, specifically) for simplicity's sake.

The 'controller' variable is also used to invoke the parent component's dragHandler( ) callback method when the separator is pressed. Although the component itself (the parent component, that is) cannot actually be dragged, this method is still invoked to give the movie a chance of setting this callback for its own use. In this case, the dragHandler( ) callback is used to swap the depths of the various movie elements so that the one that has just been clicked on is brought to the forefront.

The item component, FPopupMenuItem, is more complex. As well as a background skin, it comprises two child labels which are configured to listen to a variety of multi-text styles depending on their selected and enabled states:[150]

```
FPopUpMenuItemClass.prototype.init = function()
{
    var labelAttrs = { enableStyle:"textColor",
                       selectStyle:"textSelected",
                       disableStyle:"textDisabled" };
    var bgLabelAttrs = {  enableStyle:"",
                          selectStyle:"",
                          disableStyle:"lightShadow" };

    var hLink = "FHighlightSymbol";
    var labelLink = "FMultiLabelSymbol";

    this.attachMovie( hLink, "highlight_mc", 0 );
    this.attachMovie( labelLink, "fBackgroundLabel_mc", 1, labelAttrs );
    this.attachMovie( labelLink, "fLabel_mc", 2, bgLabelAttrs );
}
```

These multi-style names are passed to the labels via the fourth parameter of the attachMovie( ) method, as usual. The styles are chosen here (and a second, background label is used, in fact) to allow disabled item labels to appear shadowed.

Much of the functionality for this component comes courtesy of the various mouse event handlers, which call the private setSelected( ) method and also the two callback methods on the parent component. The dragHandler( ) callback method is invoked directly (since it is a function pointer and not a method name) whereas the standard change handler is invoked by way of the executeCallback( ) method defined on the FPopUpClass class:

```
FPopUpMenuItemClass.prototype.onPress = function () {
    this.controller.dragHandler();
}

FPopUpMenuItemClass.prototype.onRelease = function () {
    if ( this.enable ) {
        this.controller.executeCallback(this.index);
    }
}
```

Note the use of the 'index' instance variable here, which was set in the draw method. Each item component holds its own index in order to be able to pass it on to the callback method.

150 See the 'Implementing multiple text styles' appendix for more information on how the FMultiLabel component implements this functionality.

Both the highlight and icon skins have more than one frame, the skin elements contained in the various frames listening to different style properties. The highlight skin has two frames, labelled 'selected' and 'face', containing skin elements that listen to style properties of the same name. The icon skin has three frames, labelled 'face', 'selection' and 'disabled', but the skin elements they contain listen to the 'textColor', 'textSelected' and 'textDisabled' style properties respectively in order to match the style properties of the corresponding item labels. In fact, there is no reason why frame labels and skin element style names have to coincide, other than convenience.

In this case however, it is more convenient having the frame labels of the icon and highlight skins in agreement so that both can be set in tandem in the setSelected( ) method:

```
FPopUpMenuItemClass.prototype.setSelected = function (selected) {

     this.fLabel_mc.setEnabled(this.enable,selected);
     this.fBackgroundLabel_mc.setEnabled(this.enable,selected);

     this.fBackgroundLabel_mc._visible = !this.enable && !selected;

     var frame;
     if ( selected ) {
          frame = "selection";
     } else {
          frame = "face";
     }

     if ( this.icon_mc != undefined ) {
          this.icon_mc.gotoAndStop( this.enable ? frame:"disable" );
     }
     this.highlight_mc.gotoAndStop( frame );

     ...
}
```

There is a further test for the icon frame here, since it has a third frame corresponding to its disabled state, which holds regardless of whether it is selected or not. Note that the visibility of the background label is explicitly set – the label component having no state corresponding to being both disabled and selected, and therefore simply being hidden unless both disabled and unselected.[151] The remainder of the setSelected( ) method goes on to explicitly set the colours of the background label component and icon skin if the corresponding style properties are not set.[152]

151 This is why only the 'disabledStyle' element in the associative array passed to the background label is set, all other styles corresponding to cases where the label is simply hidden by this method.

152 The setting of the icon colours mirrors exactly the defaults used in the setEnabled( ) method of the FMultiLabel component. Again, see the 'Implementing multiple text styles' appendix for more information.

Dialog

This is another base component, extending the PopUp component and extended in turn by the MessageBox and ToolBar components. It adds a title bar and close button to the PopUp's bare, bevelled pane as well as support for multiple style properties.

The constructor checks that the '_name' property of the instance is defined in a similar manner to the PopUp component and like the init( ) method of the PopUpMenu component, the init( ) method here contains little in the way of 'boiler plate' code, apart from attaching the label component and skin to form the title bar:

```
FDialogClass.prototype.init = function() {

     FMultiStyleClass.apply(this);

     super.init();

     var titleAttrs = {multiStyle:"title"};

     this.attachMovie("TitleBar","TitleBar_mc",this.mcCount++);
     this.attachMovie("FMultiLabelSymbol","Title_mc",this.mcCount++,titleAttrs);
     this.setTitleStyle( "title", "textSize", "11" );

     this.closeButtonCount = this.mcCount++;

     this.closeLink = "FDialogCloseButtonSymbol";
     this.closeEnable = true;
     this.closeHandler = function() { this.controller._visible = false; }
}
```

In order to allow the component to directly support multiple text styles, the class methods of the FMultiStyleClass class are made available to the component by invoking the FMultiStyleClass class constructor using the apply( ) method. This is an extremely useful mechanism and essentially allows the FDialogClass class to extend both the FMultiStyleClass and FPopUpClass classes.[153]

The child label component is then created (with a 'title' multi-style), its size being immediately set using the setTitleStyle( ) method, a helper method which invokes the setMultiStyleProperty( ) method using the 'title' multi-style:

```
FDialogClass.prototype.setTitleStyle = function(propName,value) {
     this.setMultiStyleProperty("title",propName,value);
}
```

The closeHandler( ) callback method is set explicitly and the 'closeEnable' instance variable is also set, saving a call to the enableCloseButton( ) method that would otherwise force the component to be invalidated. Note also both the setEnabled( ) and enableCloseButton( ) methods invalidate the component, since both imply a change in the component's appearance. Finally, note that the closeHandler( ) method is saved as an instance method and can therefore be reapplied to the close button whenever it is recreated in the setSize( ) method as a result of the component being invalidated.

153 The FMultiStyleClass class is defined in the initialiser script for the FMultiLabel component. For the last time, the 'Implementing multiple text styles' appendix is recommended for a full explanation.

The setSize( ) method itself contains nothing but the necessary call to pass control on to the base component, all the child elements being reattached or repositioned in the private layout( ) method instead. The contents of the layout( ) method create the close button as well as configuring the title bar and since they contain no new techniques, no further comment is made on them here.

The close button, FDialogCloseButton, is held as an asset and is stored in the 'Core Assets>FUIComponent SubClasses>PopUpButton SubClasses' folder in the library. It extends the FPopUpButton component which provides a base component for all the various popup buttons. It is held as an asset by each of the popup buttons that extend it (four in total) and supports both 'flat' and 'normal' button styles, with bevelled edges of one and two pixels respectively. Both 'onPress' and 'onRelease' handlers are defined:

```
FPopUpButtonClass.prototype.onPress = function () {
     this.controller.dragHandler();
     this.pressed = 1;
     this.layout();
}

FPopUpButtonClass.prototype.onRelease = function () {
     this.pressed = 0;
     this.layout();
     if ( this.enable ) {
          this.buttonPressed();
     }
}
```

The former calls the parent component's dragHandler( ) method directly and the latter, if enabled, calls a buttonPressed( ) method that must be defined in the components that extend it.[154]

154 Not one of the four popup button components that extend the PopUpButton component contains a line of original code and none get any further mention in this chapter.

MessageBox

This component extends the Dialog component to provide a message label and support for child buttons. The multiple style properties implemented in the Dialog component are realised here, with the style properties of the message and button labels being different from those of the title. Any number of buttons can be added, the usual is between one and three inclusive, however. The close button is disabled by default, with the component usually being hidden when a child button is pressed.

Apart from explicitly disabling the close button, the init( ) method here does very little, with the init( ) methods of both the Dialog and PopUp components (not to mention the FUIComponent component) doing most of the work. The setSize( ) method is more complex, however:

```
FMessageBoxClass.prototype.setSize = function(w, h) {
     if ( this.container_mc != undefined ) {
          this.container_mc.removeMovieClip();
     }
     this.createEmptyMovieClip( "container_mc", this.containerCount );

     this.measureItmHgt();
     this.measureItmWdths();
     this.measureTitleHeight();

     this.Message_mc.setSize(w - 2 - this.padding*2,9999);
     this.Message_mc.setLabel(this.Message_mc.getLabel());

     var tmpMsgHgt = this.Message_mc.labelField.textHeight;
     var tmpHgt = 2+tmpMsgHgt+4*this.padding+this.titleHgt+this.itmHgt;

     this.width = w;
     this.height = Math.max(h,tmpHgt);

     super.setSize(this.width,this.height);
}
```

Here, after an empty container movie clip has been created (to which the buttons will be attached), various methods defined on the base components are called in order to calculate the sizes of the child elements. The child label text is then set (which ensures its text styles are updated) and the resultant text height recovered. Armed with this information, the setSize( ) method can calculate the dimensions of the component, which is duly passes on to the setSize( ) methods of the base components. The child label is then positioned and the buttons created in the private layout( ) method (or other methods called from it).[155]

155 This is a short section but there is simply nothing else to write about, so much of the functionality having been implemented in the base components.

ToolBar

This component also extends the Dialog component to form a toolbar with support for custom items as well as standard buttons. Like the MessageBox component, it realises multiple styles but these are only used if items are designed to take advantage of them.[156] The component resizes itself to fit exactly around the buttons and other items with the padding between them being hardcoded to achieve the right effect. It allows a callback method to be defined which is triggered when any of the child buttons are pressed (as well as the standard callback method invoked when they are released).

For convenience, the addItem( ) method directly supports multiple styles, the multi-style name being the optional third parameter and being added directly to the item object that is stored as an element of the items array:

```
FToolBarClass.prototype.addItem = function(link,data,multiStyle) {
     this.items.push( { link:link,data:data,multiStyle:multiStyle } );
     this.invalidate("setSize");
}
```

This value is then recovered and passed to the item movie clip (together with some others) when it is drawn in the private layoutButtons( ) method. Adding the multi-style to the attributes object passed to the item as the fourth argument of the attachMovie( ) method means that it is immediately available in the init( ) method of the built-in label class (for example) and can be applied directly to the child label created therein:

```
FToolBarLabelClass.prototype.init = function()
{
     this.mcCount = 0;

     this.attachMovie( "DarkShadow", "DarkShadow_mc",this.mcCount++ );
     this.attachMovie( "LightShadow", "LightShadow_mc",this.mcCount++ );
     this.attachMovie( "Background", "Background_mc",this.mcCount++ );

     var attrs = {multiStyle:this.multiStyle};
     this.attachMovie( "FMultiLabelSymbol","fLabel_mc",this.mcCount++, attrs );

     this.enable = true;
}
```

The 'onPress' handler must also be defined on this child component to allow the dragHandler( ) method to be invoked (even though the component cannot be dragged when a child component is clicked on in this manner).

156 As well as a default button, the component contains a child label as an asset which supports multiple styles. Note also that although several transport-like icons are contained as assets and used in the usage example, this is not simply a transport bar and any number of icons can be used instead.

3.5: The 'MultiListBox' Component

This component enhances Flash's own ListBox component with support for multiple style properties and horizontal scrolling. Apart from the setAutoHideScrollBar( ) method (which is dropped because both scrollbars are always kept visible), the base functionality remains almost identical to the ListBox component. Both the addItem( ) and addItemAt( ) methods have an optional parameter for the multi-style properties however, which are set using the setMultiStyleProperty( ) method.

The architecture of the child item components has been changed considerably, with the attachMovie( ) calls being moved out of the item's setSize( ) method and into layoutContent( ) method to avoid unnecessary redraws. Highlight and text positioning are also handled a little more cleanly. The end result is that the component often looks and performs slightly better than Flash's ListBox component, even without the added functionality.

MultiListBox

The component is comprised of three classes (apart from the FUIComponentClass class, of course) that each contribute some functionality to the whole. The topmost component class, FMultiListBoxClass, is copied directly from the equivalent class for the ListBox component, with a few changes to public methods such as addItem( ) and addItemAt( ), together with changes to the init( ) and setSize( ) methods. Its immediate superclass is FMultiScrollSelectListClass, which is similarly based on the equivalent FScrollSelectListClass class used by the ListBox component.[157]

The FMultiScrollSelectListClass class extends the FSelectableListClass class, the latter being used with only one modification. Rather than create another class based on the FSelectableListClass class in order to accommodate this one change however, the redefinition of the offending method, setSize( ) in fact, is simply added to the initialisation script of the topmost component class, thereby ensuring that it takes precedence over the original definition.[158] The main reason for this redefinition is to be able to use the 'itmHgt' instance variable a little more directly[159] but the setSize( ) method is also invoked on the item movie clips without regard for the width of the component (more on this later).

The FSelectableListClass class is responsible for drawing the item movie clips and also provides helper methods for accessing an instance of the DataProviderClass class that holds the component data (in preference to the data being held in an items array). This instance is created in the init( ) method:[160]

```
FSelectableListClass.prototype.init = function()
{
     super.init();
     this.enable = true;
     this.selected = new Array();
     this.topDisplayed = this.numDisplayed = 0;
     this.lastSelected = 0;
     this.tabChildren = false;
     if (this._name!=undefined) {
          this.dataProvider = new DataProviderClass();
          this.dataProvider.addView(this);
     }
}
```

Having created the DataProviderClass class instance, the component then invokes the addView( ) method on it, adding itself to the data provider's list of 'views', namely those components that have an 'interest' in the data and are notified whenever it is changed. The component adding itself to this list is considered by the data provider class as reason enough to notify the component immediately, in fact, with the component's modelChanged( ) method being invoked once its reference has been added to the data provider's list of views:

```
DataProviderClass.prototype.addView = function(viewRef)
{
     this.views.push(viewRef);
     var eventObj = {event: "updateAll"};
     viewRef.modelChanged(eventObj);
}
```

157 Subclassing the ListBox component is not a viable option with so many layers of functionality involved. This inevitably leads to large blocks of code being copied from one class to another – this is plagiarism on a grand scale! The alternative is to redefine the relevant methods but although I do this once with the setSize( ) method of the FSelectableListClass class, it is not good coding practice and hardly makes the use of Flash's own classes any more justifiable.

158 The redefinition of the setSize( ) method in the FSelectableListClass also has a bearing on the FTree component in the server explorer example movie, which also extends it. The changes work fine for this component too, however.

159 Without the additional adjustment, that is, which is added in the measureItmHgt( ) method instead. See the comments on the FTextLabel component in the 'Lightweight' components chapter for justification.

160 The test for the presence of the '_name' property here is unnecessary – it should be placed in the constructor, if it is to be placed anywhere.

The modelChanged( ) method, defined on the FSelectableListClass class, takes whatever action is required after the data provider has altered the underlying data and then invalidates the component. The invalidate method chosen by the modelChanged( ) method is not the usual setSize( ) method however, since the appearance of component has not changed, but rather the updateControl( ) method, which redraws the items but does not recreate or resize them (more on this in a moment).

Returning to the DataProviderClass class for a moment, the remaining methods simply add, remove or sort the items (to name but a few tasks) or allow the component to retrieve information, such as the number of items, for example. Class methods that change the data invoke the updateViews( ) method, which calls the modelChanged( ) method on all components in the data provider's list of views:[161]

```
DataProviderClass.prototype.updateViews = function(eventObj)
{
     for (var i=0; i<this.views.length; i++) {
          this.views[i].modelChanged(eventObj);
     }
}
```

Much of the remaining functionality of the FSelectableListClass class is concerned with implementing the selection mechanism for the component and since it uses little in the way of new techniques, receives no further comment here.

Since not all of the item data can necessarily be shown at once, only the item components required to fill the available space are created, these being configured to show whatever subset of the item data is currently visible. If there are fewer items than the available space will permit, the number of item components created remains the same, the unused ones simply being left blank. The (redefined) setSize( ) method creates the necessary item components:

```
FSelectableListClass.prototype.setSize = function(w, h)
{
     super.setSize(w,h);

     this.boundingBox_mc._width = w;
     this.boundingBox_mc._height = h;

     for (var i=0; i<this.numDisplayed; i++) {
          this.container_mc.attachMovie( this.itemSymbol,
                                         "fListItem" + i + "_mc", 10 + i,
                                         {controller:this,itemNum:i});

          var item_mc = this.container_mc["fListItem" + i + "_mc"];
          item_mc.setSize(0,this.itmHgt);
          item_mc._y = this.itmHgt*i;
     }
     this.updateControl();
}
```

161 This is all there is to say about the data provider mechanism, apart from noting that not once in my experience has one component registered an interest in another's data.

The 'numDisplayed' instance variable specifies the required number of item components here. This is calculated in the setSize( ) method of the topmost component class, which also resizes the component's mask movie clip and bounding box (left visible for once) to fit the component exactly.[162] Since the item components are attached to the container movie clip, masking it effectively masks the items themselves, ensuring that they do not 'spill' over the edge of the component.

It is worth noting that the items are only clipped horizontally, since they already fit the component vertically. The first parameter of their setSize( ) method is therefore ignored and the width of their child highlight (the setting of the which being the only task that this method performs) is set to be arbitrarily large.

Once the item components have been created and sized, the setSize( ) method calls the updateControl( ) method, which calls the drawItem( ) method on each item component in turn, passing the data and selected state of the corresponding data item:

```
FSelectableListClass.prototype.updateControl = function()
{
    for (var i=0; i<this.numDisplayed; i++) {

        var tmpItem = this.container_mc["fListItem" + i + "_mc"];

        tmpItem.drawItem( this.getItemAt( this.topDisplayed + i )
                          this.isSelected( this.topDisplayed + i ) );
    }
}
```

It is the item component's drawItem( ) method then, and not its setSize( ) method, that is responsible for altering its child label and highlight elements, and since this approach is considerably quicker than recreating the component from scratch, the updateControl( ) method is preferred to the setSize( ) method in the majority of cases, the former being used only when absolutely necessary (such as when the component is resized).

The FMultiScrollSelectListClass class is responsible for drawing the scrollbars, adjusting them when necessary, carrying out the required tasks when they are used and implementing helper methods to provide data on their positions and so on. The scrollbars are drawn once, and once only, in the initScrollBar( ) method but may well need to be adjusted if the underlying data or size of the component changes. To cover the first eventuality, the initScrollBar( ) method is specified whenever the data provider notifies the component that the underlying data has changed:

```
FMultiScrollSelectListClass.prototype.modelChanged = function(eventObj)
{
    super.modelChanged(eventObj);
    this.invalidate("initScrollBar");
}
```

162 The bounding box movie clip is in fact a component skin, its background portion listening to the 'background' and 'backgroundDisabled' styles.

Note that by invoking the modelChanged( ) method on the FSelectableListclass superclass here, the component ensures that the item components are reconfigured to show the required item data without a need to call the setSize( ) method. To cover the second eventuality, the initScrollBar( ) method is invoked in the setSize( ) method defined on this class:

```
FMultiScrollSelectListClass.prototype.setSize = fuction(w,h)
{
     var pos = this.getScrollPosition();
     super.setSize(w,h);
     this.initScrollBar();
     this.setScrollPosition(pos);
}
```

The scroll handlers themselves are straightforward, the vertical one simply changing the value of the 'topDisplayed' instance variable and calling the updateControl( ) method (the actual item movie clips not being moved at all); and the horizontal one adjusting the horizontal position of the container movie clip directly. With the exception of the getScrollBarWidth( ) method, the remaining methods of this class remain identical to those of the FScrollSelectListClass class and need no further comment here.[163]

Similarly, much of the functionality of the FMultiListBoxClass class remains identical to the class on which it is based, the only changes being the simplification of the setSize( ) and init( ) methods and the addition of the methods necessary to implement multi-styles.

One such additional method is the setFixedItemHeight( ) method, which allows the component's item height to be fixed without regard to the height of the constituent items. This is especially useful when new items are added that would otherwise alter the item height (because of the multiple style support) and thus change the actual component's height, something usually to be avoided.

The overridden measureItmHgt( ) method takes this fixed height into consideration, otherwise checking the height of all the items, a necessary precaution because of the multi-style support (again):

```
FMultiListBoxClass.prototype.measureItmHgt = function()
{
     if ( this.fixedItmHgt > 0 ) {
          this.itmHgt = this.fixedItmHgt;
          return;
     }
     this.attachMovie(this.itemSymbol, "tmpItem_mc", 0, {controller:this});
     this.tmpItem_mc.drawItem( {label:"Sizer: PjtTopg"} );
     this.itmHgt = this.tmpItem_mc.height;
     for ( var i = 0; i < this.getLength(); i++ ) {

          this.tmpItem_mc.drawItem( this.getItemAt(i) );
          this.itmHgt = Math.max(this.itmHgt,this.tmpItem_mc.height)
     }
     this.tmpItem_mc.removeMovieClip();
}
```

163 Like the FSelectableListClass class, the FScrollSelectListClass class contains much that is overlooked here, specifically the functionality dealing with selection and keyboard handling. The important points have been covered however, or rather, those parts that have been revised in this implementation.

Here, a temporary item component is created, its drawItem( ) method invoked and its height measured. The styles of each of the items are then applied to it one after another, again by invoking its drawItem( ) method, passing as a parameter each item object in turn. It is worth noting that nothing more needs to be done to apply a multiple style to the item component than invoking its drawItem( ) method with the required item data and indeed, passing no parameters ensures that component's default style properties are used instead.

This functionality is implemented courtesy of the displayContent( ) method of the item component's class:

```
FMultiListItemClass.prototype.displayContent = function(itmObj, selected)
{
     var tmpLabel = "";
     if (itmObj.label!=undefined) {
          tmpLabel = itmObj.label;
     } else {
          tmpLabel = itmObj;
     }
     this.fLabel_mc.setMultiStyle(itmObj.multiStyle);
     this.fLabel_mc.setLabel(tmpLabel);
     this.fLabel_mc.setEnabled(this.enable,selected);
}
```

This method is invoked from the drawItem( ) method of the item's superclass (invoked in turn by the method of the same name in the component class) and it is the setLabel( ) method here, invoked on the child FMultiLabel component, that is responsible for applying the required multi-style or using to the parent component's default style if no multi-style is supplied.[164]

The topmost drawItem( ) method, having invoked the method of the same name on its superclass (and thereby invoking the displayContent( ) method), then goes on to set the item component's 'width' and 'height' instance variables, the latter being used directly in the measureItmHgt( ) method above. The parent component's horizontal scroll offset (the amount by which the container movie clip is scrolled to show the full width of the items) is set in a similar fashion in the getItmWidths( ) method.

164 This method is discussed in detail in the 'Implementing multiple text styles' appendix.

Appendices

The Custom Tag Library

Actively generating content

The various of methods of actively generating web content can be summarised into two categories: firstly, programs or scripts that read a content file and populate it with active data, usually by means of interpreting custom tags within the file; and secondly, scripts that are embedded in the content files themselves. The first category includes Perl and Java servlets' and the second, JSP and Microsoft's ASP.

I have plumped for the first category in writing the source distribution server code because it most lends itself to portability - you can get just about any server side language to conform to this model. This is certainly not the case for the second category, which is more a collection of solutions lumped together because they all roughly conform to the same model.

For all but the smallest of projects, by far the most efficient way to process a content file with a server process is to use a custom tag library. The server process scans the content file for occurrences of custom tags and replaces them with content generated by instructions within these tags. These tags usually take the form of some degenerate XML and, ideally, they should be designed in such a way that they are ignored by the browser if they happen to slip through the server process unchanged.

The source distribution custom tag library

There are several such free tag libraries around that provide both the tag syntax and the means of interpreting it but I have gone ahead and designed my own because none of them supported a wide variety of different server side languages. The overriding consideration here was providing a common tag syntax. The actual processing done by the server processes in response to the contents of the tag is minimal. These same custom tags are also used inside the list files, in order to place certain form or configuration variables into the processed list.

The syntax of the custom tags was chosen for simple readability and to avoid any clashes with HTML tags. I could have done better here. The actual syntax is a 'double tag', namely one with two opening 'less-than' characters and two closing 'greater-than' characters. XML syntax is further overlooked by the omission of any slash before the closing characters. Here is an example:

```
<<SESSION>>
```

I have often rued the choice of this syntax since generating all the template files with XSLT because these tags are so XML-unfriendly.[165] However, there are no insurmountable difficulties and so I have never changed them. One consolation is that such double tags are easily picked out by eye, especially in the list files, where they stand out nicely.

The tags are identified by the server side processes by using regular expressions, regardless of language.[166] If you want to change the tag syntax to something more XML-friendly, by the way, all you have to do (apart from change the tags, of course) is to change the regular expression that identifies them. There are only two uses for the custom tags: firstly, to include form and configuration variables directly in the HTML templates and list files; and secondly, to place processed list files themselves directly into HTML templates.

165 In my own defence, I have to say that because of the positioning of the custom tags, it is difficult (as far as I can tell) to find any suitable combination of characters that will not break a well-formed XML document.

166 At the time of writing, of all the server side languages that I've used for the examples site, only Java didn't have native support for regular expressions. This situation was easily remedied by using one of the two GNU regular expression packages, the JAR file for which sits in the 'lib' directory of the examples source distribution. As of Java 1.4, regular expressions are part of the language. I've kept the GNU package though, for those that aren't in the position to be able to upgrade.

Interpreting the custom tags

A look at the 'template' server module in your chosen language will reveal slightly different methods for processing HTML templates and list files. The method for processing HTML files reads the template file one line at a time and looks for any custom tags on that line. On finding one, it looks at its contents. If the contents match the name of an existing, non-null configuration variable, its value replaces the custom tag. Otherwise, the contents are matched against a series of identifiers and if a match is found the relevant list file is processed and inserted in place of the custom tag. The pseudo code looks like this:

```
WHILE ( ( line = READLINE( template ) ) != _EOF )
{
  RE re = new RE( "<<([^>]+)>>" );

  line_copy = "";
  WHILE ( ( match = re.match( line ) ) != null ) {

    left = re.left();
    right = re.right();
    middle = re.middle();

    line_copy += left;

    config = CONFIG{ middle };

    IF ( 0 ) {}

    ELSEIF ( config != null ) {

      line_copy += config;
    }

    ELSE {

      line_copy += tag( middle );
    }

    line = right;
  }

  line = line_copy ? line_copy + line : line;

  content += line;
}
```

Note the use of an inner 'while' loop to allow the inclusion of several custom tags on one line, and also the call to the tag method, which is responsible for inserting list files. Custom tags that specify list files in this way are distinguished by the use of their upper-case contents, and clashes with form and configuration variables are avoided in this way, too (with any luck).

The method for processing list files is much the same except that the list file interpreter also checks for the available form variables and does not call itself if there are any custom tags representing other list files (which there should not be). It also suppresses the trailing carriage returns at the end of each variable definition in the list file, encodes the contents either side of the 'equals' sign and appends the requisite ampersands.

The list file interpreter can also handle variable values that span several lines, with the obvious (but naive) rule that a carriage return suggests a new variable definition being replaced by an explicit check for the existence of an 'equals' sign. In these cases, each line of the variable value is concatenated and the trailing carriage returns are reintroduced.[167] Note that this approach does not break the rule that Flash data must be all on one line since the carriage returns form part of the completed variable value and are encoded before being passed to Flash.

167 There is a bug in the PHP implementation of the list file interpreter (and perhaps others - I haven't checked exhaustively), which results in the end of line CRLF sequence (the default for Windows) being echoed in the variable definitions. Flash interprets this as a double carriage return and thus the paragraphs in the text blocks shown in the 'Dynamic Text' example movie (to cite a concrete example) appear doubly spaced. A workaround is to ensure that all list files are saved in UNIX format, where the end of line sequence is a single CR character. All the list files in the source distribution are already saved in UNIX format. Most good text editors in Windows (including Window's own WordPad) support UNIX format, although NotePad does not.

HTTPS

The problem with HTTPS and Flash data

Data requested by a movie may change from time to time, even if its request URL does not, so a reliable method is needed to ensure that the browser does not cache it. A quick look at the 'Utils' server module reveals that the browser is always instructed not to cache HTML content (by specifying 'no-cache' in the HTTP response header) and this goes for the Flash data, too.

Unfortunately, although setting the response headers in this way works fine over HTTP for both HTML and Flash data, and also for HTML over HTTPS, it does not always seem to work with Flash data over HTTPS.[168] Consequently, another way of guaranteeing that the server process is queried every time a request is made needs to be found.

168 This seems to be a bug with the Flash player. Adding the 'no-cache' headers stops the data from being retrieved at all in some configurations. I don't know whether there are specific rules that disallow the use of these headers over HTTPS; one would assume a secure connection would imply no caching anyway.

Generating a unique request URL

A convenient workaround is to make sure that the request URL is unique by the addition of dummy form variables, if the nature of the problem does not admit a unique URL every time without them. The problem of ensuring that these dummy variables are themselves unique is a tricky one. A movie certainly cannot be relied upon to generate such a variable. Using the random( ) method is not a viable solution – a sequence of random numbers is not the same as a sequence of unique numbers, even if a sufficiently random sequence could be generated in the first place.

A better way to guarantee the uniqueness of a sequence of numbers is simply to increment the number used each time, and this is the approach taken. Two dummy variables are in fact utilised: one generated by the server and one by the movie. A combination of both is sufficient to guarantee a unique URL every time.

The server process can easily keep track of the next number to supply to a movie by holding it in a file that it locks and updates every time it receives another request. It passes this number to the movie via the movie URL and since (as far as I know) there is no problem with the caching of HTML pages over HTTPS, a new number is passed to the movie every time the page is refreshed. The movie, in the meantime, can easily keep a global variable handy and increment it every time it makes another request for data. A typical loadData( ) method in a movie would thus look like this:

```
function loadData() {

     var uri = "";

     uri += app + "?";
     uri += "page=" + escape(page) + "&";
     uri += "data=" + escape("all") + "&";
     uri += "guid=" + escape(guid) + "&";
     uri += "instance=" + escape((instance++)) + "&";

     loadVariables( uri, loader );
}
```

The 'guid' variable, defined in the movie URL, is declared near the top of the root script.[169] The instance variable can be initially set to zero, say. The addition of these two form variables to the request URL guarantees its uniqueness. This mechanism should ensure that the Flash data is never cached by the browser. Finally, it is worth pointing out that the server process takes no interest in either of these variables whatsoever.

169 You may wonder why the server-generated variable is named guid. Before making the startling discovery that uniqueness could be guaranteed by simply incrementing the variable supplied to the movie, I took the heavy-handed approach of generating a GUID instead. GUIDs, or 'globally unique identifiers' are huge alpha-numeric combinations, sixty-four characters long, in fact, that are guaranteed to be unique. The generating algorithm achieves this by making use of variables like the current time, the ID of the computer's ethernet card and so on. The only reason I mention this is that you may want to use such numbers rather than keeping track of a unique number by means of a file on the server that can easily be deleted.

Sessions

Defining a session

Sessions are a necessity for most 'useful' websites. They allow users to be identified and their actions logged as they navigate around a site, perhaps even when they leave the site altogether and come back at a later date. The precise definition of a session is a little difficult for me to explain so I will give several concrete examples of how they are implemented and hope an implicit definition will emerge.

Sessions have nothing to do with the example movies in this book, at least not directly. The 'Simple Form' example can be considered as using sessions in the loosest sense of the word, since data is preserved from one page to the next, but in general the movies do not use sessions and the examples site is essentially stateless. However, nearly all the movies use data requested from the server and in the real world this data should, in many cases, be specific to one particular user.

For this reason, movies need to be configured to request data for an individual by supplying some kind of unique identifier (the session identifier, in fact) and server processes need to be modified to handle this extra information and supply the corresponding data accordingly. I will demonstrate this mechanism in detail first and then show how to generate the session identifier afterwards. For now, just consider it generated.

Configuring the 'Prices' movie to use sessions

In this movie, the user is allowed to submit trigger values and when returning at a later date these revised values will reappear – they are saved to a file on the server and can thus be easily retrieved.

A quick look at the list file used to generate the movie URL, namely the 'INTERACTIVE.txt' file in the root of the source distribution, shows that the movie is configured to request data from the 'submit' server process and it duly does so, passing the 'page' form variable back as a means of instructing this server process which data file to provide. If the session identifier is to be passed back as well, the first thing to do is to make it available to the movie via the movie URL. This is easily done by changing the list file for the movie URL:

```
app=<<appPath>><<procPath>>submit<<procExt>>
page=<<page>>
sessionID=<<sessionID>>
```

Remember that for now it is assumed that this 'sessionID' has been defined somehow. The loadVariables( ) method then has to be revised to include this extra variable:

```
function loadData() {

     var uri = "";

     uri += app + "?";
     uri += "data=" + escape("get") + "&";
     uri += "page=" + escape(page) + "&";
     uri += "sessionID=" + escape(sessionID) + "&";

     loadVariables( uri, loader );
}
```

A call to the 'submit' server process will now give the required data, once the server process has itself been modified.

Why is it necessary to pass the session identifier to the movie only to have it passed straight back to the server again? The reason for this is that server processes are inherently stand-alone. This is an important point and one that is not at all obvious so it is worth a little explanation – it is the job of the web server software to wait for and respond to client requests, not the job of server processes. They are simply executed, interpreted or whatever in response to specific requests and then killed off. Instances of server processes certainly do not persist from one request to another.

Specifically, the instance of the server process that generates the page in which the movie is embedded will not be the same as the one which responds to the movie's request for data, even though it may well be the case that the same server process is used to service both types of request. The latter instance must therefore be made aware of the session identifier provided by the former instance by means of the request URL.

Modifying a server process to use sessions

Once the server process retrieves the session identifier it must locate the corresponding file. The easiest way to do this is to name the file as nearly as possible after the session identifier itself. For example, instead of the file being named purely after the 'page' form variable, this variable is used to specify the directory and the session identifier is used to specify the file. So, the part of the server process that prints the response …

```
if ( FORM{'data'} == "get" ) {

   staticData = CONFIG{'rootDir'} + "data/" + FORM{'page'} + ".txt";
   submitData = CONFIG{'rootDir'} + "submit/" + FORM{'page'} + ".txt";

   print( template_data( staticData ) );
   print( template_data( submitData ) );
}
```

… is replaced with …

```
if ( FORM{'data'} == "get" ) {

   staticData = CONFIG{'rootDir'} + "data/" + FORM{'page'} + ".txt";
   sessionData = CONFIG{'rootDir'} + "session/"
                                   + FORM{'page'} + "/"
                                   + FORM{'sessionID'} + ".txt";

   print( template_data( staticData ) );
   print( template_data( sessionData ) );
}
```

Note that some of the data is not session-specific and hence its retrieval remains the same both before and after the modification. In the 'Prices' movie, for example, the positions of the sliders make up the session-dependent data and the red, static price indicators comprise the session-independent data.

It is worth leaving some initial data for the slider positions in the 'data' directory to be copied to a newly created session file when new sessions are generated. It is also worth making a clear distinction by means of directory names, say, between static and variable data. In the source distribution, the former is kept in the 'data' directory whilst the latter is kept in the 'submit' directory. Variable data specific to a particular user (session data, effectively), can be kept in a 'session' directory.

These are the only modifications necessary to enable sessions for the 'Prices' movie and this model can be used as a template for any movie. The remainder of the appendix looks at sessions themselves in detail and explains how to generate a unique session identifier.

Using form variables for persistent data

In the 'Simple Form' example, the movie passes as form variables the values of the input fields and the tick box to the server process when the submit button is pressed. Also, the values of the input fields and tick box can be set when the movie is initialised and in this way (because the server process that handles the data submittal is also responsible for printing the succeeding page), form data can persist from one page to the next.[170]

The submittal of form data by a movie and the movie's subsequent configuration when the page is redrawn is actually not the issue here – this mechanism will work just as well with standard HTML forms. It is the purpose of the 'Simple Form' example to mimic HTML forms, after all. The important point here is that as long as a page is generated actively by a server process in response to a form submission and therefore has access to the form variables, these variables can be perpetuated by inclusion in a form in the subsequent page and the process continued ad infinitum.

170 See the chapter on the 'Simple Form' example for an exact description of the data that persists.

URL rewriting

One drawback to this method is that data becomes difficult to manage as the number of items increases. It is not necessary to show each item of data in a visible form element, of course. Hidden form variables can be used to store data without the need to display it in every form but this is hardly an efficient method. Another drawback is that navigation can only be allowed via form submissions, which is wholly unacceptable in most situations. What is needed is a way of perpetuating the data by means of plain hyperlinks.

URL rewriting provides a solution, with hyperlink targets including the form variables, essentially mimicking a form GET request. HTML forms do no more than append the encoded name-value pairs of form variables to the request URL, after all. This approach is used in just about every loadVariables( ) call in the example movies, by the way. By modifying all the hyperlinks on a site in this manner, data can persist without the need to resort to form submissions, or a combination of both methods can be used.

Session files and session identifiers

To solve the problem of the volume of data that can be generated by user input, data is held in a file on the server and a unique identifier is passed around instead of the variables themselves. This is known as the session identifier. The server process can use this identifier to retrieve and modify the data file in question (look back to the beginning of this appendix for one way to associate session identifiers with their corresponding session files).

In order to generate a unique identifier for a user, two approaches can be used. The user could be asked to supply one (an email address being the most obvious choice); or one could be generated automatically. Uniqueness can be assured by a suitably large number of possible combinations and a check against all existing session identifiers in a separate file or database. In this second case, there is no need for the user to even know of the session identifier's existence.

Furthermore, if the session identifier is made available to the user either by displaying it as some kind of a 'key' or by virtue of it having been supplied by the user in the first place, the user can return to the site at a later date and 'log on' by supplying the identifier, thus gaining access to previous data and preferences. This key can be guarded by the addition of a password, the password also being held in the session file.

Cookies

Another method of saving the session identifier for later retrieval is to request that the browser saves it to a text file held on the user's own computer. Such a text file is known as a 'cookie'.

Server processes can request that a cookie be written to the client machine by including the cookie's details in the HTTP header of any response in much the same way as MIME types or caching preferences are specified.
The browser will then automatically include the cookie details in the HTTP headers of requests to the same domain.[171]
Cookies generally have a name, value and expiry time. The value can be an associative array of many name-value pairs, enabling one cookie to store a considerable amount of information.

Cookies should not replace the use of session files. They should be used to save the session identifier but not the session data. Specifically, any password that protects the session must be held on the server or it is effectively useless. The dangers of using cookies on public computers where browsers are shared amongst many users should be obvious, not least because the cookies themselves are held as unencrypted text and can easily be recovered.

Users should always be prompted to confirm their identity before proceeding with a session whose identifier has been supplied by a cookie, unless the nature of the information held in the session file makes this step unnecessary.[172]
Users must also be given the opportunity to 'log off' from a session and start a new one, as well as being allowed to specify that a computer is a public one (and therefore that it should not be used to store session identifiers at all).

171 This is an over-simplification. Servers can in fact specify that a cookie can be made more globally available and modern browsers can refuse such requests or even deny the use of cookies altogether.
172 Sessions used on the support website for the purposes of allowing users to submit data using the 'Prices' and 'Volumes' movies are not protected, for example.

Scope

Variable persistence in object scripts

Although variables cannot be defined outside of event handlers in object script, it is possible to define them inside these handlers and have them persist from one event to another. The following object script for example, defines a 'counter' variable in a button event handler and increments it every time the button is pressed:

```
on ( press ) {

     if ( count == undefined ) {
          count = 0;
     } else {
          count += 1;
     }
}
```

This method also works for movie clip event handlers, perhaps saving the declaration of variables somewhere in a frame script.

Variable scope in frame scripts

There are three ways to define a variable within a frame: as a 'global' variable, a timeline variable or a local variable. Global variables are available throughout a movie and do not need a target path. They are defined by prepending the '_global' keyword, thus:

```
_global._WIDTH_ = 400;
```

It is not necessary to prepend the '_global' keyword when referencing global variables, although doing so is not disallowed and can be used to signify that it is a global variable that is wanted.

Timeline variables are available in the timeline in which they are declared and from other timelines by prepending the relevant target path. They are defined using the 'var' keyword, thus:

```
var myWidth = 360;
```

Local variables are only available within the curly braces in which they have been declared. The syntax is identical to that of timeline variables. Timeline variables are available from within methods on the same timeline, without the necessity of having to give their full path. Local variables of the same name will take precedence, however. Consider the following root script:

```
var mcCount;

function createElement () {

     _root.attachMovie( "FmyElement", "element_mc", mcCount++ );

     element_mc._x = 100;
}
```

There is no need to prepend the '_root' keyword to the 'mcCount' variable when using it in the attachMovie( ) method here. The 'element_mc' reference is similarly used without prepending the '_root' keyword – the movie clip has been placed on the root of the movie and thus the 'element_mc' variable effectively sits beside the 'mcCount' variable. The '_root' keyword could also have been safely omitted from the attachMovie( ) method in this instance, too.

Scope in initialisation scripts

Variables and methods defined in initialisation scripts sit at the root of the movie, whether defined inside or outside of method bodies. For example, setting the debug field can be done conveniently without the need to prepend the '_root' keyword:

```
FBoxClass.prototype.init = function () {

    debug += "init()...\n";
}
```

It is important to remember to use the 'var' keyword when defining local variables and the 'this' keyword when defining and accessing class or instance variables, because of the wide scope used by default.

Profiling

Optimising applications

In order to improve an application's overall performance, two fundamental pieces of information are needed: the amount of time each of its methods takes to execute, together with how many times they are executed in the course of a program 'cycle'. To gather this information, you can run an application using a profiler, which typically hooks each method call and logs it, together with its execution time. Usually an application is run by a profiler for a few seconds (during which time its performance would be slightly impaired due to the overhead of hooking and logging all the method calls) and a text file is then generated listing all the methods that have been invoked, together with their execution times.

Armed with this information, you can improve the performance of the application as a whole by concentrating on those methods that take the lion's share of the execution time, either because of their complexity or the number of times they are called.

Applications that respond best to optimisation are those that loop continually, running through the same 'cycle' again and again. Arcade games are a good example. They use all the available CPU time and run as fast as the hardware will permit. Event-based programs do not respond as well to optimisation because the CPU will be idle for most of their execution time.

Profilers that work on compiled C programs, say, require an intimate knowledge of the operating system in order to hook method calls. Flash does not have an in-built profiler but since ActionScript is an interpreted language and therefore 'hooking' method calls a relatively straightforward task, it would be quite easy to write a native profiler.[173]

173 I hope someone does so at some point.

Using a Flash based profiler

In order to profile a movie then, a profiler has to be written in ActionScript and run as part of the movie itself. I have written a simple profiler component and used it to optimise the PDBViewer example movie. This is the only movie in the examples distribution that runs in a similar way to an arcade game and is therefore a suitable candidate for optimisation. As long as the molecule is being moved around, it is redrawn as often as possible, performance monitors showing an almost one hundred per cent CPU usage while the movie is running.

The profiler component differs from standard profilers in that it does not keep a tally of method calls and then report them on termination. Instead, totals are kept for each 'cycle' and displayed immediately on the screen. I have also included a rough 'frames per second' count and the corresponding frame time in milliseconds. Although this component does not conform to the typical model of a profiler then, it is still of considerable use.[174]

The component has been left in the PDBViewer example, albeit disabled. It can easily be re-enabled by removing the 'false' parameter from the Profiler.setEnable( ) call in the root script, however. The 'Profiler' reference here is a global one, set by the component to point to itself so that its methods can be accessed with ease from anywhere within the movie.

In order to profile a specific method, its name must be registered using the Profiler.register( ) method (usually at the start of the movie's execution), then a Profiler.start( ) call must be added to the beginning of the method body and a corresponding Profiler.stop( ) call added to the end. Alternatively, the method itself can be enclosed within these two lines. The register( ) method provides a means of turning off a method profile without having to remove the start( ) and stop( ) calls and also ensures that these methods run as efficiently as possible.

The profiler component will not keep a track of every single method call. You have to make an educated guess as to which methods are going to slow down a movie, then confirm your hunch by registering them. The easiest way to proceed is to start at the top of the function hierarchy and narrow down your search. For example, placing start( ) and stop( ) methods around the call to the molecule's draw( ) method is as good a place as any to begin with the PDBviewer, following up by examining its child methods.

174 Armed with data from the profiler component, I nearly doubled the speed of the PDB viewer.

Instantiating the profiler

The profiler must be instantiated before any methods can be called on it, obviously. It is important be sure that this happens early on in the movie's execution, since the profiler's methods are called from just about anywhere in the movie and often from within initialiser blocks. In order to be sure, it is worth investigating the various types of scripts that get executed during the normal course of a movie, and in what order.

To do this, create a movie containing the standard action and debug layers. Put the following code in the script of the first frame in the actions layer:

```
debug += "Actions/n";
```

Run the movie to check that it works. Next, draw a rectangle on the stage and turn it into a movie clip called FBox, with a linkage identifier of 'FBoxSymbol'. Make sure that the 'Export in first frame' tick box is checked in the 'Linkage Properties' dialog. Remove the resultant movie clip from the stage and edit it. Call the layer in which the graphic resides 'Graphic' and add an actions layer at the top. Add the following script:

```
#initclip

debug += "initclip...\n";

function FBoxClass () {

    debug += "FBC\n";
}

FBoxClass.prototype = new MovieClip();
Object.registerClass( "FBoxSymbol", FBoxClass );

debug += "...endinitclip\n";

#endinitclip
```

Double-check the movie clip instance has been removed from the stage, run the movie and you should see the following in the debug field:

```
initclip…
…endinitclip
Actions
```

As expected, the initialiser script is executed before the ActionScript in the root layer. The constructor is not called because no instance of the box exists. It is important to note that the initialiser block is still executed however, whether there are instances of the movie clip on the stage or not.[175]

---

175 The initialisation block is executed because the movie definition has been exported in the first frame of the movie, remember. Otherwise, it would have been necessary to leave an instance on the stage to force its execution.

The FBoxClass class has therefore been defined, even though it is never instantiated. It is also defined before any frame script within the movie is executed. Next, add the following code to the root actions:

```
_root.attachMovie( "FBoxSymbol", "box_mc", 0 );
```

The following should appear in the debug field, when the movie is re-run:

```
initclip…
…endinitclip
Actions
FBC
```

The movie clip is instantiated after the frame script is run, since it is created dynamically by the script itself. Now, remove this line from the root actions, add a 'Box' layer between the actions and debug layers and drag an instance of the FBox movie clip onto it. Run the movie again and look at the debug field:

```
initclip…
…endinitclip
FBC
Actions
```

The constructor gets called before the frame actions in the actions layer above. This is not a case of one layer executing before another: topmost layers get preference so you would expect the script to be run before the movie clip is instantiated. Evidently not, in this case. Classes associated with movie clip instances on the stage are instantiated before any script is run in that frame, regardless of layer precedence.

Placing an instance of the profiler on the stage in the first frame of the root timeline, therefore, will ensure that it gets defined and instantiated before any frame script is run, which is usually good enough. It will not ensure that the profiler is instantiated before any initialisation script is executed, however, and some methods may still therefore be invoked upon it before it is actually instantiated.

One way around this is to ensure that calls to the profiler are only made from within methods defined in initialisation scripts, and that these methods are only invoked once the profiler has been instantiated (as opposed to being called from outside of these methods and therefore being run when the initialisation script itself is executed). Creating components and movie clips dynamically will then guarantee that the profiler component has already been created, provided the methods in question are not invoked as a result of a class being defined.[176]

176 See the appendix immediately following this one for an explanation.

Optimising the movie

Because ActionScript is an interpreted language and runs in such a controlled environment, the more subtle and often most effective optimisations (such as direct calls to the hardware) cannot be employed.
However, ActionScript does admit more straightforward optimisations such as removing method calls and suchlike. These types of optimisation usually sacrifice readability and maintainability for speed.

The first rule of optimisation is that a fast-running program is a well-written one. Revise your program to your own complete satisfaction first, before optimising it. It is more difficult to make changes to a program when code is written for speed rather than readability, so optimisation should be done last of all.

By far the most important task when attempting to speed up an application is working out which low-level functions are taking up processor time. It is often the most unlikely ones which are candidates, by virtue of the sheer number of times they are called during each cycle. The profiler gives the total time that each method takes each cycle, and not the average time, for this very reason.

Maths operations are good candidates for optimisation if they are written for the most general case but are only used for specific ones. Take a matrix multiplication algorithm that operates only on matrices representing rotations:

```
FPosition.prototype.rotate = function ( mX, mY, centre ) {

     Coord.sub( this.r, this.l, centre );

/// These optimisations are based on the presumption that the matrices
///  supplied are guaranteed to have certain entries always equal to zero.
///
/// Coord.matmul( this.r, this.r, mX );
/// Coord.matmul( this.r, this.r, mY );
///
     var tx, ty, tz;
     tx = mX.l.x*this.r.x + mX.f.x*this.r.z;
     tz = mX.l.z*this.r.x + mX.f.z*this.r.z;
     this.r.x = tx;
     this.r.z = tz;
     ty = mY.u.y*this.r.y + mY.f.y*this.r.z;
     tz = mY.u.z*this.r.y + mY.f.z*this.r.z;
     this.r.y = ty;
     this.r.z = tz;
}
```

Here, the two matrix multiplication methods have been replaced by their actual method bodies with the lines that never get used being omitted. The four elements of the rotation matrices that always remain at zero admit this optimisation. Two method calls have also saved.

Another easy optimisation is to simply take out method calls where possible, even if the body of the method in question is just copied line for line:

```
FPosition.prototype.project = function ( z ) {

/// The first optimisation works because only the z coordinate is non-
///   zero. The second simply saves a method call.
///
/// Coord.plus( this.w, this.r, new FCoord( 0, 0, z ) );
/// this.distance = this.w.mag();
///
     this.w.x = this.r.x;
     this.w.y = this.r.y;
     this.w.z = this.r.z + z;
     this.distance = Math.sqrt( this.w.x*this.w.x
                              + this.w.y*this.w.y
                              + this.w.z*this.w.z )

     this.scale = kScale / this.distance;
     this.px = kXOffset + this.scale * this.w.x;
     this.py = kYOffset + this.scale * this.w.y;
}
```

Here, an optimisation is made by noting that only the z-coordinate needs to be changed in the initial translation. A further optimisation is then made by simply copying the body of the mag( ) method and thus saving a method call.

Of course, this second type of optimisation can be made all over the place but it is best left for method calls that are made frequently. This goes for all optimisations – they rarely lead to cleaner or more readable code and you must weigh up the pros and cons before proceeding. Note the copious comments. This is so important. Comments are always required when the purpose of code is not immediately obvious but never more so than when a revision seems downright backwards, as most optimisations do.

Only call constructors when necessary and use the same objects again and again if you can safely do so. Class members, whether objects or variables, are slightly more efficient than local ones. For example, the rotation matrices in the FMoleculeClass class are instantiated only once in the class constructor, then used over and again in the draw( ) method. And, of course, this usage is commented.

Avoid divisions and multiplications wherever possible they are so much more time-consuming than additions and subtractions.

One final note on the frame rate of a movie. If you have profiled the 'onEnterFrame' handler method in the FApplicationClass class you may have noticed that it does not seem to take up all the time in a cycle, despite the fact that no other methods are being called. Where is this remaining time taken up? The answer is that the Flash player stores up the information necessary to render each frame and executes it in one block, once it has finished other tasks such as invoking event handlers and running frame script. This part of the movie's execution is a closed book to Flash developers – there is no way to change the way in which the Flash player actually draws the movie. However, you will probably find that this drawing time decreases anyway as you optimise the movie.

The QuickSort algorithm

I have implemented a QuickSort algorithm that is about twenty-five per cent quicker than the Flash player's own sort( ) method. This is a most disappointing performance! The chances are that the native algorithm is based on MergeSort which, although easy to implement and a good all-round performer, is usually beaten comprehensively by QuickSort. What this comparison shows up further is that the Flash sort( ) method is not native at all – it is simply hidden code interpreted at runtime. Otherwise, there would be no competition and the native sort would beat any interpreted algorithm hands down.

Before using the QuickSort algorithm you should be aware of its deficiencies. Firstly, it performs badly for small arrays. For arrays of less than seven elements, in fact, it is best to use another algorithm or sort the array naively. Many implementations include this test and alternative as part of the algorithm but mine does not. Secondly, QuickSort performs atrociously when sorting an already sorted or nearly sorted array. This situation does occasionally arise and you should choose your algorithm bearing this in mind. Thirdly, QuickSort does not include the zero indexed element of an array in the sorting process.[177] For example, if you passed an array of twenty elements to a QuickSort algorithm it would sort nineteen of them, indexed from one to nineteen. If the call included a 'length' parameter, you would pass nineteen (the number of elements to sort) and not twenty (the length of the array). You may well have to rewrite parts of your program to take this into account and such a rewrite can cause all kinds of headaches, especially if not commented. No wonder the Flash player sticks to MergeSort!

The QuickSort algorithm is available in class form in the PDBViewer.

177 This is a point that is often omitted by commentators on sorting algorithms, who should know better but evidently don't.

The Trouble with Flash Class Inheritance

Defining an ActionScript class

ActionScript follows JavaScript syntax closely, including the way in which it handles class definitions and inheritance. The resultant syntax hardly aids understanding of exactly what classes are or of how inheritance works. Java and even C++ provide a better syntax, adhering much more closely to the actual concept of classes and for this reason, I have compared ActionScript listings with Java ones below, rather than attempt to give an introductory lesson in object-oriented programming.

Classes are implicitly created in ActionScript by defining a constructor in which you can, if you wish, make use of the 'this' keyword to declare instance variables and methods. The following Java class definition, for example ...

```
public class MyClass {

     /// Constructor
     public MyClass () {

          ...
     }

     int myVar = 0;
     public int myFunc ( int arg ) { ... }
}
```

... is equivalent to the following in ActionScript:

```
/// Constructor
function MyClass () {

     this.myVar = 0;
     this.myFunc = function ( arg ) { ... }

     ...
}
```

Note the definition of the constructor inside the class definition for the Java listing and the lack of a class definition altogether in ActionScript – in the latter case, classes are defined solely by the presence of the constructor. The 'class' keyword has no meaning in ActionScript, by the way.

Rather than define instance variables and methods inside the constructor using the 'this' keyword however, we are advised by the Flash documentation to use the 'prototype' keyword instead, since although variables and methods defined in this manner are available to all instances of a class, they are only defined once. The syntax is the following:

```
function MyClass () {

     ...
}

myClass.prototype.myVar = 0;
myClass.prototype.myFunc = function ( arg ) { ... }
```

This has the identical results to the previous ActionScript listing.[178]

178 Throughout the book, I have used terms 'class variable' and 'class method' to refer to variables and methods defined using the 'prototype' keyword, whereas the terms 'instance variable' and 'instance method' are usually taken to mean those defined by way of the 'this' keyword.

Extending an ActionScript class

Defining class inheritance in ActionScript is even more obscure. In Java, to extend the MyClass class, simply use the 'extends' keyword thus:

```
public class MySubClass extends MyClass {

     public mySubClass () {

          super();
     }
}
```

With ActionScript however, the 'prototype' keyword must be used:

```
function MySubClass () {

     ...
}
mySubClasss.prqtotype = new MyClass();
```

The 'new' keyword creeps in here, too. But for this one exception, the difference between ActionScript and other languages would be simply be a difference in syntax, and the only criticism that could be levelled at ActionScript would be that it is not as readable as say, Java. However, the presence of the 'new' keyword has some strange effects on the way that classes are initialised and with complex components in particular, this can lead to confusion.

The class with no name

Halfway down the initialiser for the FUIComponentClass class is the following section:

```
if ( this._name != undefined ) {

    ...
}
```

The contents of the braces are of no interest here. What is of interest is the test for the name of the component. A symbol on the stage will always have a name, even if it has not been assigned one explicitly. In such cases a default name will be given, something like "_level0.instance3", for example. So the '_name' property should never remain undefined, right? Wrong. A judicious trace shows that this is indeed the case, but under what circumstances?

In order to track down when exactly this occurs, follow the steps in the 'Profiling' appendix to create an FBox symbol in an otherwise empty movie. Working with this simplified movie clip will be easier than trying to get to grips with the internals of whatever Flash component has been dragged onto the stage in order to confirm the above statement.

Drag an instance of the FUIComponent movie clip onto the stage (from a project that contains it) and then simply delete it (or drag the definition straight into the library). As mentioned in the appendix on profiling, the mere presence of this movie clip in the library is enough to ensure that the associated class is defined when the movie is run, provided that it is exported in the first frame.

Next, add the following line near the top of the FUIComponent movie clip's initialisation script, not within the constructor or initialiser for the class itself but right underneath the #initclip line and banner comments:

```
debug += "FUI initclip!\n";
```

Make sure that the initialisation block for the FBox symbol has a lower precedence than that for the FUIComponent symbol by placing a '1' after the #initclip instruction at the top of the script that defines the FBoxClass class and run the movie. You should see the following in the debug field:

```
FUI initclip!
initclip…
…endinitclip
Actions
FBC
```

As expected, the initialisation block for the FUIComponentClass class gets executed before that for the FBoxClass class (because the zero after the #initclip in the FUIComponent script forces that script to execute before the script in the FBox movie clip) and then the execution continues as before. Now add the following line to the constructor of the FUIComponentClass class:

```
debug += "name is: '" + this._name + "'\n";
```

Running the movie as before should make no difference – the constructor never gets called because the class is never instantiated. Now, though, instead of having the FBoxClass class extend the built-in MovieClip class, change it to extend the FUIComponentClass class:

```
debug += "inheriting...\n";
FBoxClass.prototype = new FUIComponentClass();
debug += "...inherited\n";
```

Comment out the code in the root script that dynamically creates the instance of the FBox symbol at runtime and run the movie. Note that there are no movie clip instances anywhere, either placed on the stage, within other movie clips or created dynamically. Have a look at the debug field:

```
FUI initclip!
initclip...
inheriting...
name is: ''
...inherited
...endinitclip
Actions
```

Here is the "class with no name". Even though there are no instances of symbols created, anywhere, the constructor for the FUIComponentClass class gets called because of the presence of the 'new' keyword in the definition of the FBoxClass class. As this line of code gets executed by the interpreter, the superclass is actually instantiated there and then, and since there is no associated movie clip instance, there is no '_name' property for the class.

Add a super( ) call to the constructor for the FBoxClass class, above the debug line. This addition is necessary in order to ensure that the FUIComponentClass class constructor gets called when the FBox symbol is instantiated, and acts on the instance of the FBox movie clip. Uncomment the line in the root script that creates the FBox symbol dynamically and you will get the expected result:

```
FUI init!
initclip...
inheriting...
name is: ''
...inherited
...endinitclip
Actions
name is: 'box_mc'
FBC
```

Now, the second time the FUIComponentClass class constructor is called, the '_name' property is set to the instance name of the FBox symbol given to it by the attachMovie( ) call in the root script.

Why is this phantom instantiation of the FUIComponentClass class (the one with no name) necessary in the first place? Or, rather, precisely why is the 'new' keyword necessary? Perhaps an instance of the FUIComponentClass class needs to be created before its definition can be utilised. The use of the 'new' keyword simply forces this phantom instance to be created, then. The question arises therefore – does this same mechanism exist in other object-oriented languages? If this were indeed the case, perhaps ActionScript more closely follows the actual defining of class and inheritance than other, supposedly more intuitive languages.[179]

179 And I did suppose, above.

Working with Browsers

Compatibility issues

You should look at the compatibility section on the supporting website for a more thorough discussion than the one given here of the various issues involved in making your movies work across different browsers and operating systems. I did not feel that getting down to specifics in the book itself would be beneficial in the long run, since many compatibility issues will probably turn out to be transitory in nature and any discussion of them would soon go out of date. What follows then is just a discussion along general lines.

There may be the odd occasion when you can rely on your users to all be using the same browser and operating system. Corporate intranets are a good example. In these situations, you could rely on otherwise troublesome mechanisms once you are sure that they do indeed work on the target browser. Run the demonstration page in the compatibility section on the supporting website to check for potential problems first before committing to a mechanism that may prove to be flaky.

How a movie can interact with its surrounds

Since the Flash player provides a common platform on which movies can run, regardless of browser or operating system, compatibility issues basically boil down to the interaction of the movies themselves with their parent browsers, or the lack of it. This 'bridging', as it is known, is the main source of problems. As mentioned above, though, there are occasions when bridging can safely be used, so I will give a rough explanation.

Both the 'OBJECT' and 'EMBED' elements contain attributes that allow an embedded movie to be given a name and thus be referenced in a browser's document object model. These are the 'ID' and 'NAME' attributes, respectively. Once a movie is named, methods can be called on it from JavaScript embedded in the same web page via the Document DOM object. For example, the following JavaScript invokes the SetVariable( ) method on a movie named 'Menu':

```
function callback ( index ) {

    Document.Menu.SetVariable( index );
}
```

Going the other way, calling a JavaScript method from within a menu is a little more complex. The following ActionScript will call the JavaScript update( ) method:

```
function update ( value ) {

    getURL( "javascript:update( '" + value + "')" );
}
```

Both of these code snippets are taken from the 'Menus' article on the support website, which discusses the use of dynamic menus to change the contents of frames and so forth. The accompanying movie can be used as a template if you want such dynamic menus on your website. Even if you are sure of your target audience, however, I would suggest that you always provide a conventional alternative in the form of old-style hyperlinks to complement JavaScript based navigation.

getURL( ) – a safe bet!

It would be a sad state of affairs indeed if there were no reliable way of communicating with a browser at all and fortunately, this is not the case. The getURL( ) method provides an absolutely failsafe way of at least communicating to the browser a change in the page to be displayed. This is the same method as used above but without the "javascript:..." part. In fact, JavaScript is not used at all and the whole mechanism has nothing at all to do with the browser's document object model.

Quite why getURL( ) remains so robust across all browsers and operating systems is beyond my understanding but it seems that there is at least some common ground across all browsers with regard to the interface they provide to embedded objects for accomplishing this particular task. Indeed, all embedded players appear to have access to a method with a similar operation to getURL( ), though the name changes across the various platforms, of course. Java applets can use the showDocument( ) method of the AppletContext interface, for example.

The disadvantage of using getURL( ) to change the browser's currently displayed URL is that it does not admit the use of frames. Many (myself included) would not regard this as much as a drawback, though. I use this mechanism extensively now on all my websites and do not feel the need to provide hyperlinks as an alternative.

The connection throttling problem

All browsers allow only a limited number of connections to be open at any one time. They may close connections after a certain period of inactivity and they will limit connections both overall and per server. Some may queue a request for a limited time until a connection becomes available. The number of connections allowed differs between browsers but a general rule of thumb is around four to six, possibly more.

This has some bearing on the speed at which a web page loads and also needs to be borne in mind if your movies use the loadVariables( ) method. The good news is that in my experience, as long as there is only one embedded movie in any page requesting data, the request never fails. Ever. This is the good news.

The bad news is that with more than one movie embedded in a web page making requests, flakiness ensues. I do not know why this should be the case. Perhaps this scenario has never occurred to browser developers and there is simply no allowance made for simultaneous requests made from many embedded objects. Or perhaps the problem is with the design of the Flash player itself. And there is more bad news – the player gives no notification to the movie of a failure so there is no way for a movie to handle the situation gracefully when it does arise.

The only workaround is to periodically try the request until it is successful but this is hardly satisfactory. I have never tried it in practice and it may even have an adverse affect on the number of connections available to the browser, slowing down the loading of the web page as a whole. Waiting a certain amount of time is certainly no solution, either, since this will probably be longer than the amount of time users can be expected to sit there, waiting for something to happen.

There is some consolation in at least being able to 'chain' requests within one movie, though. Making a further request once the 'data' event has been triggered by a response to the first one seems perfectly permissible. Both the 'Line Chart' and '3D Pie Chart' example movies utilise this model; and just like the initial request from a solitary embedded movie, I have never, ever known chaining to fail.

Overcoming caching

Working with movies that need to interact with a server most of the time means testing within that environment. Although you can run a movie that interacts with the local server from within the Flash IDE, you cannot mimic the configuration of a movie via the movie URL without hard coding the values directly into the movie. For this reason, testing movies in situ, that is, embedded in the actively generated page, is probably the easiest option during development.

However, even with caching explicitly turned off, some browsers, although faithfully reloading the web page, will not automatically reload the objects embedded therein, specifically revised and recompiled movies. The only solution I have for this is to find out exactly where the cached movies are stored (you can usually specify the exact folder in the browser options) and to leave the folder open so that you can quickly delete cached movies each time before refreshing a page.

Implementing Multiple Text Styles

The FMultiLabel component

This component is used throughout both the example and component movies as an alternative to Flash's own FLabel component, over which it has several advantages. These include support for multi-lined text fields, support for 'selected' as well as 'enabled' and 'disabled' states and of course, multiple style properties.

The component is comprised of two layers, one containing a 'labelField' instance of a dynamic text field (drawn on the stage but entirely configured by the component), the other empty apart from the frame script. This script contains definitions of both the component class, namely FMultiLabelClass, together with a definition of the FMultiStyleClass class, which allows any component to implement multiple style properties and use the functionality that this component provides (more on this later).

Multiline text fields are supported by a much enhanced setSize( ) method, which configures the child text field according to how many arguments it is passed:

```
FMultiLabelClass.prototype.setSize = function(w,h) {

    if( arguments.length == 2 ) {

        this.labelField.multiline = true;
        this.labelField.wordwrap = true;

        this.labelfield.autosize = false;
        this.labelField._width = w;
        this.labelField._height = h;
    }
    else {

        this.labelField.multiline = false;
        this.labelField.wordwrap = false;

        if ( arguments.length == 1 ) {

            this.labelfield.autosize = false;
            this.labelField._width = w;
        }
        else {

            this.labelfield.autosize = true;
        }
    }
}
```

Two arguments signify a multiline text field; one, a single line text field with a definite width; and no arguments, a single line text field with variable width.

The component inherits the style properties of its parent component in much the same way as the FLabel component, this process essentially consisting of retrieving a reference to its host component and sharing the 'textStyle' instance of the TextFormat object found therein. The 'styleTable' associative array which contains the host component's non-text styles is also used, but only in the setEnabled( ) method, where the 'textColor' style can be overridden (more on this in a moment).

A reference to the host component itself is recovered by first looking at the 'controller' instance variable of the component's parent, with the parent component itself being used if this variable is undefined. There is nothing to be gained by setting the 'controller' variable of this component by means of the fourth parameter of the attachMovie( ) method, by the way (or by any other means, for that matter) - the component only looks at the value of the 'controller' variable of its immediate parent and not of itself.[180]

Some settings are configurable via the fourth parameter of the attachMovie( ) method, however, specifically the names of the style properties associated with the various 'enable' and 'select' states of the component.[181] If these names are not set (that is, they are not available as instance variables in the class constructor), default values are used. These are set in the constructor once a reference to the host component's 'textStyle' object has been obtained:

```
FMultiLabelClass = function() {

     if (this.hostComponent==undefined) {

          this.hostComponent = (this._parent.controller==undefined)
                               ? this._parent : this._parent.controller;
     }

     if (this.hostComponent.textStyle==undefined) {
          this.hostComponent.textStyle= new TextFormat();
     }
     this.textStyle = this.hostComponent.textStyle;

     if ( this.enableStyle == undefined ) {
          this.enableStyle = "textColor";
     }
     if ( this.disableStyle == undefined ) {
          this.disableStyle = "textDisabled";
     }
     if ( this.selectStyle == undefined ) {
          this.selectStyle = "textSelected";
     }

     if ( this.multiStyle != undefined ) {
          this.setMultiStyle(this.multiStyle);
     }

     this.labelfield.selectable = false;

     this.setEnabled(true);
     this.setSize();
}
```

Setting the 'selectable' property of the child text field and calling the setSize( ) method then fully configures the text field, the default setting being single line, variable width. Before looking the setEnabled( ) method, it is important to note that the 'enableStyle', 'disableStyle' and 'selectStyle' instance variables set here have nothing to do with multiple style properties, they are merely the names of the conventional styles applied to the component when the setEnabled( ) method is called. The FLabel component gives no opportunity to set these style names, with 'textColor' and 'textDisabled' effectively being hardcoded into the component.

---

180 I have adopted this practice in all of the conventional component skins throughout the book, which also look at the 'controller' variable of their parent movie clips.
181 See the configuration of the PopUpMenuItem component's child label for a usage example.

The setEnabled( ) method does nothing apart from set the colour of the text field depending on the component's 'enable' and 'select' states, effectively overriding the 'textColor' style property by querying the host component's 'styleTable' associative array directly (using the style names defined above). There is a subtle but important difference between the two approaches here: the 'textColor' style property is one of the many text styles held in the TextFormat object and is thus applied when the host component's 'textStyle' object is applied to the child text field whenever the setLabel( ) method is invoked. The three styles defined above however, are not text styles and are applied to the child text field directly whenever the setEnabled( ) method is invoked. The method itself is worth a look:

```
FMultiLabelClass.prototype.setEnabled = function(enable,selected) {

     this.enable = enable;

     var enableColour = this.hostComponent.styleTable[this.enableStyle].value;
     var disableColour = this.hostComponent.styleTable[this.disableStyle].value;
     var selectColour = this.hostComponent.styleTable[this.selectStyle].value;

     if ( enableColour == undefined ) {
          if ( this.multiStyle != undefined ) {
               var multiStyleTable = this.hostComponent.multiStyleTable;
               var multiTextStyle = multiStyleTable[this.multiStyle].textStyle;
               if ( multiTextStyle["color"]!=undefined){
                    enableColour = multiTextStyle["color"];
               }
          }
     }
     if ( enableColour == undefined ) {
          enableColour = this.textStyle["color"];
     }

     if ( disableColour == undefined) {
          disableColour = "0x888888";
     }
     if ( selectColour == undefined) {
          selectColour = "0xffffff";
     }
     var tmpColour = (this.enable) ? (selected ? selectColour
                                              : enableColour )
                                        : disableColour;
     this.setColour(tmpColour);
}
```

As well as the 'enable' parameter, this method also takes a parameter specifying the selected state of the component. It then queries the host component's 'styleTable' array directly to recover the values of the style properties corresponding to the style names 'enableStyle', 'disableStyle' and 'selectStyle'. If the corresponding values in the 'styleTable' array are undefined, suitable defaults are used (with one exception), the colour of the label field then being set directly with the setColour( ) method. The one exception is the case of the 'enableColour' variable, with multiple styles also being considered if the host component's style table entry is undefined. Also note that the 'textColor' text style is chosen as a last resort, the value of which is guaranteed to be defined for any host component which implements multiple text styles (more in this in a moment).

Implementing multiple styles

Multiple styles compliment rather than replace conventional style properties, allowing a component to store several TextFormat objects, each corresponding to a different multi-style name, rather than just the one. As well as the conventional 'textStyle' instance of the TextFormat object then, a component that supports multiple styles will contain an associative array called 'multiStyleTable' whose elements are TextFormat objects and whose keys are the multi-style names.

It must also implement the setMultiStyleProperty( ) method (amongst others) and the properties of its conventional 'textStyle' object must all be defined, whether the corresponding text styles have been set or not. These tasks are achieved by invoking the FMultiStyleClass class constructor on the component in question, using the apply( ) method.[182] The default values of the 'textStyle' object properties are set by creating a temporary FMultiLabel component and retrieving a full list of its child text field's properties using the getTextFormat( ) method, setting the corresponding properties on the 'textStyle' object if they are undefined. The reason for this becomes apparent when the FMultiLabel component's implementation of multiple styles is explained.

The FMultiLabel component supports multiple styles by containing an instance variable called 'multiStyle', usually set by means of the fourth parameter of the attachMovie( ) method, which (optionally) specifies the name of the multi-style to which it listens. In the setLabel( ) method, the corresponding TextFormat object is recovered from the host component's 'multiStyleTable' associative array and applied to the component's text field after the conventional 'textStyle' has been applied. Multiple styles are thus applied 'on top of' and not 'instead of' the component's conventional text styles:

```
FMultiLabelClass.prototype.setLabel = function(label) {

    var embed = this.hostComponent.styleTable.embedFonts.value;
    if ( embed != undefined ) {
        this.labelField.embedFonts = embed;
    }
    this.labelField.setNewTextFormat(this.textStyle);

    if ( this.multiStyle != undefined ) {

        var multiStyleTable = this.hostComponent.multiStyleTable;
        var multiTextStyle = multiStyleTable[this.multiStyle].textStyle;

        this.labelField.setNewTextFormat(multiTextStyle);
    }

    this.labelField.text = label;
    this.labelField._height = this.labelField.textHeight+3;
}
```

182 Essentially this is multiple inheritance. See the section on the Dialog component in the 'PopUp' components chapter for a usage example.

Because every one of the host component's 'textStyle' properties is defined (albeit with just a default value if the corresponding text style has not been set), applying the 'textStyle' object to the text field here will completely wipe out any trace of a multi-style TextFormat object that has been previously applied to the same label. With labels often being reconfigured to listen to several different multi-styles during the course of a movie's execution (items of a MultiListBox being one such example), it is important that their text fields are fully 'wiped clean' whenever the setLabel( ) method is invoked.

To continue, this method also retrieves the 'embedFonts' style property directly from the host component's 'styleTable' array and applies it to the text field, as well as setting the text itself and adding a few extra pixels to the height to avoid the descenders of certain characters being clipped.[183]

Finally, it is worth mentioning that to force an FMultiLabel component to update its text field with regard to either conventional or multiple style properties, the simplest approach is to call the setLabel( ) with getLabel( ) as the parameter. This is commonly done in the setSize( ) methods of components, often as a result of being invalidated when a new text style is applied.

183 A bug in the implementation of text fields means that rather than setting their height to be equal to the text height (essentially the point size of the font), several extra pixels have to be added.

Packaging Extensions

The component extensions

Each of the four sets of components discussed in the components chapters can be packaged into an extension using the extension projects provided. The compiled movie and HTML files can also be used to demonstrate the components, the projects themselves proving a useful source of usage examples.

Component projects are packaged into extensions with the extension manager. The extension project file is an XML file with an MXI extension, containing a description of the extension and references to the component project file and XML documentation files. The extension project file for the 'Lightweight' components, for example, looks like this (with the description block removed for brevity):

```
<macromedia-extension name="FFP Lightweight UI"
                      version="1.2.3"
                      type="Flash Component">

    <author name="James Smith"/>

    <products>
        <product name="Flash" version="6" primary="true"/>
    </products>

    <description>
        <![CDATA[

...

        ]]>
    </description>

    <ui-access>
        <![CDATA[

Access the components by choosing Window > Components > FFP Lightweight UI

        ]]>
    </ui-access>

    <files>
        <file source="FFP Lightweight UI.fla"
              destination="$flash/Components"/>
        <file source="FFP Lightweight UI Index.xml"
              destination="$flash/ActionsPanel/CustomActions"/>
        <file source="FFP Lightweight UI Ref.xml"
              destination="$flash/ActionsPanel/CustomActions"/>
    </files>

</macromedia-extension>
```

When the extension is installed, the 'name' attribute of the root element of the project file will appear in the component panel drop down menu and the contents of the 'description' element will appear in the main panel of the extension manager. The extension's three constituent files are referenced in the 'source' attributes of the 'file' elements, the simplest policy being to place them in the same directory as the extension project file itself.

The documentation consists of two XML files, one an index file and one containing descriptions of the component's methods. I strongly recommend that you generate these files from a common XML source file rather than trying to keep them synchronised, which becomes especially tiring as the complexity of extensions increases and new functionality is added. This also has the added advantage of allowing help files to be created in other formats simply by creating the necessary XSL transform files.[184]

When creating a new component extension, make sure that the component project is fully functional. Open it as a library and drag the components into a blank movie project to test that they bring all their assets with them and if possible, use them in real-world movies to test their functionality before packaging them as an extension.

To create the project and documentation files for a new extension, use existing ones that are proven to work. Only a few attributes and text nodes need be changed in any MXI file to convert for a new extension project. Whether you are working with a common XML source file or authoring the index and reference files directly, the safest approach is to start with one component element containing one method description, packaging and installing the extension to test that everything works before adding the remaining methods.

To package an extension, make sure that Flash is not being used, launch the Extension Manager and make sure that the extension is not currently installed. Chose 'Package Extension...' from the 'File' menu and select the required MXI project file. Click 'OK' and follow the remaining steps. If, for any reason, the extension cannot be packaged, start with the barest of extension project and documentation files. The complexity of the component project itself will never give rise to problems – it is almost always a fault in the XML files.

When the extension is packaged, install it and launch Flash. Check that the extension has been installed properly by looking at the component and reference panels. Only genuine extension components should appear in the components panel. In particular, components that belong to other extensions but that have been used in the component project either for usage examples or as part of genuine components, should not appear in the components panel. To rectify this, relaunch the component project and uncheck the 'Display in Components panel' tick box in the 'Component Definition' dialogs for the offending components. Exit Flash, uninstall and repackage the extension and launch Flash again to confirm the changes.[185]

---

184 With this in mind, the examples distribution contains the source XML and transform XSL files necessary to build the index and reference files for all the component projects. A small utility called SiteGen is also provided, together with the necessary project files to build the extension documentation. This utility is for Windows only: there is no support for Macs at the moment. Even if you decide not to use SiteGen, I would still recommend that you generate the index and reference files from a common XML source file somehow. This will save you much head-scratching in the long run.

185 I have never authored a component extension without having to repeat this process several times for one reason or another. The only consolation is that it becomes second nature after a while, and only takes a second or two.

Index

F

W

X

Y

Z

Printed in the United Kingdom
by Lightning Source UK Ltd.
99676UKS00001B/39-54

9 780954 706609